Making eHealth Work

George O. Obikoya

Table of Content

Executive Summary

E-Health has become an integral part of present-day healthcare delivery. With the

healthcare consumers, increasingly the focus of most health systems, the widespread implementation of health information and communications technologies offers cost-effective opportunities to meet their increasingly sophisticated healthcare needs. These technologies no doubt provide the enabling environment for cost-saving healthcare initiatives to work. They also promote creativity and innovation in both the development of novel yet effective healthcare services and the emerging technologies to actualize them. However, despite these and other significant benefits, the adoption of health information technologies seems excruciatingly slow even in the developed world, in particular among healthcare professionals, and other healthcare stakeholders at large. The exploration of the interplay of factors hampering the pervasive deployment and utilization of these technologies constitutes a key subject of this e-book, which also analyzes the options that healthcare providers from the primary to the tertiary care levels, governments, companies, and other healthcare stakeholders could consider in countering these factors.

Escalating healthcare costs are of major concern for even developed countries, and

which many of them seek effective ways to curb. However, these countries also must deliver qualitative health services to their peoples. The quest to achieve both objectives has led to the emergence of novel health reform approaches, including the consumer-driven healthcare model, with patients empowered to be more discerning, hence to participate more effectively and prudently in their choice of healthcare providers, treatment and in matters relating to their health in general. That the healthcare consumer needs relevant, accurate, and current information in order to be able to make rational choices regarding health promotion, disease prevention, and treatment options is not in doubt, nor is it that healthcare ICT could play a crucial role, in achieving these goals. The complex and interwoven issues that operate at the virtual interface of the healthcare consumer needs vis-à-vis health ICT deployment, fostering or hindering the widespread diffusion of the latter, hence the chances of the benefits thereof accruing to the former, or otherwise, also constitute the subject of this e-book. The author critically examines issues in a variety of domains crucial to healthcare ICT assisting in the achievement by governments, and payers in the health systems of the dual objectives of qualitative healthcare provision and simultaneous healthcare costs reduction. The e-book also discusses what healthcare organizations need to do to achieve these dual goals, particularly in the prevailing dispensation of perennially limited budgets, the funding model of the health systems in which they operate notwithstanding. By exploring these various issues in-depth, this e-book attempts to not only highlight the significance of healthcare ICT in contemporary healthcare delivery, but also some of the issues germane to moving any e-Health program forward.

Introduction

Health reform has become one of the most contentious public policy issues in contemporary times. The increasingly booming call for reform is indicative of the need for improvement in health services provision, which itself suggests some defects in current service provision. There are indeed, major problems with the health services of virtually all countries of the world, including the developed countries. One of the signs of such problems is the soaring health spending of these countries. There is nothing wrong per se in spending more on health services, but a lot is when countries are spending an increasingly disproportionate percentage of the Gross Domestic Product (GDP) on health, and in some cases, not still providing qualitative, comprehensive, accessible, and affordable health services to their peoples. Many have suggested approaches to solving the problems confronting healthcare delivery. In the U.S. for example, consumer-driven health plans such as Health Savings Accounts (HSAs) are gaining increasing acceptance, the healthcare consumer, increasingly the payer. Some contend that consumer-driven healthcare may ultimately lessen the role of third-party payers in health care transactions, but with many major health plans already offering high-deductible policies to go with HSAs, they are still likely to be in contention in the foreseeable future, nor does every healthcare provider upbeat about patient payment at the time of service. Healthcare providers doubtless have concerns about fees collection. For example, how much if at all should a doctor collect from the patient at the point of service if he/ she were a participating provider with the client's health plan? Expert advice is to handle such a situation as with any other non-contracted insurance that is, the doctor to collect the full charge before the client leaves, either via his/ her debit cards that deduct the money directly from his/ her HSA or out of pocket for later reimbursement into his/ her account. Some physicians have contracts with health plans that essentially make them participating providers and preclude them from -of-service payment, in which case, they must submit a claim to the insurance firm, wait for the explanation of benefits (EOB) that shows how much the insurer, and patient must pay, and then bill the patient for the rest. On the other hand, the contract might not bar point-of-service payment in which case, the doctor needs to know if the patient had met his/ her deductible, information sometimes obtainable for the websites of some insurers, or otherwise from the client, and if so, the doctor has to bill the health plan, or demand point-of-service payment if not. The doctor must bill the health plan for preventive services, as many plans pay for them, regardless of whether the client met his/ her deductible. Granted these complexities in the patient-as-payer inherent in the consumer-driven healthcare delivery model, the concerns some physicians have about the healthcare model are understandable. Nonetheless, it appears that the patient is right to the center of the contemporary healthcare delivery universe in many countries literally, efforts focused on meeting the ever-sophisticated demands of the patient for improved health services, and with good reasons. From the patient's perspectives, clearly to be healthy is a right, and not a privilege, hence the demand for services that guarantee this right. By extension, the patient demands safety in the process, and legitimately so, as coming to the hospital for the treatment of a sprained ankle and ending up fighting for one's life having contracted Methicillin-Resistant Staphylococcus Aureus (MRSA) while in hospital, for example is simply inexcusable. The patient also demands the privacy and confidentiality of his/ her health information, again, legitimately, as such information could fall into the wrong hands, for examples identity thieves. Meanwhile, governments, companies, and other payers also have a stake in ensuring that patients receive qualitative healthcare, considering the soaring costs of healthcare delivery that are threatening to grind whole national economies to a halt, and have already led to some companies not just firing employees en masse, but also in fact contemplating filing for bankruptcy. The situation is that dire in some case. Furthermore, the interests of both the healthcare consumer and the payers also coincide, considering the benefits of a healthy, productive, populace to economic development and the competitiveness of firms, and the opportunities for individuals for gainful employment in such a buoyant economic climate. There are thus compelling reasons in various quarters for the provision of qualitative healthcare cost-effectively, which no doubts the widespread implementation and use of healthcare ICT could help achieve, hence the shift in many countries toward electronic (e-)health. Consider the comparative advantage such shift offers for example. The Technology CEO Council, a policy advocacy group intent on seeing the U.S. become more competitive in the world arena via technology adoption recently added its potent voice to the call for more healthcare ICT diffusion, stressing that automating U.S. healthcare system is critical "not only to improving our nation's healthcare system, but also our global competitiveness." The Council, which includes CEOs from major ICT firms such as Intel Corp., Motorola Inc., Hewlett-Packard Co., Unisys Corp., NCR Corp., EMC Corp., IBM Corp., Dell Inc., and Applied Materials Inc., has even developed an e-Health Readiness Guide, a roadmap and policy suggestions for healthcare ICT implementation and monitoring. The companies, which generate up to US$300 billion in revenues yearly and employ over 800,000, plan to take the call to Congress. The Council specifically advocated the adoption of interoperable technology and common data standards; urged the U.S federal government to accelerate health ICT diffusion in its capacity as a large provider of and payer for health services; and firms and state Medicaid programs to base healthcare purchasing decisions and reimbursement, respectively, on providers using ICT to improve quality, value, and performance. The Council also suggested pay-for-performance for Medicare and Medicaid programs, and recommended a review of current federal, state and health network systems and practices to ensure data sharing and the security of patient information. Most would agree that inventions and innovations underpin an enduring comparative advantage, superior value-added endeavors, and value accumulation. It follows therefore, that a country's technological resourcefulness and capabilities must at least be in tandem with the prevalent intensity of global competition, what some would describe as the frenetic pace of technological progress, and a more suave and demanding market, to remain competitive, let alone thrive. Cost-effective information and knowledge acquisition, use, and sharing, create short-term tactical benefits with durable overall strategic advantage, for example at the point of care, accelerating recovery, hence reducing length of stay in hospital, and ultimately operational, even capital costs. Progress in transport technologies has redefined travel, national borders, the movement of goods and services, and the elements of value creation, and in information technologies (IT), is fostering knowledge creation and utilization, intellectual property (IP) assets, and technological and management value-added innovations that increasingly define comparative advantage. This comparative advantage currently is quite profound between developed and developing countries but increasingly blurred among the former, mostly knowledge-based economies. With many erstwhile planned economies becoming decentralized and more diversified in the developing countries, lifting tariffs and other trade barriers, infused with foreign direct investment (FDI), and cross-border intercourse in manufacturing and services increasing, is it plausible to conjecture that the comparative advantage even between the two groups may passé? Indeed, even now, patients are not only traveling from one developed country to another to receive medical treatment or undergo surgery, they are also traveling to developing countries and vice versa for these purposes, costs playing a significant role in the former, advanced expertise and technologies, the latter. Let us for the moment consider only where the competition is stiffest, among developed countries, where building cross-sector and pan-regional networks and collaboration at local, regional and meta-regional levels in order to enhance competitiveness is gaining currency. The Bay Area, Massachusetts, and North Carolina in the U.S, for examples, have developed a respectable critical mass few regions elsewhere can match. However, developments in Europe and elsewhere in the developed world are threatening to shift the fulcrum. In the Nordic-Baltic region for example, governments, companies, and public agencies are joining forces to establish a globally competitive and affluent meta-region made up of Sweden, Denmark, Finland, Iceland, Latvia, Lithuania, Norway, Estonia, Poland, north-west Russia, and northern Germany. Its protagonists expect this budding meta-region termed, the ScanBalt BioRegion, to be world technology leader in biotechnology, health, and life sciences, the key crucibles of knowledge-based economies. The ScanBalt BioRegion, which receives substantial financial support from the Nordic Industrial Fund, has 11 countries, 85 million people, 60 universities, and over 700 biotechnology-related firms, including large drug companies such as Astra Zeneca in Sweden and Novo Nordisk in Denmark. The region plans to focus on such Health ICT-related areas as nanotechnology, biomaterials, tissue engineering, molecular diagnostics, genome analysis, stem cells, and bio-banks, among others, and early indicators suggest that its projects are enhancing its competitiveness. Is it any wonder that Finland, for the second time in a row, is the most competitive economy in the world, and in 2005 also the least corrupt? Measured with two different indicators, the results of the Global Competitiveness Report of the World Economic Forum (WEF) showed that the country placed first on both the Current and Growth Competitiveness Index. Last year, it did on the former, but was sixth on the latter, which measures factors that support the growth of the gross domestic product (GDP.) The U. S placed first last year, with Canada, and Singapore next to Finland in that order in the Growth Competitiveness Index rankings, and two other Nordic countries, Norway and Sweden, placing sixth, and ninth, respectively.

Commenting on the 2005/06 report released on September 28, 2005, the Chief Economist of the World Economic Forum and Director of the Global Competitiveness Program, Augusto Lopez-Claros said," In many ways the Nordics have entered virtuous circles where various factors reinforce each other to make them among the most competitive economies in the world". He also noted, " .highly trained labor forces, in turn, adopt new technologies with enthusiasm, or, as happens often in the Nordics, are themselves in the forefront of technological innovations . Other developed countries must be wondering what this intra-regional dissection, which seems like an emerging balkanization of existing alliances, as most of the region s members are already in or slated to join the European Union, or have some affiliation with it, portends, and whether it was not time to revisit their Health ICT policies.

Problems with the macroeconomic milieu of the U.S are at variance with its

technological prowess and compromising its global competitiveness, in particular, its fiscal deficit in 2005 of over 4% of its GDP for the fourth year in a row, according to the International Monetary Fund (IMF), with minor fiscal adjustments expected through 2010; and its worsening public finances. ICT could remedy both problems, the latter directly via reducing health spending for example, and the former, indirectly via among other measures, institutional reforms. In the Health sector, the reforms including for examples elements such as the Health Insurance Portability and Accountability Act (HIPAA), the Medicare Prescription Drug, Improvement and Modernization Act (MMA), and the Sarbanes-Oxley Act, compliance with all of which requires significant but cost-saving ICT implementation. Such laws will likely ultimately make health care more affordable, prescription drug coverage universal and the choice of health plans less restricted. They will also likely improve access to healthcare particularly for rural folks, and the overall health of the peoples, and they have the potential to enhance productivity, foster job creation, and enhance the country s competitiveness. These benefits are immediately obvious with the MMA, but also hold true for the HIPAA, and the Sarbanes-Oxley Act. In the former, by protecting health insurance coverage for workers, and their families in case of job change or loss, and by facilitating ICT use, improve the efficiency and effectiveness of the health system, and in the latter, by fostering good governance, and discouraging fraud. The macroeconomic picture of Canada differs from that of the U.S., as it does that of the U.K, or any other developed country for that matter. Yet in none of these countries is the effective deployment of Health ICT unlikely to improve healthcare delivery, the health of its peoples, and its competitive edge, at the same time containing health spending, and freeing scarce resources for funding other sectors of the nation's economy. Further, Canada or any country that hopes to remain competitive in the global economy also needs institutional reforms, particularly in the health sector, on which many of the developed countries spend a sizeable percentage of their resources, with these health expenditures, rising yearly. Whether they run a public, or private, or hybrid health system, regardless, making health ICT diffusion integral to their health reforms, hence moving e-Health forward, for example through such legislation as those in the U.S. mentioned earlier, will not only improve health delivery, but help contain their health costs. For example corruption, what some term the unofficial economy, including bribery, money laundering, exists globally, and costs the world an estimated at US$1 to US$1.5 trillion annually. Both the public and private sectors are responsible for stamping out corruption and laws such as the Sarbanes-Oxley Act could help foster good governance, and ethical practices, and curb corruption. Further, research has shown that eliminating corruption increases prosperity, accelerates economic growth, and contains costs. By encouraging fiscal transparency, public disclosures of accounting practices, and other positive rather than negative measures, such laws increase the prospects of achieving the objective of reducing the levels of corruption, and not creating opportunities for even more. It is unlikely that anyone would dismiss the benefits derivable from such laws and of the reforms that they aim to accomplish. Indeed, ICT could help minimize corruption, and enhance a country s competitiveness in many other ways. For example, two recent reports showed that governments could use a national health information network and electronic health records to combat healthcare fraud, which costs the U.S. government between $51 billion and $170 billion annually. Commissioned by the Office of the National Coordinator for Health Information Technology, and the Department of Health and Human Services (HHS), the reports examined how automated coding software, and a nationwide interoperable health IT infrastructure, could help detect and prevent healthcare fraud. The reports looked into such frauds as false reporting of diagnoses or procedures to boost physicians fees, bogus diagnoses and billing for services and "ghost' patients, among others. The task force of providers, payers, IT vendors, and government heads that wrote the reports recommended some guiding principles on fighting fraud with IT. They include establishing a Nationwide Health Information Network (NHIN) to "proactively prevent, detect and reduce healthcare fraud rather than be neutral to it". It also recommended that electronic health records (EHR), and information obtainable via the NHIN should fully conform with federal and state laws and the criteria for reliability and admissibility of evidence, and the need for a standardized definition of a legal health record for EHR. Researchers have also developed an economic impact model that could provide a framework for tracking fraud and non-fraud related costs, the benefits of interoperable EHR, and a nationwide infrastructure for exchanging them. In an increasingly diverse and global economic milieu, the overrepresentation of economic discourses belies the significant health problems different parts of the world face, some truly global in nature, even if specific health problems have local flavors. Health authorities in the U.K conducted pathological examinations on a parrot that not long ago died in quarantine at the Heathrow airport to determine if the much-feared Avian Influenza A (H5N1) Virus caused its death. Even then, none of them was likely thinking that the virus would not travel eventually to the U.K, which examination on dead birds found on Scottish beaches later confirmed it did, as it has now to North America. Avian flu or any other "pandemic" aside, there is the problem of meeting the health needs of the increasing seniors' population living not just in the developed but also in developing countries, a quarter of world s expected to live in China alone in about two decades. With purchasing power parities (PPP) adjusted exchange-rate-based GDP per capita, a reliable measure of living standards low, projected per capita income remaining low, and pension schemes rudimentary and yearning for reform in many developing countries, their competitiveness pale in significance to the enormity of the health problems they struggle to tackle. Nonetheless, these countries also need and many are implementing the basic health ICT suited to their needs and which their limited infrastructures can support, and in many instances getting encouraging results. No country, developed or developing, has anything to lose by implementing Health ICT. On the contrary, enhancing competitiveness, hence comparative advantage, improving governance, eliminating corruption, containing health spending, improving healthcare delivery and the overall health of its citizenry are indubitable benefits any country derives by so doing. The benefits of widespread healthcare ICT diffusion are indeed legion. We will be examining these various benefits, not only to the individual healthcare consumer, but also to governments, private enterprises, and indeed, to countries, in this e-book. We will be looking at the various issues involved in facilitating this diffusion, and those that hinder it. There is little doubt that without the widespread implementation of these technologies among a variety of healthcare stakeholders, our objectives of delivering qualitative health services at affordable costs, which a national e-Health program could help achieve, would simply come to naught. Our exploration of these various issues in this e-book will no doubt reassure us that moving our e-Health dream forward is a doable proposition.

Prospects and Challenges of a National Health Information Network

The US Veterans Affairs Secretary, Jim Nicholson recently called the Veterans Affairs

Health System "a model for our nation". In a "state of the VA "speech on March 27, 2006, he cited the use of electronic medical records (EMR), an important component of a national health information network (NHIN), as one of the reasons for the success of the VA health care system. Specifically, the Secretary noted that EMR enabled doctors and nurses to obtain health records and treat uninterrupted patients transferred from VA facilities in New Orleans to those in Houston, during Hurricane Katrina. A survey taken of evacuees in Houston after Katrina showed that 50% had no health insurance; 41% reported suffering from chronic conditions, such as heart disease, hypertension, asthma, diabetes, and cancer. With New Orleans large state-run hospitals, Charity and University, shut down since the storm, private clinics lost to flooding, evacuees swamped the few facilities still operating. At one point, visits to outpatient clinics at Baton Rouge s Earl K. Long Medical Center skyrocketed 50%, from 8,000 patients a month to over 12,000. Many individuals could not receive needed care due to shortages of hospital beds, staff, and drugs, but most crucially, because doctors could not access their paper-based health records the floods had washed away, information therein for examples, medications, and their dosages, and lab records, among others, many could not remember. Could this have happened had the health facilities the storm destroyed that had these records, like the VA hospitals, implemented electronic medical records? Even the cell phone would help avert in future, the sorts of problems with healthcare delivery encountered post-Katrina. Indeed, the cell phone will play an increasingly important role in healthcare delivery in general not just in the U.S but also worldwide. Cell phones are now able to monitor heart and respiration rates, detect blood alcohol, and glucose levels, and to analyze ECG patterns and transmit the information to a call center. Besides making calls, people will be carrying cell phones around in future for other reasons, including watching their favorite TV programs and monitoring their health. With cell phones already commonplace even in many developing countries, its potential to deliver targeted health information and to perform other health-related functions is immense. The increasing convergence of cell phone and other applications will not only create opportunities to improve workflow processes in the health domain, but also facilitate the utilization of wireless technology convergence. Doctors and authorized healthcare professionals for example will be able to gain access to patient health records at any point of care (POC), on their way home, at home, and wherever they need to know what is happening to their patients. This will no doubt improve patient care, reduce medical errors rates by making accurate and timely information available, and has the potential to save many lives, and healthcare costs. The technologies that could constitute an electronic health record (EHR) system are as varied as they could be numerous, the essential thing being to establish a communication link via which health information sharing and communication could take place. The cell phone, for example, will in future be an excellent storage medium for personal health records (PHR), access to which individuals could authorize doctors and other healthcare professionals, including via voice-activated technologies, and even biometrically in the event that the individual from Miami has lost consciousness say on a vacation in Las Vegas. It could also be invaluable for the delivery of targeted health information, to high-risk individuals, subscribers, and to all, who also need to know about important new medical knowledge that people could find useful in helping themselves and others understand health issues and take the necessary actions. Obsessive-compulsive disorders, for example, is a major source of distress for those that suffer from the condition and those around them, including family, friends, even colleagues at work. Some people have intrusive thoughts they want to rid themselves of but cannot, or embarrassing hand washing and other rituals, and some hoard almost everything ending up with little room even to move around at home, and even sleeping in the verandah sometimes due to lack of space, their children, perhaps as young as twelve years having to leave home. Scientists at the National Institutes of Health's (NIH) National Institute on Alcohol Abuse and Alcoholism (NIAAA) have identified a hitherto unknown gene variant that increases someone's risk for obsessive-compulsive disorder (OCD) twofold; the findings expected

for publication in the May 2006 issue of the American Journal of Human Genetics. The new functional variant, or allele, is a part of the serotonin transporter gene ("SERT"), site of action for the selective serotonin reuptake inhibitors (SSRIs) commonly used to treat OCD, other anxiety disorders, and depression. According to Dr. Ting-Kai Li, Director, National Institute on Alcohol Abuse and Alcoholism, "Improved knowledge of "SERT s" role in OCD raises the possibility of improved screening, treatment, and medications development for that disorder . . It also provides an important clue to the neurobiologic basis of OCD and the compulsive behaviors often seen in other psychiatric diseases, including alcohol dependence. Would new medical knowledge such as this not benefit some people targeting it at them? About 2% of U.S. adults (3.3 million people) have OCD. The condition is the fourth most prevalent mental health disorder, in the U.S. These findings could offer hope, and potential treatment options for patients with this condition and could it not facilitate screening and early diagnosis, which might improve treatment outcome? How much could the country save in human and material terms of the benefits overall of these findings reaching those who need them and their healthcare providers? The researchers, who discovered the linkage aided by new functional analyses of the "SERT" genetic variant, found that the OCD patients were twice as likely to have the variant on comparing the genotypes of 169 OCD patients to those of 253 controls in a large U.S. patient population. They also studied the transmission and non-transmission of the variant in a Canadian population of 175 OCD parent-child trios (two healthy parents and a child with OCD). In this phase of their study, they also found twice-likely risk variant transmission from parent to child with OCD, specifically, of 86 informative trios, 48 and 26 children had and lacked the new risk variant, respectively. Says Dr. Goldman, "Whereas most genetic diseases are caused by variations that lead to reduced gene function, we found that a common "SERT" variant that increases "SERT" activity also increases risk for OCD". The location of the new variant is a well-known site of the "SERT" gene, also known as HTTLPR, known to have two variants, S and L that change how "SERT" manifests, loss-of-function of the former resulting in minimal effects on someone's risk for anxiety, depression, and suicidality, particularly in response to environmental stressors. The S allele causes a more significant effect on the intermediate neurobiology of anxiety and depression, namely, by disrupting the structure and functional coupling of key brain regions. Contrariwise, gain-of-function of the L allele, increases "SERT" activity and functional coupling, and seem to inhibit links between emotion and repetitive behaviors and such executive brain functions as task switching. There is likely to be convergence of technologies to explore further, such genetic variations, and their interactions with the environment, including technologies for genomics and proteomics, and other technologies for example, sensor technologies, and the information emerging thereof proper constituents of future electronic health record systems. The applications of sensor technology in healthcare delivery, for examples in readily tracking and monitoring patients and their health parameters, fed into and shared in electronic health records, could likely lead to the accumulation of a mass of valuable data and information over time, whose judicious use could benefit healthcare delivery immensely. Experts are already examining the possibilities of integrating sensor networks with data mining, facilitating more in-depth understanding of health information, including revealing the early warning signs of disease epidemic.

Indeed, the convergence of wireless technologies will help speedier information sharing

and communication, including text messaging of lab results to patients, and facilitating treatment of their conditions, appointment scheduling, and billing, reading medical journals, contacting clinical trial participants, and tracking hospital beds and wait lists, among others, all with potential costs savings. Cell phones will make it easier to manage the elderly at home, monitoring whose health parameters constitute a crucial aspect of such domiciliary care. They will also help in managing chronic diseases and enable individuals to participate in fitness and wellness programs from any location. The concept of electronic health records (EHR) systems is not new, nor are the benefits of implementing these technologies unknown, yet their acceptance appears slow in coming, the health industry by experts estimates lagging behind other information-intensive industries such as the banking industry by at least a decade. Take ambulatory care for example. A Retrospective, serial, cross sectional study, conducted at Colorado and Northwest regions of Kaiser Permanente, a US integrated healthcare delivery system, and published in the March12, 2005 issue of the British Medical Journal set out to evaluate the effect of implementing comprehensive, integrated EHR systems on use and quality of ambulatory care2. The researchers used total number of office visits and use of primary

care, specialty care, clinical laboratory, radiology services, and telephone contact as the main outcome measures and Health Plan Employer Data and Information Set to assess quality. The researchers found that two years after full implementation of EHR, age adjusted rates of office visits and age adjusted primary care visits decreased by 9% and 11% respectively, in both regions, and specialty care visits fell by 5% and 6% in Colorado and in the Northwest regions, respectively, all decreases statistically significant. The percentage of members making $\geq$ 3 visits a year fell by 10% and 11% in Colorado and in the Northwest, and the percentage of members with $\leq$ 2 visits a year rose. In the Northwest, scheduled telephone contact also rose from a baseline of 1.26 per member per year to 2.09 after two years, although the utilization of clinical laboratory and radiology services remained essentially unchanged, as did intermediate measures of quality of healthcare. The researchers concluded, "Readily available, comprehensive, integrated clinical information reduced use of ambulatory care while maintaining quality and allowed doctors to replace some office visits with telephone contacts". They also noted that changing usage patterns indicate lesser inappropriate or marginally productive, ambulatory care visits. Are these findings also not likely to yield healthcare cost savings? Let us examine another study on the benefits of electronic health/medical records[3]. Osteoporosis causes high morbidity and mortality[4], its burden in human and societal expected to rise with the population aging. Furthermore, older women with a history of fractures are at higher risks for future fractures[5], hence to who targeting, via health information for example, or any other

appropriate approach, fracture prevention education, would clearly be cost-effective. According to current clinical guidelines, older women who have had fractures should take calcium and vitamin D supplements, and indeed, pharmacological treatment with for examples, bisphosphonates alendronate and risedronate, estrogen, raloxifene, calcitonin, and teriparatide, all Food and Drug Administration (FDA) approved, if osteoporosis is apparent. Otherwise, they should have bone mineral density (BMD) measurement followed by treatment based on the BMD[6]. Despite these recommendations, research showed that less than 50% of these women had osteoporosis treatment or BMD measurement[7]. What might this state of affairs portend for the health of the women, and

the burden of care on their families and on healthcare costs, all of which following the guidelines might have prevented? How could we reverse this situation, particularly as the management of osteoporosis after a fracture became the basis of a Health Plan Employer Data and Information Set quality-of-care measure recently, and will likely interest clinicians and health-care managers more with times[8]? Researchers recently assessed

methods to increase guideline-recommended osteoporosis care post-fracture. The study, conducted at a Pacific Northwest nonprofit health maintenance organization involved 311female patients aged 50 to 89 who suffered a fracture in 1999 and did not receive bone mineral density (BMD) measurement or medication for osteoporosis, and their primary care providers, 159 of them. The researchers sent patient-specific clinical guideline advice via electronic medical record (EMR) message or electronic reminder to the providers, and an educational letter mailed to each patient. They assigned participants randomly to usual care or one of two interventions. The researchers found that provider reminder led to 51.5% of patients receiving BMD measurement or osteoporosis medication, at six months, provider reminder plus patient education, 43.1%, and usual care, 5.9%, during the same period, all statistically significant. There was no statistically significant difference between the effect of provider advice plus patient education versus provider advice alone, and patients aged 60 to 69 were 18% likelier to receive BMD measurement or an osteoporosis medication than those aged 80 to 89. The study not only supports the value of targeted health information, be it to patient or provider, in this case that patient-specific post-fracture advice to the provider through an EMR message significantly increased BMD measurement and osteoporosis medication. With more EMR adoption by healthcare providers, this intercession no doubt would help improve osteoporosis management for many post- fracture patients, and other high-risk groups, with significant reduction in healthcare costs in addition to enhancing the quality of life of these elderly women and others at risk for osteoporosis. The above examples are just a few of the documented benefits of EHR/ EMR. Considering these benefits, why would few U.S. residents want to pay more for higher-quality healthcare as a recent Harris Interactive poll reported in the March 28, 2006 issue of Wall Street Journal Online, revealed? According to the online poll, to which 2,123 adults responded, 33% and 13% support and oppose, respectively, higher reimbursements from health insurers for hospitals and medical groups that provide higher-quality care, with 54% of respondents, undecided. On the other hand, 55% of respondents would not pay significantly higher health insurance premiums for higher-quality care, which requirement, 57% in fact said is unfair. Could it be that more information needs to reach the public on the mechanics of cost sharing in the health system, and on the roles of healthcare ICT, for example, in eventually bringing down health insurance premiums with the user rationalization that the wider diffusion and more appropriate applications of healthcare ICT would engender? Does this not again speak for the need for targeted information on all aspects of healthcare delivery? Is the seemingly continuing information asymmetry that the public still endures not one of the significant challenges to pursue and overcome were EHR implementation to succeed? The findings of a recent study published in March 30, 2006 issue of the new England Journal of Medicine₉ that compared the claims patterns of seven Federal Employees Health Benefits (FEHB) plans from 1999 through 2002 matched with control health plans that did not have benefits equivalence with mental health and substance-abuse benefits via a difference-in-differences analysis are instructive. The idea of the FEHB Program was to ensure the parity of mental health and substance abuse benefits with general medical benefits to improve insure coverage for the former, starting in January 2001 the plans geared to manage care. The researchers examined the rate of use, total spending, and out-of-pocket spending among users of mental health and substance abuse services. This study found that health insurance plans that offer mental health and substance abuse coverage are not only not any more costly than less comprehensive plans, but that of the seven plans examined, only one, the one that did not use managed care to try to control how often subscribers used the benefits, was actually costlier than conventional plans. According to Howard Goldman, a professor of psychiatry at the University of Maryland and the study's main author, the findings indicate the possibility of offering mental illness and substance abuse in a package covering physical illnesses "without any adverse impact on cost and quality". Indeed, the researchers found an association between the implementation of the parity policy and significant reductions in out-of-pocket spending in five of seven plans, and concluded that when tied with management of care, implementation of parity in insurance benefits for behavioral health care can improve insurance protection without increasing total costs. Now, besides Medicare, and private health insurers, most of which still limit coverage for mental health services, should the public not have this information? Would insurers continue their reluctance to pay for mental health problems, which incidentally cause substantial health burdens for families and society, on the excuse that they are difficult and costly to treat having this information? Is there something about managed care responsible for these findings, for example, the rationalization of service utilization via the appropriate use of health information systems such as electronic health records systems? Would it in fact therefore be necessary in the long term for people to pay more for higher quality services, were the appropriate information technologies deployed within a technology-backed management milieu, both of which could help cut costs? Does this not in fact speak to the increasing need for more widespread adoption of not just electronic medical records (EMR), and personal health records (PHR) but of payer-based health records (PBHR), and their eventual integration? Such integration, which would require multi-level authentication protocols, strict rules of engagement, standardized interoperability, and high levels of security, would bring together a wealth of clinical, claims, demographic, public health, laboratory, even health surveillance data. With such sophisticated data mining technologies, such data could reveal important information that would be useful to government, to improve healthcare delivery and reduce healthcare costs, and to the health and insurance industries, for example to reduce medical errors, and to improve premium pricing and claims management, among other healthcare stakeholders.

Countries such as the U.S. Canada and the U.K. are investing heavily in their national health information networks. President Bush on February 6, 2006 presented to Congress, his $2.8 trillion budget proposal for FY2007, with plans to purge or considerably shrink over a hundred federal programs, but two years prior, he announced an initiative that by 2014 will make EHRs accessible to most Americans. The Office of the National Coordinator for Health Information Technology (ONC) essentially oversees the government s healthcare ICT plans, with numerous projects already launched and others in the offing. Standards, interoperability, privacy, and security issues are some of the most pressing concerns of government funded via ONC, which would receive $116 million in FY2007, up by $55 million. For the same year, the President plans to develop national standards for speedier patient access to EHRs, and the portability of health information data, developing prototypes for National Health Information Networks, and the architecture for PHRs, are among major healthcare ICT projects for which the president has requested $169 million, $58 million more, in FY2007. The federal government also plans to give Centers for Disease Control and Prevention (CDC) $102 million including to broaden the scope of its near real-time disease surveillance technologies, to reach more users, and $109 for public health informatics to standardize and facilitate data and information communication and sharing between reporting and surveillance systems, hence prompt response to disease outbreaks. The Agency for Healthcare Research and Quality (AHRQ) will receive $50 million to promote healthcare ICT diffusion and patient safety including the of cutting-edge reporting systems technologies, computerized physician order entry (CPOE) and decision support systems (DSS.) Importantly, AHRQ will earmark $29 million for the Ambulatory Patient Safety Program, plus $6 million for general patient safety. This is particularly significant as the country's health system places increasing emphasis on ambulatory and domiciliary care, both of which would require significant healthcare ICT deployment for their success. The President's budget proposal acknowledges the ongoing commitments of the Indian Health Service (IHS) to implement new healthcare ICT, thereby facilitating patients' accessibility to health records and to track and streamline insurance billing processes, full implementation of IHS s EHR system in all its facilities expected in 2008. In FY 2007, an allocation of over $11 million for HIS implementation of its Unified Financial Management System (UFMS), will allow "IHS facilities to operate in a more business-like manner and improve their collection of health insurance." This aspect of health information systems is just as crucial to reducing the overall healthcare costs of the U.S. as the more clinical health information systems, both systems integral aspects of a national health information network. The Pittsburgh Tribune Review on March 23, 2006, for example, reported a PNC-funded survey of 150 hospital, insurance, and health system executives that found that 50% of U.S hospital executives indicate that they could save up to $10 million annually, and cut patients costs were more insurance claims handled electronically. Although electronic fund transfers are not new, only about a 30% of U.S. insurance companies utilize them, most preferring to pay hospitals by check, according to PNC Financial Services Group Inc. representative Paula Fryland, who also lamented the small number of hospitals that have synchronized their payment systems with those of their insurers. A study published in Health Affairs in February noting that Americans spent $571 billion on hospital care in 2004, and with only 50% of health insurers processing and 30% paying hospital bills electronically, there is no doubt that more widespread synchronization would help reduce the administrative costs of healthcare delivery in the country, and in effect overall healthcare costs. In his FY2007 budget plans, the President also gave the Health Resources and Services Administration (HRSA)'s Telehealth program $7 million, and the Food and Drug Administration FDA, $272 million, $11 million more than the previous year, to support patient safety and effectiveness of medical devices. These figures show that the U.S government is not only investing substantially on its national health information networks, but on healthcare ICT in general, and not just on the technologies, but also on such issues crucial to the smooth running of an integrated health information system in the country such as standardization, certification, patient safety and security. These are all issues that also have technical, legal, ethical, and costs underpinning, important considerations in enhancing the prospects of implementing national health information networks, and the challenges they face in a variety of domains. One of the key benefits of electronic health records is in preventing medical errors and adverse events, by making accurate and timely information available to healthcare providers at the point of care (POC). The U.S. Institute of Medicine (IOM) report in November 29, 1999, "To Err Is Human: Building a Safer Health System," revealed the extent of the problem of medication errors in the U.S, and sparked a keen interest on the subject among the public, healthcare professionals, and policy makers, among others[10]. Interest in this matter, with estimated mortality due to hospital-related

medical errors in the U.S between 44,000 to 98,000 per year, many of which were preventable, led to a research project sponsored by the Canadian Institute for Health Information (CIHI) and the Canadian Institute of health Research (CIHR). Conducted by Ross baker and Peter Norton in 2004, to estimate hospital-based adverse events in Canada, their findings showed that 1 in 13 adult patients admitted to acute care hospitals in Canada in fiscal year 2000 experienced adverse events, reigniting interest in patient safety. A month later, another CIHI report, Health Care in Canada 2004, provided additional information on how often different types of events, ranging from medication errors to hip fractures in hospital, occur in the country and relative to other countries[11]. Indeed, CIHI is

collaborating with *Safer Healthcare Now!* (SHN), a pan-Canadian grassroots patient-safety campaign, launched in April 2005, in response to the challenge medical errors pose, with a focus on six proven strategies, aimed at achieving measurable reductions in unnecessary morbidity and mortality[12]. The effectiveness of these targeted interventions in patient care

based on research evidence that showed that their appropriate implementation and practice could result in reduced mortality and morbidity, no doubt requires substantial healthcare ICT input. Consider the first, namely improved care for Myocardial Infarction (AMI), for example, which requires the immediate administration of medications including Aspirin, and a thrombolytic agent within thirty minutes, of patient arrival in the ER. Would it not be useful for the ER doctor to have prompt and accurate information on the patient's medication history, including drug-drug interactions, some of which could potentially be fatal, particularly as the patient might not be able to give history, being unconscious or in excruciating pain? Indeed, another of the interventions is MedRec, which aims to prevent adverse drug events (ADEs) by implementing medication reconciliation, which again underscores the need for the health information communication and sharing the EHR, and other aspects of a national health information network would facilitate. Canada also recently witnessed the launching of the Canadian Obesity Network with an initial $800,000 federal government investment over two years under the Networks of Centers of Excellence program. With Canada experiencing a growing epidemic of overweight/ obesity affecting 18 million people, and costing the Canadian health care system in excess of $4.3 billion per year, this indeed, is a welcome initiative. However, there is no doubt again, that such a program requires significant healthcare ICT involvement, in particular that of electronic health records (EHR) within the framework of a national health information network, for the success of its overweight/ obesity prevention research collaboration and public education and other initiatives, which would help reduce the health and economic burden of these conditions[13]. A national health information network would be a veritable conduit for the

dissemination of general and targeted health information, for example that of new research findings on the benefits of reducing cholesterol levels earlier in life protecting against later heart disease. New research from UT Southwestern Medical Center shows that lowering "bad" blood cholesterol earlier in life, even modestly, significantly protects someone from coronary heart disease. The research, published in the March 23, 2006 issue of The New England Journal of Medicine, found that individuals with genetic variations, found in a recently discovered gene termed, PCSK9 that make them have lower low-density lipoprotein (LDL) cholesterol in their blood from birth stood less chances of developing coronary heart disease later in life than those lacking the variations[14]. The

researchers tracked over 12,000 multiethnic subjects aged between 45years and 64years for 15 years. They found that individuals with cholesterol-lowering genetic variations that reduced their LDL level by about 40 mm/ dL had eight times less chances, and by about 20 mg/ dL from average, a two-fold chance reduction, to develop coronary heart disease than those without the mutations. According to Dr Helen Hobbs, senior author of the study, and director of the Eugene McDermott Center for Human Growth and Development, "These data indicate that a moderate, life-long reduction in LDL cholesterol is associated with substantial reduction in the incidence of coronary events, even in populations with a high prevalence of other cardiovascular risk factors." Dr. Hobbs and colleagues at UT Southwestern had previously identified specific mutations in the gene called PCSK9 linked with lower LDL cholesterol levels in individuals with the mutations. There is also no doubt that the present study underscores the benefits of maintaining a low cholesterol level throughout life, including ensuring one takes less of saturated fats and cholesterol and maintains a desirable body weight, and in high-risk individuals, the additional use of cholesterol-reducing medications such as the statins. Is it not important for the public and in particular, individuals at high risk for developing coronary heart diseases (CHD) to have this information, which means, not to have to seek it, which many might not do, but delivering it to them via the national health information network and its components? Could such an endeavor not save substantially in human and material terms? Prior research had indicated that individuals with a high level of LDL cholesterol in their blood are at increased risk of developing CHD, risk which this study suggest is preventable via life-long reductions in LDL cholesterol could significantly lessen. Does this not suggest the need for targeted health information on this subject to children and adolescents too? Would this not be nurturing a healthier future adult population, which would help reduce future healthcare costs? Would investing in a national health information network not facilitate such targeted health information dissemination? The PCSK9 gene produces an enzyme that controls the number of LDL receptors that line the surface of liver cells, receptors that attach to LDL and remove it from the blood, hence genetic mutations that inactivate PCSK9 resulting in lower levels of the enzyme, and in turn, increased levels of LDL receptors. This means that the liver is able to remove more LDL, hence lower its blood levels in individuals with the mutations. Contrariwise, the higher the PCSK9 levels, which incidentally statins, currently used to lower LDL blood levels may cause via increasing the levels of the PCSK9 enzyme minimizing the effectiveness of these drugs, the higher the blood LDL levels. A different approach to not only reducing LDL levels but also increase the efficacy of statins is to develop new medications able to inhibit PCSK9. Coronary heart disease is a major cause of mortality, particularly in the developed world, and increasingly in other parts of the world. This study offers a chance to reduce the prevalence of this condition, and reduce its health and economic burden, and the use of healthcare ICT, via the numerous technologies associated with a national health information network, offers immense opportunities for ensuring that important information such as that evident in this research as a cost-effective approach to achieve this critical goal.

Mobile and wireless networks, for example, are offering many opportunities for healthcare service provision, in particular with the emergence of a new generation of mobile ehealth services, for example, applications such as SMS (text message) patient reminders, which could be useful for appointment and medication reminders. Patients failing to keep appointments could have a significant economic impact on service provision, escalating costs. A national health information network would facilitate automated mobile communications between healthcare provider and patients, and could streamline communication and information sharing among a healthcare provider team, including for example the social services department. This could help with care planning and with coordinating care and ensuring compliance to treatment, which would improve the chances of disease outcome. Other applications such as diet analysis, vital signs monitoring, blood sugar monitoring, alcohol breath analyzer, and capsule endoscopy would gain increasing currency in healthcare provision, creating immense business opportunities for healthcare software and ICT vendors. A national health information network would be crucial to the evolution of the network of healthcare services that will characterize future service delivery. This is more so with the shift in healthcare delivery emphasis toward ambulatory and domiciliary care as more diseases become preventable via healthcare ICT-backed initiatives, overall also helping to reduce healthcare costs. Could such prevention for example not help avert the sort of problems General Motors and Ford Motor Co. currently face regarding health benefits to their workers and retirees, problems that have led to massive lay-offs of workers, with palpable consequences for not only the welfare of these workers and retirees but also those of their dependents? Could such lay-offs not further make access to healthcare inequitable, and even worsen the nation's overall financial and economic health? GM, which is the world s largest private provider of healthcare, won a federal judge's approval to go on with $1 billion reductions to retirees benefits in a March 31, 2006 ruling by U.S. District Judge Robert Cleland in Detroit. The ruling followed the Judge s preliminary approval on Dec. 22, 2005. GM and its largest union, the United Auto Workers (UAW) reached an agreement earlier in

October 2005, in a bid to reduce the firm s health-care spending, an agreement that apparently also resolved an earlier lawsuit the UAW filed against GM's planned cuts in retirees benefits. The UAW and Ford Motor Co., agreed to a similar plan on Dec. 10, 2005 to save Ford healthcare costs. The approval GM received in the courts essentially means that over 475,000 GM retirees and their dependents will have to pay part of their health insurance premiums for the first time, up to $752 per family annually. GM wants to reduce its healthcare costs on its 1.1 million active and retired employers and dependents by as much as $7 billion annually, as part of its remedy for recent posted losses, $10.6 billion in 2005. An important aspect of cost sharing in healthcare provision is that the healthcare consumer likely be more discerning in his/ her choices of health services utilization. Consumers would likely prefer a competent over an incompetent healthcare provider, would not encourage or condone "defensive Medicine" in which healthcare providers order unnecessary lab tests and expensive CT scans and MRI's for wrist sprains, for examples, because the are paid "fee-for-service" and/ or want to avoid malpractice suits, as some contend. The discerning healthcare consumer would also want to be actively involved in his/ her care management, including knowing all about the diagnosis, treatment options, and possible outcomes of the illness that he/ she needs to know. Such knowledge would empower the healthcare consumer who is then able to make rational, evidence-backed choices. However, would the consumer be able to do this lacking information? Does this not speak to the importance of targeted and indeed, general health information provision to the public, and of course healthcare providers, and other healthcare stakeholders? Would a national health information network not be an invaluable resource in these information-dissemination efforts between healthcare providers and consumers for example? With the consumer equipped with accurate and current information, would healthcare providers and suppliers not have to ensure that they provide higher quality services? Would the ensuing competition not modulate prices, and make healthcare more affordable, and hence accessible, to for examples, retirees, and indeed, everyone else? Coupled with increased Health Savings Accounts (HSA) for example, and less regulation of the healthcare and insurance industries, would the healthcare consumer not be even better able to afford their choices of healthcare providers and insurers? The merits and demerits of a free-market approach to healthcare provision is a subject debated in many countries, including the U.S, where some actually advocate "socialized medicine" as the solution to the country's healthcare woes. Others, for example, Christopher J. Conover, an assistant research professor with the Center for Health Policy, Law and Management in the Terry Sanford Institute of Public Policy at Duke University, even contest aspects of free-market healthcare provision such as overly regulating it. According to the professor, in a policy analysis article, titled, "Healthcare Regulation: A $169 Billion Hidden Tax" published by the CATO Institute on October 24, 2004, a "top-down" approach, puts a "back-of-the-envelope" annual estimate of health services regulation at $256 billion, with a range of $28 billion to $657 billion), hence could increase overall regulatory costs by over 25%. A more accurate "bottom-up" approach puts the estimates at over $339.2 billion, including regulation costs of health facilities, health professionals, health insurance, drugs and medical devices, and the medical tort system, and of "defensive medicine". Moreover, this approach allows for a calculation of some important tangible benefits of regulation15. The professor concluded that even after subtracting $170.1 billion in benefits, the net burden of health services regulation was still $169.1 billion per year, outweighing benefits by two-to-one and costing the average U.S household more than $1,500 annually. Given this background, and with U.S. Federal spending having increased 45% in the last five years, healthcare costs are soaring, the population is graying with expected even higher healthcare and other welfare programs' costs, is it any wonder that many are calling for government to be more frugal, including capping not just discretionary but entitlement spending? Entitlements account for over half the federal budget. Given that they are, for example, Medicare, guzzling federal funds, and creating what seems like a looming, if not already a crisis situation, would investing in a national health information network and the required technologies to make it work effectively and efficiently not be one important way to help reduce these healthcare costs considering its benefits some discussed above? Canada's Advisory Council on Health Infostructure identified the electronic health record (EHR) to be of fundamental import to the patient-centered healthcare delivery approach in an integrated health care delivery system hence the EHR is has top priority for Health Canada as a major aspect of a Canadian health infostructure. Indeed, the Canada Government has been investing in EHR and other e-Health initiatives since the 1997 Federal Budget, including federal pledges towards First Ministers Agreements (September 2000 and 2003). The country is actively promoting the use of electronic health records, within the context of a national health information network via various initiatives sponsored by Canada Health Infoway. EHR plays significant roles in health information communication and sharing, continuing medical education, and public health education and awareness campaigns, and increasingly deployed in hospital, primary care and home care settings, will likely play even greater roles in healthcare delivery in the country. The renewed emphasis on population health for example, suggests greater efforts on disease prevention, and health promotion. Greater emphasis on ambulatory and domiciliary care would involve more remote consultations that telehealth would facilitate, increased home monitoring of chronic conditions such as diabetes and asthma and renal dialysis monitoring. These shifts in direction of healthcare delivery would require substantial investments in healthcare ICT, including a national health information network, but would not only make healthcare delivery more accessible, yet qualitative, but also delivered more cost-effectively, which would help reduce the country s increasing healthcare costs, which many consider unsustainable. Recent five-year trends, for example, indicate that the country s Medicare will consume over 50% of total revenues from all sources in most of the provinces and territories by 2022, about 70% of their total revenues in 2032, eventually 100% by 2050, according to Paying More, Getting Less 2005, released today by The Fraser Institute on October 31, 2005. . Five, eight, and 30-year trends all indicate that health spending has been growing faster on average than total revenue in all provinces, also outpacing inflation and economic growth. The end-result of this disparity is that health care is taking up an increasing share of provincial revenues over time[16]. According to the report, five, eight, and 30-year trends all show health

spending that is growing faster on average than total revenue in all provinces, and outpacing inflation and economic growth. The likely consequence of this development is to make healthcare increasingly unaffordable to the government a situation that likely increased healthcare costs that the country s aging population will engender would likely worsen. Rather than face stark options such as spending less on other public priorities as healthcare costs wallop an increasing share of available revenues annually, or raise taxes, or further limit access to medical services, should the governments, provincial and territorial, not investment more in and develop healthcare ICT relevant to their needs? Should they not invest more efforts and resources to building their regional health information networks and harmonize them to a national network? Considering the cost-saving benefits of these measures, would they not prevent the need to restrict access to health services, which could prolong illnesses, and further increase service utilization, hence further increase health spending? One cannot in fact, gainsay the importance of healthcare ICT, including a national health information network, as the example of the suicide problem in Northern Ireland shows. Health Minister, Shaun Woodward recently announced, according to a March 30, 2006 BBC report that the government will spend over £4m tackling suicide in Northern Ireland over the next two years. According to Northern Ireland s General Registrar s Office, suicide rates increased 50% in 2005. Indeed, the government is refocusing on improving its entire mental health services. Mr. Woodward launched a government, suicide prevention strategy on March 30, 2006, entitled "Protect Life', costing almost £2m, a further £2.4m earmarked for the government s suicide prevention strategy for 2007/ 08. Experts insist that part of the reason for the increased suicide rates, particularly in some of the most deprived parts of Northern Ireland, was that young people were waiting up to three months to see a counselor. Could healthcare ICT not play a role in educating youths and others on depression, its manifestations, and what to do in suspected cases? Could such counseling the youngsters had to await for so long not occur via healthcare ICT-backed programs, for examples, via the telephone, or VoIP, particularly with evidence suggesting the effectiveness of such approaches as telephone cognitive behavioral therapies (t-CBT), an important treatment modality for depression? Could depressed youths that might be apprehensive revealing their identities due to the shame of sexual abuse for example, receive help anonymously via healthcare ICT-based programs within a national health information network (NHIN)? Part of government initiative is to involve the British Medical Association (BMA) in the development of a depression-awareness training program for GPs. Could such training programs occur without interfering significantly with the routines of the general practitioners, with a NHIN in place. Would this perhaps not save many patients the trouble of cancelled or delayed appointments with their GPs, who had to leave his/ her office to attend such training programs? Would this not save costs for the GP, the patient, and government someway in the end, and is this not an example of the potential versatility of such a network? Also in the U.K, a recent study by Wolverhampton-based researchers suggested that individuals that have diabetes are having unnecessary lower limb amputations, because too few were receiving the right foot care. Individuals with diabetes are 15 times at increased risk of lower limb amputation than those without the condition, which is the UK s second commonest cause of lower limb amputation. In fact, Diabetes UK data reveals that up to 70% of people die within five years of having an amputation. Experts attribute part of the problem to lack of education. A recent survey showing that of 30 persons with diabetes, aged between 60 and 80 years that had amputations, 90% had been considered high risk in the period leading up to the procedure, due to the presence of one or more risk factors such as a history of ulcers, nerve damage, circulation problems and foot deformities. However, over one fourth of such high-risk persons do not receive any kind of specialist care, the Wolverhampton study suggested, and two in five, not educated on ways by which they could prevent and treat infections that could result in amputation. Could healthcare ICT not a play role in educating these high-risk patients, via for example, targeted health information, which a NHIN could facilitate, or could they not receive it even via their GPs, if connected to such a network? More than 30% of these individuals did not have any sort of review of their diabetes to assess how they managed it and to ensure they did not develop any other complications hence preempt the amputation. Many of these patients could receive care at home, and do not have to end up hospitalized for amputations were measures such as mandatory foot care plans place to ensure that they all receive the right care and education, taken to prevent complications such as infections that could eventually lead to amputations. Would having a NHIN not facilitate such domiciliary, even ambulatory care, enabling strict monitoring of their diabetes, and enhancing the delivery of standard foot care practices, including at least an annual foot check, hence possibly helping to reduce the amputation rates by as much as 40%. Would this not result in substantial savings in healthcare costs for the U.K not mention the improved quality of care and reduction in the burden of illness for the patients and their families?

D espite its immense benefits, implementing a national health information network

could pose major challenges in several domains some technical, others cost related, and yet others with its administration, and its reception by the end-user. One could also conceptualize these challenges as occurring at the service delivery level, for example, problems with providers accepting, implementing, and utilizing the network, and referral and communications reluctance and failures. Another level would be at the policy and strategic management level for examples issues such as, the type and degree of regulation of various aspects of the use of the network, for example, whether it should be just within Canada, or shared cross-border, with the U.S; coordination between healthcare delivery players, and interoperability. Furthermore, the challenges could surface prior to, during, and post-implementation, hence the need to anticipate them and develop the appropriate approaches to addressing them well in advance. No health information network would deliver on expected results without due diligence to quality issues, from both delivery and management viewpoints, for examples, effectiveness, efficiency, accessibility, and timeliness. The network also has to be acceptable, safe, secure, equitable, evidence-based, and client centered. The issues point to the potential complexity of these quality-related challenges that straddle technical, policy, and management issues among others, hence the need for an intersectoral approach to confronting them. This approach would indeed, be important to adopt in tackling many of the other challenges of implementing a national health information network. End-user reluctance to accept the network for example could be due to technophobia, which itself could be due to inadequate education on the technicalities of the use of the network, poor user buy-in from project commencement, or simply an inherent disinterest in all technical matters. All of these problems are amenable to change, albeit involving experts in different fields, for example, IT and change managers, using different approaches, yet collaborating toward achieving the same end-result. There will be the need for inculcating in those that manage and use the network alike, a solid quality improvement mentality necessary to ensure its implementation, and its continuing optimal usage. This will assure the realization of the full benefits of the network in improving the quality of healthcare delivery and ultimately reducing healthcare costs without comprising the quality of these services. Thus, countries implementing a NHIN should aim at extensive and long-term quality improvement based on rational choices of the most appropriate approaches for their particular circumstances, for examples including annual national and regional accreditation processes for the networks and their administrative and technical components. Healthcare ICT will itself play a major role in process quality evaluation, and different organizations would need to follow strategic guidelines albeit with as much flexibility as their peculiar contexts warrant. In other words, adherence to quality could be flexible but not necessarily variable. Particular organizations for example might need time to implement certain aspects of the network due to financial constraints but will still need to do so according to stipulated standards when they are ready. Put differently, they should not have to implement substandard features simply because they want to please the accreditation committee. This likely explains the decision on March 21, 2006, of the Electronic Health Records Work Group, one of four advisory groups formed in fall 2005 in the U.S to advise the American Health Information Community on ICT issues. The Work Group decided it best to promote the use of electronic laboratory data through an incremental approach starting with support for the expansion of current electronic communications between labs and physicians, then moving on to centralize lab data collection and dissemination. Although its primary responsibility is to promote EHRs in general, the Group must first recommend on the promotion of lab data exchange to AHIC by May 1, 2006. Expectations are for the group to recommend a patient-centric system that would deliver both current and historical data to providers in multiple locations, as opposed to lab-centric model, which simply stores test results that providers could access via interfaces with lab computer systems, or a provider-centric model, with providers or physicians doing the storing. Jason DuBois, vice president of government affairs for the American Clinical Lab Association advised the workgroup to recommend the recognition of the EHR-Lab Interoperability and Connectivity Standards under industry development with the support of the California HealthCare Foundation. The workgroup also discussed the effect of state privacy regulations on data flow, again underlining the interplay of technical, ethical and policy issue, and the need for intersectoral collaboration in resolving them. One approach to quality improvement could also involve focusing on complex capacities such as multi-level program integration, another, for example, could couple specialized vertical functions such as disease control programs with extra healthcare ICT-based quality control procedures. In the U.S., the Centers for Medicare and Medicaid Services (CMS) is providing technical assistance to physicians' offices regarding ways to adopt healthcare ICT tools to improve quality via the Doctor's Office Quality Information Technology (DOQ-IT) project. Initiatives on standardization continue apace for interoperability of health information systems including EHR, e-prescribing and other healthcare information technologies. From 2007, there will be requirements for hospitals to participate in a pay-for-performance system coupling performance to distinct quality measures, with penalties stipulated for noncompliance, for example a 2%-point reduction in the annual basket update, which would be expeditiously effected by the new payment systems CMS is developing and implementing to support higher quality care. Indeed, the Medicare website now includes quality data enabling clients to be more discerning regarding their choices of hospitals, nursing homes, home health agencies, and dialysis facilities, for example, based on performance and prices. These measures will likely foster competition among these providers and eventually modulate their pricing, forcing the prices down, and making access to improved and qualitative services more affordable. There is no doubt that technical issues could bog down the implementation of a national health information network, and Senate on March 16, 2006, of a reserve fund for Healthcare ICT, part of its FY2007 budget resolution, attests to its commitments to facilitating the removal of all obstacles in the way of healthcare ICT diffusion nationwide, including tackling technical issues.

The approval would allow Congress to pass a healthcare ICT bill in 2006 that provides money for related projects, the funds also allowing performance-based payments for providers who meet certain standards of care, a crucial incentive for quality improvement in for example the country's NHIN, that will augur well for the entire health system. The very idea of a network implies a conglomeration of communicating systems of varying similarities and dissimilarities. An EHR for example on its own could comprise a variety of technologies including an electronic medical record system, customarily used to delimit health information technologies used in doctors practices, personal health records (PHR), that could be virtual-based that the health consumer essentially controls but access to which he/ she could give healthcare providers or anyone else. It could also have a computerized physician order (CPOE) system, to ensure safe and promote rational prescribing, laboratory and radiology information systems, including Picture archiving and communications systems (PACS), and a host of others. The EHR itself would a component of the regional or local information network, which will aggregate into a national health information network. The most crucial thing is for these various components to be able to communicate with one another, and to do so means strict compliance with set interoperability standards. Agreeing on and establishing such standards would be a crucial first step in making the NHIN work seamlessly and effectively, and these agreements may not just be among experts in one country but might require international collaboration and agreements too. This is one reason that within-country intersectoral collaboration is a necessary first step, as this would make it easier to deal with the vagaries of international agreements on such key issues as Internet governance. There are moves for example by some countries to internationalize the management of the Internet s core resources, namely, the domain name system, Internet Protocol (IP) addresses and the root server system that might have important significance for the technical infrastructure and tactical operations of a country s NHIN. There is a host of other technical challenges. They include issues relating to standardization, interoperability, privacy and security, and integration of disparate systems that require attention, and of course issues regarding maintenance and quality control. These technical challenges would require attention at different levels, for example, implementing electronic medical records (EMR) at the physician practice or healthcare provider level, computerized physician order entry (CPOE) at the hospital level, or radio frequency identification (RFID) system at ambulatory and domiciliary care level, the chief technical concerns different for different technologies even at individual levels. The following example illustrates the point. In a PRNewswire press release on March 28, 2006, MobileMD(TM), a leading provider of healthcare ICT announced that it has successfully implemented its MobileMD(TM) Health Information Exchange (HIE) at Centura Health, which is the largest health care system in Colorado and one of its biggest private employers. The exchange, an outsourced service, receives clinical information such as lab results, transcription, and radiology reports from all 12 Centura Hospitals, which it transmits in real time, into the electronic medical record (EMR) systems of subscribed Centura physicians. Should this sort of connectivity not be the norm in contemporary healthcare delivery, enabling providers to gain real time access to patient information at the point of care (POC)? Would this not improve the quality of care delivery including patient safety, reducing eventual morbidity and mortality and saving healthcare costs overall? Would it also not in fact reduce practice-operating costs for subscribed physicians to receive vital patient information, via electronic-rather than snail-mail? Does it not speak to the important benefits implementing such connectivity on a larger scale in a regional and national health information network? Yet, it is essential that the exchange communicates and seamlessly too with the electronic medical records systems of the subscribed physicians, each of who might have different systems purchased from different vendors. Here is where the need for standardization to facilitate interoperability is one of the key technical challenges of implementing a NHIN perhaps even of higher priority than privacy, about which concern would be limited were there no information transfer and sharing. To complicate these technical challenges, there is not always consensus among the experts on all aspects of these technical issues. For example, Karen Bell, director the Office of Health IT Adoption within the Office of the National Coordinator for Health IT, urged the EHR workgroup mentioned earlier to recommend a patient-centric EHR model to AHIC when its recommendations on the promotion of lab data exchange are due in on May 01, 2006. On the other hand, Jason DuBois, vice president of government affairs for the American Clinical Lab Association noted that a better option would be to promote and expand the existing peer-to-peer communication patterns between labs and physicians. On a different note, the American Hospital Association (AHA) has raised concerns over a planned certification process for inpatient EHR, noting that the process should consider a product s ease of use and reliability, and that it would oppose a process to certify IT interoperability across organizations. The association made these observations in a letter it sent March 23, 2006 to the Certification Commission for Healthcare Information Technology (CCHIT), in which it also asked CCHIT to from a workgroup to seek ways to certify the usability of IT products. Noted Rick Pollack, AHA executive vice president, "Hospitals spend inordinate resources on IT system maintenance and still face system disruptions that can adversely affect workflow, patient care and clinician acceptance of IT," in the letter. HHS in 2005 awarded a contract to CCHIT, which will also certify the infrastructure and network components required for inter-provider data exchange, to develop product certification for electronic records used in ambulatory and in-patient environments. CCHIT is also preparing certification criteria for EHRs in hospitals and other in-patient environments. The AHA has concerns about the planned focus on inter-organizational interoperability rather than as it prefers on systems that connect pharmacy, laboratory, and radiology systems to clinical data repositories and administrative systems within a hospital although in general endorses CCHIT's staged approach to certification. The AHA opposes certification of hospitals' implementation of IT systems, arguing that it would place an "undue burden on a field that already undergoes significant scrutiny through accreditation, surveys, and other processes". The association also does not support the idea of certification for hospitals and health systems with advanced IT systems due to its lack of clarity. Technical issues inherently pose their own challenges but such lack of consensus on these technical issues as described above, pose even more significant challenges to the implementation of a national health information network in any country and its constituent parts and need speedy resolution to move the program of implementing the network forward.

Thomas Jefferson University Hospital in Philadelphia will distribute 100,000 CD-ROMs

containing personal health records (PHR) software, made by the CapMed division of Bio-Imaging Technologies Inc., Newtown, Pa., according to a news report on March 28, 2006. Besides making it possible for patients to create a personal health record (PHR) for themselves and family, the software will include the hospital's patient registration and health history forms, provider directory, and age-specific health management guidelines, and an alert/ reminder system. The hospital plans to brand the PHR software and distribute the CD-ROMs to patients through by mail, coupled with newspaper and Web site advertisement giving the software away gratis on request. Furthermore, senior managers at the hospital will test the vendor's Personal HealthKey, a USB flash drive device for storing and transporting medical information, to determine if the hospital should also distribute the devices to patients. This gesture demonstrates the need for efforts to encourage end-users to embrace healthcare ICT, including the PHR components of the EHR system that is an integral part of a national health information network. It also shows that not just healthcare providers need such encouragement. There is no doubt that changing the attitude of the end-user toward embracing healthcare ICT is a major challenge in the implementation of a NHIN. Besides healthcare providers, many who still shun healthcare ICT for a variety of reasons including disinterest in technology in general, fear of compromising the much-cherished doctor-patient interaction, billing concerns, implementation costs, and worries about process change, among others, healthcare consumers also have their own concerns. Privacy and confidentiality issues for examples are of major concern to the public, which makes it especially a smart move to encourage the public to use healthcare ICT as the above example shows. A recent study set out to examine users' attitudes to implementation of an electronic medical record system in Kaiser Permanente Hawaii. Conducted by four primary healthcare teams in four clinics, and four specialty departments in one hospital, on Oahu, Hawaii, Kaiser Permanente stopped implementation of the initial system in favor of a competing one, shortly prior to the interviews for the study, in which 26 senior clinicians, managers, and project team members, participated. Published vol 331 of the British Medical Journal in 2005, the study showed that users saw the decision to adopt the EMR system as flawed, and that software design problems increased resistance to its use17. It also found that the system compromised doctors productivity, particularly earlier on in the implementation phase, and called for role clarification, aggravating resistance, and engendering conflict. The researchers noted the need for ensuring early proper project perception, and system selection, testing, and adaptation, and for strong leadership, even that a transient climate of conflict was might not be that harmful to the system' s adoption. No doubt, other countries could learn from the findings of this study in implementing EHR. The English National Program for IT has similarities for example with what Kaiser Permanente tried to do in Hawaii and the plans for the English NHS, the overall goal, to implement an integrated electronic medical record for use by all clinicians. This study clearly showed that organizational issues are also important for the success of EHR implementation. Leadership, consultation, communication, defective decision making, education and training, and in effect, change management, are also critical aspects of any EHR success story, and on the contrary the lack of attention to which, as the study also showed, could lead to implementation failure. One should not expect automatic success of an implementation effort simply because funds and technical expertise are available. The initial decision to implement the Kaiser Permanente project was remote from the clinical user base, deficient product design created resistance, and indeed, the implemented system reduced clinical productivity, the exact opposite of what it set out to achieve, all these potent evidence of the importance of end-user buy-in for project success. The authors' suggestions for averting these problems tally with those of Nancy Lorenzi, president of the International Medical Informatics Association and a change management expert. They include setting and communicating unambiguous goals and formulating a modifiable strategic plan, fostering end-user plan ownership, not shunning shifts in organizational culture in favor or opposed to the plan and attempting to encourage a positive attitude toward it. It is also important to nurture formal and informal change leaders and champions, and to be patient, stay focused on the task, communicate effectively, seek and appraise feedback, and take the necessary action on it, and plan ahead for the next phase of change18.

Costs are also major issues that stall or even prevent the implementation of an NHIN, and in particular of its components technologies among healthcare providers. Some of these components are quite expensive, and beyond the reach of many physician practices, particularly the solo practices. Governments in the U.K, Canada, and the U.S., are investing significantly on EHR. The U.K for example plant to spend US$10.9 billion on its electronic data initiative. Canada Health Infoway has received $1.2 billion thus far in total funding from the Government of Canada in three phases. It received $500 million in March 2001, the money earmarked to develop and ensure the use of common, pan-Canadian information standards and compatible communications technologies. Infoway received $600 million in July 2003, consequent upon consensus by the First Ministers in support of a nationwide EHR and support for Infoway in the wake of the Romanow and Kirby, which both called for a pan-Canadian EHR. The money was also to fund Telehealth systems in the country, and in June 2004, Infoway received $100 million, meant for developing a pan-Canadian Health Surveillance System, the SARS crisis a key trigger for the funds. The U.S is also spending significantly on its national health information network, and related technologies. Nonetheless, considering the increasing calls for automating healthcare processes to increase patient safety and reduce medical errors, it is a major challenge to implementing a NHIN finding ways to reduce the costs of these technologies or other ways to increase their adoption rates by healthcare providers and other healthcare stakeholders. Pharmacy information systems, for example, are important in realizing this goal of improved patient safety as they help to not only reduce medical errors by providing opportunities for physician order entry, but also improve nurse-pharmacy communications, and offer integration and interoperability in closed-loop drug administration. Some also offer a mobile bar code that facilitates bedside point-of-care application via the provision of electronic verification and record of the medication administration process, further enhancing patient safety. However, many physician practices might find the costs of these systems, as they currently stand, prohibitive. The same goes for CPOE, and some other health information systems that are integral parts of an EHR, which will in turn operate in the wider health information network. Some governments in Canada, for example, offer incentives to general practitioners and family physicians to encourage them to implement EMR, which they could do incrementally, purchasing and implementing features most valuable to their practices one after another, spreading out the costs. Health Plans in the U.S and other private sector organizations, both for-and not-for-profit offer such incentives. Programs such as Bridges to Excellence, a not-for-profit coalition of employers, health plans and others, are helping to reward doctors for quality outcomes, rather than providing funds for healthcare ICT adoption. However, some experts speaking to a Capitol Hill audience on March 23, 2006 queried such practices, insisting that reform of the healthcare payment system is the key to driver healthcare ICT adoption, despite its benefits that some employers and healthcare providers are starting to report. United Parcel Service (UPS) for example, participates in Bridges through the Georgia Diabetes & Obesity Program, a project the Center for Health Transformation coordinates. Cigna analysis showed participating physicians reporting $350 in gross diabetic care costs savings per patient, bonuses they receive expected to add up toward future investment in healthcare ICT. Employers might not be keen to fund healthcare ICT in physician offices, but want to reward efforts to improve care quality, which reward would make it likelier for physicians to continue to deliver as they later purchase and implement their healthcare ICT. Some disagree, insisting that healthcare ICT investments alone do not guarantee improved service provision by physicians. Most concerns center around physician productivity, which proponents of this view argue the technologies hardly improves, although they reduce transcription costs and improve patient/ doctor communication, among others. This is one indication of the need for more research into developing cutting-edge decision support systems (DSS) for example that could help improve physician productivity. There are challenges here too, for example, overcoming the problems inherent with knowledge-based systems (KBS) such as the lack of effective methods for ensuring their quality and reliability, particularly with regard to the verification and validation of the knowledge bases utilized. CareFirst BlueCross BlueShield is testing a Bridges program planning to reward up to $100,000 over three years for practices with demonstrable quality improvement. Some have criticized the

Bridges to Excellence program as limited in its rewarding quality, focusing only on rewarding patients with certain conditions, for example diabetes, and argued for focus to be on improving healthcare quality and not just on healthcare ICT adoption and use. The costs challenge remain one of the most difficult for healthcare ICT adoption in general, and for implementing the technologies any national health information requires to function effectively and produce the desired results of improving overall healthcare quality while simultaneously reducing healthcare costs. One point of view is to let market forces to prevail in determining the costs of these technologies. However, this would require the achievement of a critical mass of healthcare ICT diffusion, for healthcare ICT vendors to reduce their prices in order not to outprice their companies from the market. Perhaps such incentive programs as described above and other such programs would help facilitate the attainment of this critical mass. The announcement on April 02, 2006 by Data Strategies, Inc., a leading provider of practice management software and Exscribe, Inc., an innovative pioneer in Orthopedic documentation, of their agreement to their key products Data Strategies'elligence practice management system and Exscribe's E-Record EMR, to create an integrated digital office solution for orthopedic surgeons, is significant. This is so because it could also help promote healthcare ICT adoption among healthcare providers. By developing such integrated systems able to perform the functions a physician would have had to purchase two or more systems to perform, physicians would likely save some costs and be more willing to implement healthcare ICT. The integrated system resulting from the agreement mentioned earlier for example, exploits industry standards including MS Windows and HL7, supporting bi-directional sharing of clinical and administrative data. This way orthopedic practices would benefit from an improved information flow, with less effort duplication, hence significantly reducing the time and costs of patient charts, billing, administration, and reporting. This is besides the all-inclusive documentation E-Record creates, including a library of over 500 templates for orthopedic documentation, facilitating compliance with Medicare and other regulatory bodies. Such targeted EMR and other healthcare information systems will likely continue to gain currency in the industry, again, encouraging the increased adoption of health information technologies as doctors could tailor their healthcare ICT purchases to their specific needs. These developments will likely help solve the challenges costs pose to healthcare ICT diffusion, including the implementation of a national health information network. Canada Health Infoway recently announced its corporate business plan for 2005-06, in which among others it wants to speed up EHR implementation in the country, the entire plan costing an added $9 billion, interoperability, and by extension, standardization, key goals. The business plan envisages the emergence of widespread network of interoperable electronic health record systems, linking healthcare providers, hospitals, laboratories, and pharmacies, making accurate and timely patient health information available when needed thereby substantially improving healthcare delivery accessibility and quality, and ultimately reduce health spending. However, costs also pose major challenges to Canada Health Infoway, having only received $1.2 billion of the $10 billion it needs from the federal government. Some have criticized Infoway's business plan based on an Infoway-commissioned report from US consultants Booz Allen Hamilton[19], which estimated acquisition costs for a national EHR system at $10 billion, total implementation costs, between $7.9 and $16 billion, the benefits, based on the assumption of 100% population coverage, and an enhanced mandate for Infoway, $6.1 billion annually, with a cautionary note. There is little doubt about the benefits of a nationwide electronic health record system, which as previously noted is an integral part of a national health information network. Indeed, it would be one important step toward solving the hospital wait-times problems of the country's health system, by making available updated information and registries of wait lists including surgeon's availability wait-times duration, and other information that would make rational referral easier, hence, workloads more evenly distributed. Yet, some remain concerned about the country s preparedness for the massive organizational change that implementing such a large scale, electronic health records system warrants as the Teasdale commentary on the Hawaii Kaiser mentioned earlier indicates. Other concerns include managing the typical delayed implementation, cost overruns, system reliability issues, deficient end-user buy-in, and security, and privacy issues, which some consider challenges the country needs to ponder over before making such huge financial commitments to a countrywide EHR project. Costs will likely remain a major challenge in any country that could derail plans for a national health information network, hence the need to continue to seek solutions to overcome them within the context of each specific country.

One key issue that many believe would be an important cost driver in healthcare

delivery in the future is the aging of populations particularly in the developed world. Indeed, many cite the aging of baby boomers as reason for the quick rise in U.S. hospital construction a recent research study showed that population aging will play a relatively small role in rising demand for inpatient hospital care over the next decade. The study, by Center for Studying Health System Change (HSC) researchers, appeared on March 28, 2006 as a Web Exclusive in the journal Health Affairs. The study estimates that between 2005 and 2015, the population aging will increase the use of inpatient services by only 0.74% annually, or 7.6% over the entire ten-year period, compared with a projected overall 64.8% rise during the same period[20]. The researchers added that local population

trends and medical technology advances would be far more crucial in forecasting community needs for more inpatient hospital capacity than population aging. Co-author of the study, Dr. Paul B. Ginsberg noted, "The findings are a cautionary tale for hospital administrators to look before they leap into large-scale expansions based on the notion that an aging population will drive big increases in demand for inpatient care". Contrary to what many believe that the U.S population is aging fast, the study noted that the country's average age would only increase from 36.5 to 37.9 years, or an average a yearly increase of 0.37% during the same decade, during which it will play a greater role than in the preceding decade, although with a relatively small overall effect. There would also be differential utilization of inpatient services, cardiovascular and orthopedic conditions likely to be more reasons for their use, aging with paradoxically likely to result in stable, or declining use of other services, for example, related to childbirth and mental illnesses. Concluding the authors note, "Although aging will likely have an important impact on spending, its magnitude will be dwarfed by the impact of advances in technology and other factors that affect medical practice patterns." This study has important implications for policy formulation on resource allocation, for example, the building of hospitals. Should we be building hospitals at all, and if so, should we be building only those that focus on certain types of activities, for example on the treatment of cardiovascular and orthopedic conditions? In other words, should we revisit the idea of centers of excellence, which in fact, some governments, for example, the Quebec government in Canada are already doing with the concept of complementarity? What effect would this have on funding the training of doctors and other healthcare professionals, and in particular on specialists training? Should government be examining such research directions in formulating policies on such issues? Why would inpatient utilization not be as high as previously thought according to this study, and are the advances in medical technology it mentioned those that would help prevent the chronic diseases commonly resulting in increased use of inpatient hospital services? This last question also raises another important one that of the role medical technology really plays in the soaring healthcare costs of many developed countries, or there a misconception somewhere on this role? There is little doubt that certain medical technologies are expensive, and their implementation and usage some would argue, irrational. Now, this combination of factors will increase costs, no doubt. The question then is if the reversal of these factors, for example, implementing these costly technologies where there is demonstrable need for them, and not ordering MRI for an ankle sprain, would make a difference to the effect of the technologies on overall healthcare costs. Furthermore, would investing in those technologies, for example, those required for a national health information network to operate effectively and efficiently, reduce the need for these more expensive technologies, because of the prevention of the conditions the latter are most suited to treat? Is this what the study mentioned above is really saying? Does this not speak to the need to pursue disease prevention and health promotion m ore vigorously, including investing in the appropriate healthcare ICT that would facilitate the achievement of this goal? Regarding other factors that affect medical practice, besides the prevalence and distribution of diseases mentioned above and of course their outcomes, which healthcare ICT could help shape significantly, for example via prevention activities, issues such as developments in the insurance industry and government policies would also count, and could pose significant challenges. The idea of consumer-driven healthcare delivery for example, has its roots in health economic policy, yet some would insist also in shifts in medical paradigms, for example, toward better appreciation of the value of focusing on health as well as on disease. The idea also shows the complexity of the interplay of factors that could create significant challenges to healthcare ICT implementation including the success or otherwise of a national health information network. For example, in a recent opinion piece in the Washington Times, Alex Gerber, a clinical professor of surgery emeritus at University of Southern California notes, " The answer to our health care dilemmas is single-payer, government-sponsored universal health insurance", or Medicare for all age groups. He insists this is the way to end the current state in which one-fourth of ˆcurrent total health care costs are eaten up by the insurance industry's overhead expenses", comparing it to Medicare that has overhead expenses of less than 5%. Gerber adds that Canada that runs a single-payer health care system "spends one-tenth as much as U.S. insurance providers spend for overhead" and "functions at almost one-half the cost of ours yet boasts lower infant and maternal mortality and longer life expectancy". Others in the U.S. insist that the health care industry only needs to be committed to embracing the core principles of the free-market for the country s health system to improve. Each school of thought has its strong and weak points, but there is something common to both, which is the fact that neither could hope to achieve its objectives, which incidentally is common to both, of improving the quality of healthcare delivery and reducing escalating healthcare costs, ignoring the crucial role that healthcare ICT would play in achieving these goals. This is a key policy challenge to the implementation of a national health information network for example. There is no doubt that about the numerous research findings on the benefits of EHR systems for example, but there have also been those that question the ability of these technologies to deliver the desired results in a variety of specific domains, for example, regarding physicians' clinical productivity. For example, a recent study of four physician practices revealed the variety of intended and unintended effects introducing electronic health records into physician practices could have. Although not that one could make far-reaching judgment of these technologies based on findings of such a limited scope, the findings nonetheless are instructive, or perhaps would not be for some physicians that believe for example in writing their clinical notes long hand. The qualitative study, published in the March 2006 issue of the *Annals of Family Medicine*, analyzed the effect of EHRs on several factors for patients and physicians at four primary care practices in Oregon. Each practice utilized GE Medical Information System's Logician EHR, which the researchers found affected "multiple cognitive and social dimensions of the clinical encounter". Examples of these effects include large, fixed monitors in the corner of the examination room causing consternation among physicians and patients, although not so, flat-screen monitors on mobile arms, and cost concerns influencing whether doctors typed or dictated office visit notes into the EHR. Most of the doctors also considered EHR notes concise but lacking in the depth of narrated notes, EHR still considered in early developmental stages after six years of use. This study certainly point to a number of challenges such as user buy-in, and training, and the design of future EHR technologies to make them more user-friendly, but should they dissuade policy makers say, a hospital's management board, from pursuing the implementation of these technologies? Should we not see more such studies that interested healthcare stakeholders could sponsor, to reveal important challenges, hindering the success of these technologies? There are also management challenges, for example regarding healthcare ICT governance, including issues relating to accountability. These are genuine issues considering not only the significant costs of implementation for example, a national health information network, but also those of its failure due to mismanagement in terms of missed opportunities to improve the quality of healthcare delivery, with its attendant worsening of the overall health of the populace, which in turn would further increase healthcare costs. Aspects of the Sarbanes-Oxley Act and the 1996 Health Insurance Portability and Accountability Act (HIPAA) in the U.S for examples aim to ensure such accountability in a variety of ways. Other countries also have similar legislation and expectedly take these issues seriously. Yet, a March 18, 2006 report in The Columbus Dispatch that the state Supreme Court ruled the previous day that Ohio s law guaranteeing people access to government records supersedes a federal law that shields personal health information clearly shows that challenges exist even on such issues. In a Cincinnati case involving the Cincinnati Enquirer's request to examine lead-paint citations the local health department issued, justices ruled unanimously that the department could not use federal privacy guidelines to seal records that are public under state law. There is little doubt that this ruling, the first of its kind, will significantly affect the federal law, which some contend has been already mystifying health-care providers, government officials and the news media alike. At issue in Ohio was the refusal of the Cincinnati Health Department to allow access to a decade's worth of lead-paint citations, because they contained children's private health information as they listed the addresses of homes with lead hazards. The newspaper insisted that the city citations does not have medical information, or list the children s names, ages or any other personal information, and that even if they did, HIPAA does not preclude access to information to which other laws, for example, The Ohio Public Records Law, require access. To be sure, HIPAA requires disclosure of records made public under other laws, but Ohio s open-records provisions excused those safeguarded by federal laws, and exempts medical records from public view. The effects that these laws might have on the already controversial privacy issues regarding electronic health records for example, remains speculative, although some would argue, likely negative. Privacy issues therefore should remain on the agenda, with the relevant technological, ethical, and legal issues that surround important challenges finding the solutions to which are clearly urgent, among others, to minimize the management mayhem of healthcare ICT such as a NHIN, not doing so could engender. Managing a national health information network could be indeed, Herculean, and some, for example Gordon Atherly, in an article titled, The Electronic Health Record: *A National Endeavour or Bureaucratic Nightmare?* wonder for example whether governments should be placing billions of dollars in the hands of an independent, not-for-profit, organizations such as the Canada Health Infoway to manage the country's health information networks or seeking other "bottom-up" approaches[21]. Accountability will always pose challenges wherever

funds are involved and should be of legitimate concern, but this is also why all concerned should ensure transparency in the use of resources, which would ensure everyone's satisfaction with funds disbursements. The challenges implementing a national health information face are indeed, legion. However, there is no disputing the fact that the days patients medical records reside in manila folders are ending, and healthcare ICT, including national health information networks, will gain increasing currency with the resolution of the various obstacles in the way of implementing these valuable technologies, currently and that will emerge.

References

1. " Serotonin Transporter Promoter Gain-of-Function Genotypes Are Linked to Obsessive-Compulsive Disorder' appears in the current online version of the American Journal of Human Genetics at www.ajhg.org. Expected publication in the May 2006 print issue (Volume 78, Number 5)

2. Garrido, T, Jamieson, L, Zhou, Y, Wiesenthal, A, and L. Liang. Effect of electronic health records in ambulatory care: retrospective, serial, cross sectional study *BMJ* 2005; 330:581 (12 March), doi:10.1136/bmj.330.7491.581

3. Feldstein, A, Elmer, PJ, Smith, DH, Herson, M, Orwoll, E, Chen, O, Aickin, M, Swain, MC. Electronic Medical Record Reminder Improves Osteoporosis Management After a Fracture: A Randomized, Controlled Trial *J Am Geriatrics Soc*. 2006; 54(3):450-457. ©2006 Blackwell Publishing

4. Cummings SR, Melton LJ. Epidemiology and outcomes of osteoporotic fractures. *Lancet* 2002; 359:1761-1767.

5. Ross PD, Genant HK, Davis JW et al. Predicting vertebral fracture incidence from prevalent fractures and bone density among non-black, osteoporotic women. *Osteoporos Int* 1993; 3:120-126.

6. Physicians Guide to Prevention and Treatment of Osteoporosis. Washington, DC: National Osteoporosis Foundation, 2000.

7. Elliot-Gibson V, Bogoch ER, Jamal SA et al. Practice patterns in the diagnosis and treatment of osteoporosis after a fragility fracture: A systematic review. *Osteoporos Int* 2004; 15:767-778.

8. National Committee for Quality Assurance. NCQA Releases HEDIS® 2004, 10 New Measures Address Public Health, Service Issues [on-line].

Available at www.ncqa.org/communications/news/Hedis2004.htm
Accessed March 29, 2006

9. Goldman, HH, Frank, RG, Burnam, MA, Huskamp, HA, et al, Behavioral Health
Insurance Parity for Federal Employees. *NEJM* Volume 354:1378-1386, March 30, 2006
Number 13

10. Kohn LT, Corrigan JM, and Donaldson MS, eds. Institute of Medicine Report: To Err
is Human: Building a Safer Health System. Washington, DC: National Academy Press;
November 29, 1999.

11. Health Care in Canada 2004. Available at:

http://secure.cihi.ca/cihiweb/dispPage.jsp?cw_page=PG_263_E&cw_topic=263&cw_rel
=AR_43_E
Accessed on March 31, 2006

12. Available at: http://www.saferhealthcarenow.ca/Default.aspx
Accessed on March 31, 2006

13. Available at: http://dailynews.mcmaster.ca/story.cfm?id=3922
Accessed on March 31, 2006

14. Available at: http://www.docguide.com/news/
Accessed on March 31, 2006

15. Available at: http://www.cato.org/pub_display.php?pub_id=2466
Accessed on April 01, 2006

16. Available at: http://www.fraserinstitute.ca/shared/readmore.asp?snav=nr&id=693
Accessed on April 01, 2006

17. Scott JT, Rundall TG, Vogt TM, Hsu J. Kaiser Permanente's experience of implementing an electronic medical record: a qualitative study. *BMJ* 2005; 331: 1313-6.

18. Teasdale S. Shaping sands, shifting services [editorial]. *Inform Prim Care* 2005;13: 81-2.
Available at: http://bmj.bmjjournals.com/cgi/content/full/331/7528/1316#REF3#REF3
Accessed on April 1, 2006

19. Creating Healthy Connections, Annual Report 2004-2005. Montreal: Canada Health Infoway. Canada Health Infoway.

20. Available at: http://content.healthaffairs.org/cgi/content/abstract/hlthaff.25.w141
Accessed on April 2, 2006

21. Atherly, Gordon. The Electronic Health Record: *A National Endeavour or Bureaucratic Nightmare?*
Available at: http://www.fraserinstitute.ca/shared/readmore.asp?sNav=pb&id=829
Accessed on April 2, 2006

Healthcare ICT and the Law

$\mathbf{M}$ore doctors are making house calls in the U.S according to the April 04, 2006 issue of

USA Today, more Medicare beneficiaries receiving medical care at home since Medicare increased payments for house calls in 1998. Medicare paid for about two million such home visits in 2005, or about 1% of outpatient visits for medical care. Indeed, Medicare now has a three-year pilot program enabling 15,000 chronically ill elderly patients in California, Florida, and Texas, many with restricted mobility and dementia, with otherwise slim chances to see a doctor except via ambulance to the ER, to receive round-the-clock medical care at home that board-certified physicians deliver. This is at no extra cost to recipients than their customary fee-for-service Medicare premiums. The problem is that there are not enough doctors to meet the demand for these house calls, due to a nationwide shortage of primary care doctors and geriatricians, generally deemed less lucrative medical areas. There is no doubt that it is ultimately more cost-effective to treat these seniors at home, thereby reducing their ER and hospital bed utilization, besides receiving treatment in the comfort of their homes and among their loved ones enhancing their quality of life (QOL.) Is it therefore not worth seeking solutions to the problem, and what could these solutions be? According to Bonnie Kantor, an Ohio State University gerontologist," Technologically, we can do so many more things in the home than we were able to do." Could the more widespread use of healthcare information and communications technologies (ICT) be one way to solve the problem? A major recent development in the healthcare of seniors in the U.S is the Medicare prescription drug benefit. On April 03, 2005, the Wall Street Journal reported that private health insurers sponsoring Medicare prescription drug plans would no longer be able to offer more than two plans with effect from 2007, save some insurers offering plans that fill drug-benefit coverage gaps. These latter might have the opportunity to offer three plans as some insurers do this year, although the number of choices reportedly overwhelming for some beneficiaries. The intent of Part D for Medicare drug plans, drugstores, and other stakeholders is to save money for seniors and ensure their access to the drugs that they need. What role, could aiming healthcare ICT-enabled information to the seniors play in their fuller understanding of the workings of the plans, and could such understanding facilitate the achievement of goals of the plan? Indeed, the findings of a survey that the Medicare Rx Education Network released on March 03, 2006, support the need for such efforts at information dissemination. The findings showed that 87% of beneficiaries who voluntarily enrolled in the drug benefit consider the program works well, about 50% of beneficiaries actively planning to enroll in a plan indicate that lack adequate information to chose, and about 60% of beneficiaries not enrolled see choosing a plan as difficult. Would it not be easier for seniors to choose between plans armed with sufficient information to make such choices, and for the concept of empowering the health consumer to be meaningful, hence able to achieve its eventual goals of fostering competition in the healthcare market? Would such competition not drive prices down, ultimately, making healthcare even more accessible, and affordable? Many pharmacists complain of low reimbursements and payment delays, with some actually opting out of the plan for these reasons. Could more widespread adoption of healthcare information systems, for example, that enables more efficient information exchanges between pharmacies, pharmacy benefit managers, Medicare drug plans, and CMS, help prevent such problems? Lawmakers in Massachusetts recently approved a health care reform package that considerably expands coverage for the state s uninsured, protagonists of which hope it is one bill will become a model for the entire country in the near future. The idea is to employ a mix of financial incentives and penalties to expand access to health care over the next three years, thus making healthcare accessible to the current 500,000 uninsured in the state. However, critics, argue that such individual mandates for healthcare coverage would encourage pervasive regulation of the healthcare industry, and political intrusion in personal health care matters, not to mention its costs, at a time healthcare costs are soaring, and possible unanticipated fallouts. A Cato Institute policy analysis, titled, Individual Mandates for Health Insurance-Slippery Slope to National Health Care, by Michael Tanner, Cato s director of health and welfare studies, published on April 05, 2006 examined the idea of an individual health insurance mandate. This is a legal obligation that every American obtains adequate private health insurance coverage, those not receiving such coverage via their employer or some other group required to buy one on their own, or be subject to fines or other penalties1. The author argues that

although the idea might help address the problem of those uninsured that regardless receive treatment passing their costs to taxpayers or the insured, enforcing such mandates would pose significant tactical problems, costs and the bureaucratic intricacies of tracking, sanctions, and subsidies, chief among them. The author also expressed concern about the implication of such mandates being tacit acceptance of the idea that ensuring each person has health insurance is government's responsibility, which as noted earlier, could unwittingly result in overly government regulation of the healthcare industry, particularly if such mandates were federal. This might be the start of "a slow but steady spiral downward toward a government-run national health care system", the author contends. With the trend toward the consumer-driven healthcare delivery model, such regulations some would insist are antithetical to free-market principles, including the competitiveness that characterize free markets, which expectedly would reduce prices, making healthcare more accessible and affordable, and curtailing government health spending, and companies' health benefits for examples; in other words, worsening an already problematic situation. There is hardly any doubt that even the free market does not have free reign and that government must from time to time rein in discordant market tendencies in the best interest of the overall market. The question many would probably be asking therefore is not whether there ought to be regulation, but rather how much regulation and political interference there should be? Should there not be regulations, for example, protecting the privacy of patients health data and information in the wake of the electronic health records (EHR) systems? However, should there be laws mandating individuals to purchase health insurance, the answer to which for some would be negative? Others consider the imminent Massachusetts law, which only awaits the signature of Governor Mitt Romney, a major achievement that policy-makers in Washington and the entire country could not for so long. Once signed, the law will require all the state s citizens to have health insurance as of 1 July 2007, giving the state the status of the first in the U.S to achieve close to universal healthcare, with the almost all of the half a million currently uninsured having coverage. Are we going to see more of such bills in state legislatures in the U.S. in the months and years ahead? Maine, for example, appears to be following suit, as are Illinois and Hawaii, although none has made it a legal mandate for its citizens to have health insurance coverage. An important aspect of the Massachusetts law is that it enjoys bipartisan support, accommodating the positions of Democrats and Republicans, regardless that the Governor is a Republican. The bill comprises subsidies and incentives for the poor and middle classes, but also some penalties. It provides for the establishment of a new state body that will assist the lowest earners purchase heavily subsidized policies for almost nothing in premiums or other costs, with provisions also to help the not so poor for who health insurance policies prove unaffordable. The bill will fine private enterprises with over 10 workers that do not provide their workers coverage $295 (£170) per worker per year, and persons considered able to afford but do not buy health insurance, up to $1,000 a year. The state expects the bulk of the cost of the program to come from the federal government, and its enormous current costs on emergency health care for its 500,000 uninsured to peter out in the main. Some would ask what the effect on the federal government absorbing the costs of such programs from all the other states would be were these states to pass such laws, some would ask, considering its already high health spending. On the other hand, would it not eventually save the state and federal governments and other healthcare payers, significant healthcare costs for citizens to have affordable and accessible healthcare? Would the country as a whole not benefit from a healthier and more productive citizenry? These are no doubt desirable scenarios, but would the bill on its own be sufficient to achieve these goals, or would it need consideration of certain other crucial factors in order so to do? How could we still prevent adverse selection, for example, premiums for the ill being more, perhaps even out of reach, while in general raising premiums for all, making them unaffordable, for even those not so ill? Would there be over-utilization, or abuse of healthcare services by some, because they are paying almost nothing for health services? Would the taxpayer still not bear the costs of such service over utilization some would ask? How would this program interface with Medicare and Medicaid, particularly in terms of monitoring and enforcement? Although a Federal program, the states operate Medicaid, which offers health care coverage for some low-income people unable to afford it, such as the aged, blind, or disabled or some individuals in families with dependent children. Would the state change eligibility criteria and the scope of service provision? These are all questions that highlight the role healthcare ICT, one of the key other factors that such a bill would need to achieve its goals, in addressing the various problems involved in healthcare delivery not just in the U.S. but elsewhere in the world. From the perspective of the state, it wants to provide healthcare services to all of its citizens, and to save substantially in costs doing so. It is even prepared to help those of its citizens that cannot afford health insurance in order to ensure that everyone receives needed healthcare. The problem is that unlike in a publicly funded health system, there are motley service providers operating differing healthcare delivery models, with variable nature, size, focus, and technological sophistication. These variations, for example, in plan choice of a fee-for-service plan, a health maintenance organization (HMO), or a preferred provider organization (PPO), have important cost and coverage implications, with some services going to be unaffordable for certain individuals, despite that they need them. In other words, these individuals would still not have access to services that they need. The question then arises if the state would be willing to pay for them via the subsidies, and would they have to endure their plans restricting access to certain services for example, expensive imaging studies, or life-saving cutting-edge surgeries on cost grounds. These concerns also raise another important contemporary healthcare delivery issue, that of patient-choice. In other words, would patients be able to exercise the choice of service provider for example if offered limited services? Clearly, those that can afford sophisticated services such as those mentioned above would for example be able to use fee-for-service plans, but not those that cannot, would have to use HMOs, or PPOs, where service utilization receives greater scrutiny and control. Having to pay a monthly premium, deductibles, and co-payments is not what many find easy, particularly when they have chronic illnesses. Would such persons not therefore end up either not receiving healthcare or in the ER to seek it, depending on how fast their deductibles run out, where their insurance cap, the maximum they would need to pay yearly on insurance bills, is at, and how large is their co-insurance? Workers on group insurance, including the lowest earners the state subsidies would in particular assist, would lose their group coverage if laid off or they took voluntary retirement at some future point in time even with the provisions of COBRA. The Consolidated Omnibus Budget Reconciliation Act of 1985 or COBRA is a federal law enabling many to continue their group health coverage for sometime but they would have had to work a business of 20 or more employees and could only continue to receive health coverage for at least a year and a half. Even with Medicare, which caters for seniors aged 65 years and older, and some disabled Americans, only Part A, its hospital insurance part is free, while seniors have to pay a premium for Part B, or supplementary medical insurance, which pays for doctors, the supplies they order, and related services. Because Medicare usually operates on a fee-for-service basis, although in some places, beneficiaries now could use HMOs, and other prepaid health care plans, and with service utilization usually quite high among seniors, some services might carry substantial cost implications. The point here is that healthcare costs will likely remain an issue for many people that limit or prevent their access to health services, and that need addressing, and the solution, just like the issues involved, will likely be multifaceted. Underlying them all, however, is the key role healthcare ICT will play in the success of these many solutions in resolving the twin objectives of qualitative healthcare provision for all while simultaneously curtailing the healthcare spending that is spiraling out of control in the U.S. as indeed in many other countries, particularly in the developed world. Healthcare ICT could help achieve these goals in many ways, for example, via the more widespread use of electronic health records (EHR) systems.

The efforts of various governments to implement an EHR are indeed, commendable, millions of dollars already pumped into diverse initiatives and projects in the U.S., Canada, Australia, U.K., New Zealand and other countries, toward achieving this goal. Electronic health records would for example provide the communication link that could make it easier for healthcare consumers to make more-rational choices regarding their service providers, participate more effectively in their treatment plans, including the lab investigations, medications, and ancillary services their doctors order, and indeed, in their overall lifetime health care choices. These opportunities, which a variety of healthcare information technologies could facilitate would likely make healthcare more affordable to individuals, including the 46 million Americans currently uninsured[2], even those on company-sponsored group plans, who armed with the appropriate information could leverage it in collective bargaining for provider choice for example. The more affordable healthcare coverage is, the lesser for example, governments would have to subsidize their citizens health bills, thereby reducing their health spending, yet still achieving their goals of qualitative health services provision to their citizens. Yet, several factors hinder the widespread diffusion of healthcare ICT, which is essential for the full realization of the benefits of these technologies, which brings the issue of the interface of healthcare ICT implementation and the associated legislative issues to the fore, even their ethico-moral dimensions, sometimes have cryptic legal encumbrances. Consider the issue of the privacy and confidentiality of patient data and information, which has dogged the idea of the EHR from the start, and does not seem to be going away, but rather is escalating. In the U.S for example, a coalition of 26 organizations, representing bipartisan constituencies wants Congress to endorse a patient-centered EHR system with patient privacy rights central to any national healthcare ICT law. Yet, some might argue that it is fundamentally an ethical breach, in itself sufficient deterrent. However, are ethical principles such as patient confidentiality binding, when newly qualified doctors in some medical schools no longer even have to swear to the Hippocratic Oath? Should they not therefore have legal teeth? Would such legal backing not reassure the public about the privacy of their cherished personal health information? Would such reassurance not open the way for more widespread deployment of EHR, and facilitate the realization of its full potential, including qualitative service provision and health spending curtailment? The question posed earlier however remains, and that is even if government regulation makes sense in certain situations, how much of it should we have? When does government regulation put free-market principles in jeopardy in relation to healthcare ICT implementation in particular? As argued above, healthcare ICT could help governments achieve their goals of providing healthcare services to their peoples, as for example, that of Massachusetts is trying to do. Indeed, the contrary is also true, that is, it would be difficult to achieve this goal and worse still that of curtailing healthcare costs without the widespread diffusion of healthcare ICT. In fact, this defective or lack of healthcare ICT diffusion would achieve the opposite results, inefficient and ineffective healthcare services, with resulting escalation in health spending. There are many who would argue that compelling individuals to buy a product or service is anathema to the very core of democratic principles, and others that would oppose other forms of healthcare services mandates, for example, those compelling companies to provide healthcare services to their workers to stipulated extents. However, few will likely contend the noble motives of these laws in promoting the interest of all in the end. Therefore, at issue really is not whether these statements about healthcare ICT are true, as they are, but the modus operandi for realizing the full potential of these technologies, and in particular, and in this discussion, in relation to the issue of the use of legislation and government regulation in achieving that goal. Is the benefit of healthcare ICT disputable for example, with regard a recent Canadian-led research that finally settled the controversy over the potential of vitamin B to lower the risk of cardiovascular death, hence to benefit coronary patients? This study, the Heart Outcomes Prevention Evaluation (HOPE)-2 trial, the results presented at the American College of Cardiology annual meeting and published at the same time in the online version of the New England Journal of Medicine, did not support the prevailing view on this vitamin and cardiovascular health. This is the idea that the reduction in plasma homocysteine levels by the use of folic acid and Vitamins B6 and B12 supplements has significant benefits for the heart. The HOPE-2 trial revealed that the daily use of 2.5mg folic acid, 50mg vitamin B6, and 1mg vitamin B12 together over five years reduced homocysteine levels in high-risk patients with vascular disease. However, it did not lower major cardiovascular events in this cohort of 5,522 patients, 55 years and older, with vascular disease or diabetes, randomized into two groups, that took the supplements or placebo groups. According to Dr. Eva Lonn, professor of Medicine at McMaster University in Hamilton, "The failure to show a difference in the risk of cardiovascular death in patients on vitamin B regimen and patients on a placebo diet mean that greater attention should be focused on established treatments for secondary prevention." The professor added, "…..the focus should be on what has been proven to work-namely a healthy lifestyle, including fruits and vegetables, exercise, and for those who already have had an event, certain drugs such as Aspirin, beta-blockers, and angiotensin-converting enzyme inhibitors, which have proven benefit." There is no doubt the public, which hitherto have consistently heard that a vitamin B regimen could help prevent myocardial infarction and strokes in high-risk patients by reducing homocysteine levels, which research studies have shown to be an important coronary risk factor, should have this information. The HOPE-2 trial showed that mean plasma homocysteine levels indeed fell by 0.3mg/l in the vitamin group and increased by 0.1mg/l in the placebo group. However, myocardial infarction, stroke and death from cardiovascular causes, occurred in 519 patients in the active therapy group (18.8%) and 547 patients in the placebo group (19.8%), a non-statistically significant difference. However, the reduced risk of stroke in the treatment group (4% versus 5.3%) and the higher risk of hospitalization for unstable angina (9.7% versus 7.9%) that the trial also revealed, reached statistical significance. The results of the HOPE-2 trial tallied with those of another study conducted in Norway, the Norwegian Vitamin (NORVIT) trial, also published in the New England Journal of Medicine. The Norwegian study also found that lowering homocysteine levels with vitamin B did not prevent myocardial infarction in patients. The results of these clinical trials would no doubt be valuable to the public in understanding the much praised benefits of these supplements in preventing angina and heart attacks is now in question, which should make people seek more effective ways to prevent these diseases. Would such understanding not in fact eventually result in the reduction of the risks for cardiovascular diseases, with people focused on the proven ways to reduce such risks? Would this not mean less morbidities and mortalities from these conditions, less service utilizations and less healthcare spending? Do government and other healthcare stakeholders not therefore have an interest in ensuring that such information reaches its intended audience? One of the major themes this author has touched upon is the idea of targeted health information, which essentially is delivering valuable, current, analyzed, and contextualized health information to high-risk and other individuals rather than waiting for them to seek the information. The premise for this idea is that medical knowledge is evolving at a very fast pace, at which not even healthcare professionals could realistically expect to keep track of important developments in the field. Furthermore, the is confounding the information glut that is already creating retrieval problems with a search for any simple medical term on an Internet search engine for example coming up with thousands of search results. Is a busy mother of two juggling office with housework, in between, taking the children to school, the school gym, and piano lessons, likely to spend an hour searching for the health benefits of folic acid and the B vitamins? Would she not more likely read such information delivered to her via any of the many electronic channels currently available for such information transmission, in a concise, contextualized manner? Indeed, there is research evidence to show that people favor such targeted health care, including information delivery. In Europe, a new video-telephony system underscores the value of e-care with about 60 million older Europeans suffering from chronic diseases and, or that need care indicating their interest in online help delivered to their homes. Video telephony enables instantaneous domiciliary contact, enabling individuals to receive home care and reduces home visits by healthcare professionals, saving costs. First tested in Europe in the early 1990s using analogue cable, even then, it proved popular among seniors. The IST@HOME project set out to develop an affordable and usable video-telephony system, cumulatively on previous efforts in a series of European Union-funded projects to design home and care-provision systems for seniors. An assemblage of a small movable camera, a set-top box for a TV and a handheld service pad, enables audio-visual, real time professional help over the Internet. Users are able to communicate with their care givers from anywhere in their homes, including receiving targeted health information, and other services via a TV set rather than a PC, the video quality, 256 kbits/ second. Funded via the European Commission s IST program, 600 homes in Germany, Belgium, Spain, and Portugal have had full system installation and six months testing. Despite problems identified, such as with alarm integration, eye-to-eye contact, asynchrony of lip movement and speech, and audio quality and technical interruptions, most of the participants, including the caregivers welcomed the service. According to the project partners, contemporary wireless networks are not so efficient for larger homes, particularly regarding video quality, and future systems should aim for better integration, for example of alarm systems or with mobile devices that record vital signs such as blood pressure, pulse, and temperature. Indeed, individuals can now receive make this contact via TV on their cell phones. At the April 5-7, 2006, Las Vegas convention of the Cellular Telecommunications and Internet Association (CTIA), Motorola announced plans to offer DVR-to Mobile service, its latest technology that will enable multiple devices wherever in a home to access a single Motorola digital video recorder (DVR) through set-top boxes, utilizing OCAP, the cable industry s standard interactive-service software, in 2007. This depends on the resolution of rights management issues. SlingMedia released its Sling Player Mobile in early April 2006, joining the increasing number of telecom firms developing the capability to provide broadcast content on cell phones. Sling Media Player, compatible with any Microsoft Windows mobile phone, would enable owners to watch live TV, and DVR-recorded content, and to program their Slingbox DVRs, all remotely. These and other evidence of the value of targeted information, and even healthcare delivery, and their acceptance by not just seniors but many other individuals, and the increasing interest in for example, personal health records (PHR), however, increasingly highlight the need for ensuring the privacy and confidentiality of patient health data and information. Again, this brings forward the real issue, which is how to ensure this privacy. There is no doubt that this would involve technical maneuvering, but just as with its ethico-moral perspective, would this ensure compliance even with policies determined by IT experts to ensure privacy? Would there still be the need for regulation to ensure such compliance, and if so, to what extent, and to who should the regulation apply? Should the mandate be on the IT staff, the end-users, or the patients? Should government be setting standardized criteria for ensuring privacy to which a law mandates healthcare consumers to demand that their healthcare providers prove compliance, by say signing a pre-prepared document affirming such compliance, a copy of which both keep, for the records? Should there also be some law requiring healthcare providers to ensure the continued security of such information for entire duration that the law requires them to have safe custody patient information, and cannot discard such information? Hardly any would dispute the importance of these issues and many others that lie at the interface of healthcare ICT and the law, and the need to address them in order for the shift toward e-health to proceed apace. Privacy issues no doubt remain obstacles to such progress, even from the perspective of caregivers, most of who are justifiably concerned about the chances of lawsuits and their potentially damaging effects on their professional reputations and on their finances. However, they are not the only ones that need urgent legal attention in relation to moving e-Health forward. There is also the issue of patient safety, including medical errors and their disclosures. Public interest in medical errors increased significantly with the publication by the U.S Institute of Medicine in 1999, entitled, To Err Is Human: Building A Safer Health System that as many as 44,000 to 98,000 people die in hospitals each year due to medical errors, medication errors alone causing 7,000 of those deaths. Besides these needless deaths, these errors cost the U.S., about $37.6 billion annually, about $17 billion due to preventable medical errors, 50% of the latter, spent on direct healthcare costs[3]. In

approaching the subject, should we not first be looking at why there are so many medical errors, most preventable at that? Many such errors occur in hospitals, but not all do, and in fact, many also occur outside the hospital setting, including improperly filled prescriptions by pharmacists, in nursing homes, community health centers, physicians' offices, and in ambulatory and domiciliary settings. Besides the setting, we also need to know who is responsible for these errors, and if doctors, nurses, pharmacists, or any other group of professionals are? No doubt, these professionals make mistakes for such errors as diagnostic errors, misreading of medical orders, but should they take all the blame? Poor doctors handwriting could result in misreading of orders, which implementing a computerized physician order entry system, or any other form of e prescribing, could help prevent. Should there not be a law therefore mandating e prescribing? Some patients have the wrong limb amputated, but implementing an electronic medical records (EMR) system that makes patients records available at the point of care (POC) could help prevent this. Should there be a law mandating the implementation of this technology?

Patient safety is also recently in the spotlight in the U.S. with the signing into law in July 2005 of the US Patient Safety and Quality Improvement Act of 2005 (S. 720 and HR 663), which mandates the Department of Health and Human Services to establish a process for the voluntary and confidential medical errors reporting. Indeed, legislative focus on medical errors is not new. This Act only complements a series of laws previously introduced or passed by the US Congress and Senate. For example, the Medicare comprehensive quality of care and safety act of 2000. H.R. 5404 amended title XVIII of the Social Security Act to establish and implement an all-inclusive system under Medicare Program to assure quality of care Medicare beneficiaries receive, and reduce the incidence of medical errors. The Medication error prevention act of 2000 H.R. 3672 amended the Public Health Service Act regarding voluntary reporting of medication errors by healthcare professionals in order to aid relevant public and non-profit bodies to develop and share information and ideas on preventing medication errors. The objective of the Medication errors reduction act of 2001 H.R. 3292 was the establishment of an informatics grant program for hospitals and skilled nursing facilities in order to stimulate IT research and progress among health care providers via a Medical IT Advisory Board, which will develop and disseminate standards for the sharing medical information electronically. The enactment of The Patient Safety and Quality Improvement Act of 2005 is evidence of the persistence of the problem of medical errors and testimony to the desire of US lawmakers to stamp it out. The question is; will this new law fare better? Since the revealing studies of Drs Leape and Bates in the early 1990s, supported by the Agency for Healthcare Policy and Research, renamed Agency for Healthcare Research Quality (AHRQ), awareness of the problem of medical errors has been increasing steadily. President Clinton created a 32-member Advisory Commission on Consumer Protection and Quality in the Health Care Industry to recommend measures "as may be necessary to promote and assure health care quality and value, and protect consumers and workers in the health care system." The Commission's report "Quality First: Better Health Care for All Americans," submitted in March 1998, identified medical errors as one of the four major challenges the US faced in improving health care quality, and recommended steps to provide a "national commitment to improving health care quality." The November 1999 report of the Institute of Medicine (IOM), To Err Is Human: Building A Safer Health System, seemed to raise the tempo of public awareness of medical errors to a new high, with its shocking revelation of medical errors resulting in as many as 44,000 to 98,000 deaths in US hospitals yearly. A national survey conducted in 1999 showed that the report was the health policy story that caught public interest the most that year, and repeated US surveys since then confirmed Americans' concern for patient safety. In light of the recommendations of Advisory Commission, President Clinton established the Quality Interagency Coordination Task Force (QuIC,) to coordinate quality improvement activities in Federal health care programs, and asked it to recommend measures to improve health care quality and ensure patient safety in response to the IOM report. The president also signed an executive order in December 1999, mandating federal agencies and departments to develop, within three months, a list of activities to make patient care safer, which resulted in many government agencies initiating new patient safety programs. The Task Force submitted its report in February 2000. Should we therefore have more such executive orders rather than laws, and would an executive order for example, that every government agency delivers targeted health information via office emails, or other efficient electronic means to all its staff be easier to enforce? Such health information could of course be printed on posters and pasted all over office walls, but would this not be messier, and costlier, including repainting costs, and would it not require printing hundreds of posters for new health information? The private sector is also active in the efforts to promote patient safety, most prominently Leapfrog, a coalition of major large health care purchasers, which launched its "safety leaps" campaign for the use of computerized physician order entry (CPOE), evidence-based hospital referrals, and physician staffing in the intensive care unit to improve service delivery and ensure patient safety. The National Quality Forum has compiled lists of patient safety measures, and the Joint Commission on Accreditation of Healthcare Organizations, requires compliance with patient safety measures for accreditation. Some would argue that perhaps this, what some would describe as a gentler, persuasive approach would work better to ensure compliance with standards than legislation. Indeed, one would have thought that these developments in both the public and private sectors would herald a new era of patient safety but alas, a recent research study published in the November 11, 2004 issue of the New England Journal of Medicine showed that five years after the 1999 IOM report medical errors are still rampant in American hospitals. To put the issue in perspective, thousands of patients are still dying yearly in US hospitals due to preventable medical errors occurring not just in hospitals but in physician offices, pharmacies, nursing homes, even with health services delivered at home. Medical errors cost American taxpayers about $37.6 billion annually according to the IOM report, roughly $17 billion of which is preventable. Indeed, a 2004 Kaiser Family Foundation survey revealed that 55% of Americans are currently dissatisfied with the quality of the country's healthcare system, 40% think it has worsened, and over half had concerns about the safety of their medical care. Why is the US health system so unsafe? How can it become safer? Does it need current patient safety laws enforced or does it need new laws to meet the challenge of the times? There are many possible answers to these questions, some of which may spark vigorous debates. However, few will dispute the lack of the use of ICT, inadequate or lack of medical error reporting, a general lack accountability, fear of malpractice suits, personnel and training, and nonconformity with regulations as issues germane to patient safety. There is no doubt that more widespread use of ICT such as CPOE, electronic health records (EHR,) electronic prescribing, knowledge-based decision support systems, and bar codes, by healthcare providers can help prevent medical errors. Adherence to evidence-based practice and the prompt and accurate reporting of medical errors will help in preventing medical errors now and in developing proactive measures to prevent them in future, respectively. Incidentally, these measures will also likely reduce the rate of malpractice suits. Many US hospitals now have policies on telling patients and their relatives about medical errors. Implementing systems-based changes, for example reducing or spreading-out the workloads of healthcare personnel, and shoring recruitment and training efforts will also reduce medical errors. The issues surrounding patient safety, are therefore multifaceted, some for example, the increased chances of overworked ER staff to make mistakes, some of which could cost lives, inherent in a health system that needs to revisit its staff recruitment and retention policies. Professional bodies would better handle and impose the necessary sanctions on their members in regard certain ethical lapses than state or federal laws, and the latter others, for example, that transgress the criminal code. The point here is that there are instances where legislation might improve patient safety and others where other approaches to improving patient safety would work better. Medical errors and adverse events have different causes as previously noted, and require different solutions. Hence, each healthcare organization needs to establish its own task force to identify specific issues and problems it deems as their causes, and recommend and implement measures to prevent them from occurring in future. Indeed, the IOM report stressed that medical errors are systems problem, and that making necessary changes to healthcare delivery systems will reduce medical errors. However, absolving individuals from blame for medical errors simply because human beings are not perfect is anything but helpful in preventing another family from having to endure unnecessary hardship and sorrow due to a medical error or adverse event. How does one absolve a healthcare professional from medical errors that adamantly rejects measures known to reduce medical errors, for examples electronic prescribing, yet whose illegible writing often results in patients being given the wrong doses of medications? Should there be a law to sanction such a doctor, should a medical professional body handle it, or should the hospital have policies mandating e-prescribing and stipulating consequences for their breach? These are issues that need teasing out if we were to make significant progress not only ensuring patient safety, but also accelerating the more widespread use of healthcare ICT in healthcare delivery. It is on record that a hospital in Veterans Affairs Department reduced medication error rates by 70% after it deployed hand-held wireless IT and bar codes. Indeed, who would absolve a doctor from blame in that hospital that refused to use the devices and ended up causing the death of a patient due to medication error or in another that did not follow standardized policies and protocols for preventing nosocomial (hospital-acquired) infections that subsequently resulted in a patient s death? System changes are important, but will be ineffective if the individuals that operate within the system refused to embrace those changes. This highlights the significance of the new Patient Safety and Quality Improvement Act of 2005, which has the potential to supersede state laws on patient safety, including not just medical errors/ adverse events but nosocomial infections and medical outcomes reporting. This will undoubtedly bode well for reducing ensuring patient safety and for improving the quality of care delivery. The 2003 IOM report on data standards for patient safety (Patient Safety: Achieving a New Standard of Care) stresses the importance of a culture that encourages revealing rather than concealing errors. The lack of accord among policy makers, healthcare professionals, and even the public, on which events need public reporting and the system changes needed to prevent avoidable medical errors has been an obstacle to dealing with the problem of medical errors effectively. The Patient Safety and Quality Improvement Act of 2005 should help change all that.

As noted earlier, one of the major concerns regarding electronic health records (EHR) is ensuring the privacy and confidentiality of patient information. Add this to the threat of malicious logic, often termed viruses, including worms, Trojan horses, trap doors, and denial of service and the future of EHR will likely look anything but rosy. It is inconceivable that we will all continue to lack the high quality service provision in healthcare that we take for granted in less critical domains of our lives simply because of worms. Yet, medical information systems (MIS), including hospital information systems (HIS), radiology information systems (RIS), picture archiving systems (PACS), and other clinical-related information systems, are prime targets for hackers on the prowl for exploitable software and end-user logical or physical access vulnerabilities, among others. Hackers are increasingly developing hybrid programs for multi-pronged attacks, making counter-offensives against them more tasking. It is crucial for healthcare organizations to secure the integrity and confidentiality of patients' information in their care, and so is it for MIS vendors to support them in doing so. Should we simply expect these things to happen, or should there be degree of responsibility on the parts of these different groups, and others that handle patient information, for example health insurers, to keep hackers at bay. Should part of software licensing agreement include a guarantee that the software is impenetrable, or that the vendor would be liable in the event hackers breach its security, and for how long should this guarantee be, after all, there is some form of warranty on many other goods? Should there be laws requiring hospitals and others in custody of patient information to disclose publicly when someone breaches the security of their databases, and should be penalties for such breaches? The need to keep patient information from falling into the wrong hands is even more compelling in these days of rampant identity theft. Patients' health information now moves freer and faster electronically among healthcare professionals and facilities, some in different cities, even countries. Such information available in real time at the point of care (POC) is potentially life saving. On the other hand, its corruption by malicious software can result in data damage or loss, or can degrade the system to the point of compromising service delivery, even putting patients in jeopardy. Viruses and other malicious software not only damage software they can also destroy hardware, for example by switching a disk drive off but not parking the read-heads. Identity theft, when unauthorized persons using malicious logic pose as authorized recipients of data, can result in a breach of confidentiality. Denial of service attacks, which may exploit system vulnerability, or overload it with malicious data, can result in system malfunction, or even shutdown. A worm can target the hospital s email system, disrupting sometimes-critical information flow. The manner notwithstanding, the result of an attack by viruses and other malicious software on MIS can be catastrophic for the patient. Preventing viruses from gaining access into MIS is crucial to securing the systems integrity. The question remains, however, how much risk a system is still at, with its software not built in-house, in a sterile milieu, stand-alone and service-free, and with flawless access control. This perfect scenario hardly exists in real life. Someone somewhere in the hospital is more likely to access the system with a data-laden floppy disk or CD, which data may also have a Trojan horse masquerading as an authentic program only to effuse its malicious content on deployment. What sort of regulation could we impose at this level, just technical policies, and if so, how do the hospital s IT staff, enforce the policies? Could the IT administrator not prevent employees downloading software with cryptic malware? Could he or she also not prevent employees sharing patient information with unauthorized persons via email, for example, within or even outside the hospital? At what point would such policies become intrusive into employees privacy? Further, via its connection to the Internet, or any external network, the ports and modems of MIS can create easy entry portals for both harmless and unauthorized data. There are several other ways malicious programs may attack MIS, which is inherently risk-prone to a certain degree. This is why healthcare organizations need to take the matter seriously and mitigate the risk to the best possible extent, with the active collaboration of their vendors. How can the healthcare organization protect its MIS? Systems not connected to any other are less vulnerable although they still face possible internal attacks and need protection. The corollary is also true: the more the systems connected in MIS, particularly the more those sharing the same port, or software platforms, the more vulnerable they are, as hackers striving to achieve maximum damage often seek such systems, which will therefore attract more hackers, further increasing the system's vulnerability. It is useful to perform enterprise risk and threat analysis to ensure rational and optimal resource deployment prior to adopting any preventive measure. The healthcare organization should also conduct risk analysis and plan approaches to mitigation. It should establish security policies and procedures and have disaster preparedness and damage control plans. It should also train its staff on its security protocols, and should consider using key-locked cabinets, and in general make physical and logical access to the systems strict. It should configure its network routers and other devices for antivirus protection and implement a multi-layered defense system including the use of firewalls, virus scan, intrusion detection system, privacy service, and activity logging and analysis, among others. Should we trust hospitals and others with access to electronic health records to carry out these measures, or should we have ways to mandate them to do so, and if we did, could we enforce the regulation effectively? On the other hand, would hospitals have to ensure that they did if they had to face lawsuits if they did not and someone happened to be unhappy about his or her health information going public? Healthcare organizations should require vendors deploying MIS to ensure the system is secure via a number measures. The vendor should also start with use risk and threat analysis. Among other measures, it should compute, compare, digitally sign checksums, and conduct systems profiles. It should scan the systems throughout its entire life cycle with properly configured and maintained virus scanning software, and build buffer overflow prevention, detection, and removal into the system's design. It should conduct software inspection and audit, and ensure knowledge of and access to updates of security patches, which it should develop and make available to the client. Again, would they implement these measures on their own? Collaboration between vendors and health organizations is important for these measures to succeed, which no doubt will help enhance system integrity and reduce its vulnerabilities to malicious attacks, and reassure the public about the safety of patient information, which would facilitate healthcare ICT diffusion. Would such collaboration become inevitable, as healthcare consumers increasingly demand their rights to assurance on the safety and security of their personal health information? According IOM, medical error is the failure to complete a planned action as intended or the use of a wrong plan to achieve an aim, whereas an adverse event is an injury caused by medical management rather than by the underlying disease or condition of the patient. Both are clearly preventable, for example via the implementation of healthcare-ICT backed, evidence-based practice that standardize treatment policies and protocols, and of pharmacy information systems or even programs such as epocrates that doctors and nurses could download onto their personal digital assistants (PDAs). Some would not surprisingly be asking by now how many laws we would have legislating the use of every valuable technology, and if in fact, this is the right approach to solving the problems of patient safety and medical errors, which however, no one would likely dispute its importance and the need to address. Should we be looking at the problems from a system's viewpoint, in other words as a system's failure rather than that of individual healthcare professionals for example, or should be seeking solutions including regulations that target both? Is it the responsibility of a hospital to provide its doctors with PDAs for example, if say the law mandates it to improve its system by implementing an EHR system that make patient information available to its doctors at the POC? Would the hospital be liable if a patient sues for negligence because one doctor made a grievous error due to not accessing vital patient information that could have prevented the drug allergy that led to a life-threatening angioneurotic edema, even when it had an EHR system in place? Many governments are spending millions of dollars implementing a national health information network (NHIN), of which an electronic health record system is an important component. Would these governments need to mandate the implementation of electronic medical record systems (EMR) in physicians' offices in order for the latter to be able to hook up with the information networks? How else could government achieve its objectives spending so much on these networks without such legislation? Other would ask if such legislation do not interfere with free-market operations and could turn out to be counter-productive. Yet others would argue that how could we stop thousands of healthcare consumers dying of medical errors and adverse events, for example, nosocomial or hospital acquired infections, without ensuring that healthcare professionals, and hospital systems, in general, follow certain standards of care provision? Many hospitals have policies but are these sufficient to change the attitudes of healthcare professionals to for example, embracing healthcare ICT, and in any case, do these policies aim to censure the hospitals themselves, or do they need annual accreditation? Should these accreditation panels be evaluating compliance with the laws aimed to improve patient safety in addition to other preset standards they audit? The U.S.

Food and Drug Administration (FDA) announced on April 06, 2006, for example, that it would review wireless-phone safety consequent upon following a recently published study that reopened concerns about an increased risk of brain cancer. Swedish researchers indicated in March 2006 that the use of mobile phones over a long period could increase this risk, findings that contradicted some previous studies and are "difficult to interpret," according to the FDA, on its Web site. Nonetheless, the FDA is pressing ahead with its plans, and to continue to monitor studies for possible health problems emanating from exposure to radio frequency energy. The Swedish National Institute for Working Life researchers compared data from 2,200 cancer patients and the same number of healthy patients. The results, published in the International Archives of Occupational and Environmental Health, noted that individuals that used wireless phones heavily that is, 2,000 or more hours, or about one hour per day for 10 years, had a 240% increased risk of a cancerous growth on the side of the head that they often used their phone. This is clearly a user safety issue that some would even argue require legislative intervention, but should government, the telecommunication industry, and other interested stakeholders such as the health and insurance industries not be keen to commission further research to elucidate this subject? In other words, should such considerations be important in some cases rather than or at least before sweeping legislation? As previously noted, there are compelling reasons to support some measure of legislation to assure the safety and security of patient information, for example, and of patient safety, both of which the implementation of appropriate healthcare ICT could ensure. These laws therefore would relate to issues of implementation and the required use of these technologies in order for the attainment of their full potential to facilitate qualitative and affordable healthcare delivery and help to contain healthcare costs. Consider the following research findings a team of scientists from Los Alamos National Laboratory in New Mexico, the University of Washington, and the Fred Hutchinson Cancer Research Center in Seattle presented in the April 3-7, 2006 online, and April 11, 2006 print issues of the Proceedings of the National Academy of Science. These researchers with grants from the Department of Homeland Security and the National Institute of General Medical Sciences MIDAS (Models of Infectious Disease Agent Study) program, used supercomputers to respond to a potential national health emergency thereof developed a massive, stochastic simulation model that predicts the possible future course of an avian influenza pandemic, given current environment of worldwide connectivity. This model gives a clear picture of how the H5N1 virus would spread across the country were it to mutate and become transmissible between humans. The simulation gives a city- and census-tract-level picture of the virus spread through a synthetic population of 281 million people over 180 days, also looking at the effect of interventions such as antiviral therapy, school closures, and travel restrictions, while vaccine development speeds up. The researchers concluded that "Based on the present work... we believe that a large stockpile of avian influenza-based vaccine containing potential pandemic influenza antigens, coupled with the capacity to rapidly make a better-matched vaccine based on human strains, would be the best strategy to mitigate pandemic influenza." They added that while simply limiting contact with measure such as travel restrictions, school closures, and quarantine might be impractical to contain a potential pandemic, they might be effective in buying time to produce and distribute enough vaccine and antiviral drugs. They recommend dual measures such as stockpiling vaccines, even if only moderately effective ones, and antiviral drugs, and contact limitation. Both these measures and the surveillance measures necessary to track the movement and evolution of the virus and the disease, all require significant healthcare ICT input. Would anyone contest the need to ensure that healthcare providers and others responsible for these activities have the necessary technologies implemented to ensure their successful conduct? Should there be a legal requirement to have these technologies in the interest of the entire public? The discussion thus far has raised important questions about the need or otherwise for laws to compel the use of healthcare ICT by a variety of stakeholders under different circumstances in order to ensure that individuals and the entire country realizes the immense benefits of these technologies. In the March 7, 2006 issue of Pediatrics, a study revealed that about a third of Ontario children under two years old are lagging behind in their vaccination schedules. Experts noted that the absence of a national immunization surveillance system and shortage of doctors, which could compromise continuity of care are to blame, although contend that perhaps the most significant problem might be the number of young patients each physician attends to, in other words, the less this number, the less the number immunized. Children that have healthcare providers stand a better chance than those whose parents take to walk-in clinics, of follow-ups and reminders about their immunization schedules, although this is not even necessarily foolproof for the former.

Some experts contend that this state of affairs might not typify Ontario. Does this not again speak to the need for targeted health information mentioned above, in this case reminders to these children's parents via for example, email, or text messages on their cell phones of the due dates of their children's immunization schedules? Some providers already use reminders and trackers but should this be mandatory and at what level, policy, regulation, or law? The point here and in the discussion so far is that there is a need to define the concept of intervention in implementing healthcare ICT, or any health related technologies for that matter. Some cell phones are now able to measure blood alcohol levels. Should all youngsters or indeed anyone have to compulsorily purchase such a cell phone to alert him or her to when to stop drinking, and perhaps even more importantly, when not to drive after having been drinking? This may sound implausible but many governments have banned underage drinking, and smoking in public places, and the imminent Massachusetts law mentioned above will compel all its residents to purchase health insurance. On the other hand, should it be a company's policy to request that every worker log on to a webcast relaxation exercise program at a specified hour on particular days? Should government regulation mandate all departments to have such health promotion programs for its staff? All of these measures would require significant healthcare ICT input, and it is unlikely that many would question the wisdom of these measures, or indeed, the interventions. Interventions should therefore be contextual, in some cases, with legal backing. Not immunizing children for example could lead to a health crisis, with many children contracting diseases they should not have. We have not completely eradicated Rubella and measles for examples, although the Measles, Mumps, and Rubella (MMR) vaccine has significantly reduced their prevalence. Dr. Joanne Embree, chair of the Canadian Pediatrics Society's Infectious Disease and Immunization Committee, who practices in Manitoba, observed that EHR offers one of the best means for a physician to track a child's vaccination status. According to Dr. Embree, shots that a child registered in the province born on or after January 01, 1980 go into a program called Manitoba Immunization Monitoring System, every doctor or nurse that has vaccinated a child required to key the data into a database. This makes tracking possible and efficient, as even a child's new caregiver only needs to call the data up, upon authentication, electronically, to know his/ her immunization status. Should each Canadian province not have such a system and should family practitioners in Manitoba and in other provinces and territories not have electronic medical records (EMR) that would enable them communicate with such a system and be able to access the database in real time? Should a province that has spent millions of dollars implementing such a system not care about its children not immunized because primary healthcare providers, including family doctors, nurses, and others, are not purchasing the corresponding technologies to enable communication with the system? Should that province or territory legally compel these healthcare providers to implement the required healthcare ICT? How many lives could the pop-up reminders, features that these EMR have save, and how much could it save the provinces and territories in terms of healthcare costs to treat the diseases the children could have not immunized? Is this an instance where legal intervention compelling healthcare providers to implement healthcare ICT would stir no ripples? To underscore the importance of these vaccines, an outbreak of rubella occurred in Ontario in May 2005, which many experts contend started in a small community high school, only 60% of whose students had vaccination. Over a hundred people became ill, and it could have been worse. This was the largest outbreak of rubella in Canada since 1998, hence of a disease that really should be becoming rarer. This incident demonstrates how not immunizing children could put the entire populace at serious health risks, and the importance of reminders for the parents, via targeted health information, or through their family doctors, either way, healthcare ICT playing a crucial role. While many might not quarrel with legal intervention in the above instance, a pilot project is underway at St. George s Hospital in Stafford U.K to help individuals that compulsively hurt themselves, who research has shown have difficulties simply quitting this dangerous behavior. This "harm-reduction' approach involves a nurse offering these individuals safer options, such as an ice cube to hold, or a rubber band to wear. By not forcing them, and combining these options with other treatments such as cognitive behavior therapy (CBT) and other treatments, the caregivers, hope these persons would eventually quit the behavior. Could someone not have simply said that these persons have no business trying to commit suicide and should compulsorily take even telephone or t-CBT, which some studies have proven effective, for depression for example, at least for those of them with that diagnosis? This of course seems an extreme example of the instances in which coercion does not work, but it illustrates the concept of contextual intervention quite clearly. In other words, it shows the clear indication or lack thereof for legal intervention depending on the nature and context of the issue in question. As mentioned earlier, system issues are important reasons for the high rates of medical errors and adverse events. Not too long ago, research indicated that doctors and nurses could become so busy in certain hospital units attending to so many different patients that they cannot afford the luxury of washing their hands for the average these studies found of about two minutes. Experts therefore recommended that to ensure that these professionals wash their hands after attending to every patient, the processes needs to be speedier, hence the emergence and widespread use of alcohol-based hand cleaners in hospitals, which by the way some object to because they do not drink alcohol for a variety of reasons. There is no doubt that it is important to try to prevent the spread of germs in hospital settings, and the recent outbreaks of C. difficile and the so-called super bug, Methicillin-Resistant Staphylococcus aureus (MRSA) in the U.K attests to this. Yet a recent employee poll that the U.K. Healthcare Commission, a public health advocacy group carried out showed that almost 40% of the 200,000 workers surveyed noted that they lacked adequate access to soap, water, and alcohol wipes in their hospitals. Should the government not therefore mandate its hospitals to provide not just these materials but periodic training on nosocomial infections, perhaps healthcare ICT-enabled, for examples via web-based continuing education that they could access whenever they are able, to minimize service disruption? Such training becomes even more important in light of a recent study on the same subject that showed that only a few of the alcohol-based hand cleaners are effective. The study, published in the March 2006 issue of Emerging Infectious Diseases showed that these hand sanitizers should have 60% alcohol, minimally, to be able to destroy most harmful bacteria and viruses. Would such periodic training exercises not provide healthcare professionals this important update, and would it not help in a hospital management's choice of hand cleaners to recommend to its purchasing department? Many would argue for professional bodies regulating such training for certification and recertification purposes, yet, others would insist that it is entirely within an employer's purview to stipulate hiring requirements, either way another example of the complexity of the issues involved that require consideration to decide upon an intervention approach. This is perhaps one reason the Massachusetts bill is generating such intense debates.

As many as 46 million Americans remain uninsured, or 15.7% of the population. Eight

million children in the U.S. are also uninsured. The country spends $1.9 trillion annually on healthcare, 16.5% of its Gross Domestic Product (GDP), and rising. Many in the U.S. do not just want more people to have access to healthcare, which indeed, is desirable, but also the country to find ways to reduce health spending. Massachusetts says its spends up to $1 billion annually on uninsured individuals receiving free health care or whose health bill one way or another taxpayers ultimately bear. The State Governor insists it will not have any net increase in health spending subsidizing the poor, which it plans to fund with that saved not paying health bills for those uninsured that use health services free. Unlike states that have large numbers of uninsured, Massachusetts smaller numbers and excellent health facilities also work in favor of making the program work. The state will ensure every state resident has not universal, but nonetheless comprehensive healthcare. The state envisages that individuals would be able to buy high deductible, high co-payment, health insurers with providers having a network of services. The problems that some have with this development concern the core issue we have been discussing, that of the nature of intervention in healthcare matters, and in particular in relation to healthcare ICT implementation. Another dimension to this intervention type has to do with the issue of responsibility, a theme of central importance in another topical health issue, namely, the consumer-driven healthcare delivery model. Some see the Massachusetts bill as wanton use of government power, others as the state s resident taking responsibility for their healthcare, although how many of the state s estimated 500,000 uninsured would be subject to the individual mandate, in other words those that make enough money to purchase health insurance but do not remains unknown. The bill gives the poor, single adults that earn $9,800 or less annually, access to insurance with no premiums or deductibles. The law, expected to take effect in July 2007, will require all that file a state tax return, starting in 2008, to say if they have health insurance, and Medicaid and private insurers to give the state lists of their enrollees monthly, with whoever deemed able to purchase insurance, but remains uninsured, slammed with rising penalties. An example of such penalties is loss of ability to claim a personal exemption on their state tax returns in the FY, which could cost one person up to $189 and a couple filing jointly, $378. Since the bill concerns essentially those uninsured, one could ask if those currently insured also benefit from the bill or would not? As discussed earlier, simply having health insurance does not translate into improved health and freedom from diseases, both of which are sine qua non for service utilization to fall, which might make it possible for the Massachusetts for instance curtailing its health spending as it hopes this bill would help it also achieve. However, if people only see health insurance as for treating, and not preventing diseases, they will sooner than later use up their deductibles and co-payments, even if high. The state or employer, or the person will then have to start paying for their medical or treatment expenses, albeit it, part of it, which some might not be able to afford, and will end up seeking free treatment at the expense of the taxpayer, which bill. The state ultimately picks these bills up, or passes them on to the taxpayer in higher taxes. This where the question of responsibility comes in, and indeed, what the idea encompasses. It is also why it is important to recognize the key role that healthcare ICT could play in these issues and why the debate on whether to mandate by law this role or intervene in ensuring that it plays the role is important. The core principle behind consumer-driven healthcare is to empower the healthcare consumer, and with power naturally comes responsibility. For the power of the healthcare consumer to serve him or her, the consumer has to be able responsible enough to make rational choices about healthcare providers and to participate in the management of his or her illness actively, including involvement in decisions on the lab investigations and treatment ordered. Only having the ability to do these things could one unequivocally say confers true power on the healthcare consumer. In fact, they could be crucial determinants of the outcome of the consumer's illness. However, how could the consumer make those decisions without the necessary information to assist in doing so? How could the consumer know which regularly forgets swabs in his/ her patients' abdominal cavity, or amputates the wrong limb, without mechanisms in place for adverse events reporting at the very least, if not other information regarding doctors and surgeons that the public could access? A healthcare consumer is unlikely to know which healthcare provider to patronize on account of the costs of say an elective appendectomy he/ she intends to do, on the recommendation of say his/ her family doctor, with pricing information not made public. Healthcare consumers also need health information on disease prevention, and healthy lifestyles, and on medical progress regarding certain diseases from which they or some persons they know suffer, or are at high risk of so doing. In short, healthcare consumers need information to make the rational choices implicit in the consumer-driven healthcare model. This underscores the need for widespread healthcare ICT diffusion, possibly by fiat, at least under certain circumstances as our discussion thus far indicates. Many argue further, that healthcare consumers need additional reasons to make such rational choices, namely, having to pay part of the medical bill. In other words, what prevents a healthcare consumer over-utilizing or abusing services if they had nothing at stake. Could one not prefer to visit a nearby plastic surgeon for surgery on Sunday evening after watching his favorite soap opera, for consultation perhaps even surgery on a chronic in-growing toenail, rather than choosing the less expensive chiropodist s clinic across town the next day, if not sharing the costs? This is an added dimension of responsibility that many argue health systems around the world, particularly in the developed countries need to curtail their soaring health spending. Here again, the need for healthcare ICT becomes evident, as the costs the consumer will likely incrementally reduce armed with the required information to make the right choices not just regarding treatment, but also in healthy living and in preventing diseases. Furthermore, not only will having the necessary information enable the consumer to be more discerning, the freedom to choose would engender competition among healthcare providers and with market forces kicking in, will eventually force prices down, making healthcare more affordable, hence reducing the consumer's health spending, and that of the country overall. In other words, healthcare ICT would facilitate the achievement of the dual objectives of providing the populace with comprehensive an affordable healthcare, while simultaneously reducing the state/ country's health spending. These general principles of course entail detailed exploration to adjustments to suit individual environments, hence for example the discussion over the nature and extent of intervention to facilitate the use of these health information technologies in order to speed up the achievement of these goals. The important point is that these goals are desirable irrespective of whether the health system is a publicly-or privately funded system, although as noted earlier, while the strategic objectives may tally, the tactics and mechanics of achieving them are necessarily contextual. In March 2006, Sunnybrook and Women's College Health Sciences Center in Ontario, Canada launched a new electronic Continuity of Care Record (CCR) system, aimed at streamlining the delivery of health information between healthcare providers and at empowering healthcare consumers to manage their personal health information. Internet-based and using XML language, the

CCR encapsulates patient health data including illness history, patient diary, lab and imaging results, and treatment notes. It is accessible gratis to the patient or any person the patient authorized and valuable in particular when one has a chronic disease, for example, diabetes, and has to see numerous experts. Such a patient could post blood glucose readings daily, which his/her doctors could access even on the go, facilitating management changes that might be necessary. Patients cold collate historical lab data and view them in graphical or tabular form to have a clearer idea of progress or otherwise made with treatment. They could book appointments online and record allergies, immunization records, blood pressure, and weight, for examples in the diary section. There is no doubt that the CCR empowers patients by enabling them to become active participants in their health affairs. Besides, would the availability of patient information when needed not help improve the quality of care delivered? Would it not save precious time the family doctor or specialist cardiologist would spend waiting for patient information requested via fax or even snail mail, and would this not save costs for the doctor? Considering the ubiquity of the Internet, is this not a cost effective way to communicate and share patient information, which is entirely under the patient's auspices? One of the major problems that doctors have with electronic health records systems is that the technologies impede workflow, but does this not facilitate workflow by offering direct real-time access to valuable information at little or no costs, and should many more doctors not embrace the idea? Indeed, some might even ask if there ought not to be some form of intervention mandating doctors, perhaps even legislation, to have the technologies, in this case a computer with access to the Internet, to access authorized patient information of this sort. The public that is volunteering personal information that the healthcare professionals and others that handle health information share should naturally be the ones to have the greatest concern about on whose laps such information lands. One could argue that if the public could overcome its concern and embrace the CCR, why should the healthcare providers shun it, in particular considering the immense benefits it offers both? Now, should the Ontario government not step and mandate the use of CCR by its doctors? With chronic illnesses such as diabetes major drivers of healthcare funds, and the province's desire to improve the health of its residents, would this it be at all surprising if it did? Perhaps the intervention would be something other than law, but would it surprise anyone that Ontario is promulgating laws to facilitate the implementation of other healthcare ICT that would help it achieve the dual objectives and that the province is in Canada, which has a publicly funded health system? With Ontario's projected 2005 health expenditures 10.6% of the province's GDP, 10.3% in Saskatchewan, and even 13.8 in Prince Edward Island (P.E.I), and rising, and 10.4% for Canada. Projected total health spending for the country, approximately $142 billion for the same year, and projected to increase even higher is striking. Should it surprise anyone that the country and its provinces and territories would be seeking ways to curtail health spending while ensuring the provision of qualitative healthcare to its citizens in accordance with the provisions of the Canada Health Act, even if it warranted passing new laws? Considering that a 2004 study by Ross Baker and Peter Norton showed that 1 in 13 adult patients admitted to acute care hospitals in Canada in fiscal year (FY) 2000 had adverse events, it is no surprise that patient safety looms large in the country. Healthcare ICT plays a major role in ensuring patient, and mostly systems issues, medical errors need a variety of health information technologies to reduce their prevalence, and not only implemented at the system's level, but individual healthcare providers. An example of the former is the Ontario Mental Health Reporting System (OMHRS), which the Canadian Institute for health Information (CIHI) is developing on behalf of the Ontario Ministry of Health and Long-Term Care (MOHLTC). This is a new system comprising for examples, clinical, administrative and resource information to support inpatient mental health services planning in hospitals that have adult inpatient mental health beds in the province, via data collection and reporting for all admissions with effect from October 1, 2005. Thus, the Ontario Ministry of Health and Long-Term Care (MOHLTC) is mandating mental health reporting utilizing the RAI-MH data collection system (Resident Assessment Instrument–Mental Health, version 2.0) in all hospitals with designated adult inpatient Mental Health beds. According to the Canadian Institute for health Information (CIHI), the mandate includes about 74 facilities in Ontario, general hospitals with designated adult inpatient mental health beds, and specialty psychiatric hospitals and provincial psychiatric hospitals, among others, all required, under the mandate, to start data collection using the RAI-MH, by October 1, 2005. Is this not an appropriate level of intervention, one whose enforcement would likely be unproblematic, and which would likely be cost effective, and does this not underscore the idea mentioned earlier of intervention being tailored to meet respective needs?

The situation is not much different in other developed countries such as the U.K,

Australia, and New Zealand, despite their disparate health systems. The fundamental question regarding whether legal constraints are important and to what extent in ensuring the delivery of qualitative healthcare and at affordable costs for both the individual and the payer. Consider a recent study that showed that Men and women with elevated blood pressure that make healthy lifestyle changes, sustained for up to a year and a half could reduce their high blood pressure rates significantly, potentially lessening their heart disease risk. High blood pressure rates fell from 37% to 22% among participants given behavioral counseling, and that adopted a healthy eating plan, called DASH, and exercised more, in a study that the National Heart, Lung, and Blood Institute (NHLBI) of the U.S National Institutes of Health (NIH) conducteds. The study, called PREMIER, published in the

April 4, 2006 issue of Annals of Internal Medicine, "underscores the value of lifestyle changes, namely improving diet and increasing physical activity, in reducing high blood pressure, an important public health problem", noted NHLBI Director Elizabeth G. Nabel, M.D. She added, "For the millions of Americans with prehypertension and hypertension, this shows that individuals can make healthy lifestyle changes to keep blood pressure under control without use of medications." That about 65 million American adults, one in every three, have high blood pressure, a further 59 million adults, prehypertension, above-normal blood pressure levels that increases risk of heart disease and stroke, there can indeed, be no gainsaying the value of this study. Let us examine the details of this study a little more. The researchers assigned eight hundred and ten men and women aged 25 years and older with either prehypertension (120-139mmHg/80-89mmHg) or stage 1 hypertension (140-159mmHg/90-95mmHg) but not on blood pressure control medications randomly assigned to three groups. Participants in two of the groups attended 18 counseling sessions during the first six months, 14 group meetings and 4 individual sessions, and 12 group meetings and 3 individual sessions in the last 12. They had to meet certain goals, namely, for weight loss, physical activity, and limits on sodium and alcohol intake. One of these groups also had guidance on carrying out the Dietary Approaches to Stop Hypertension diet (DASH), an eating plan rich in fruits and vegetables, low-fat dairy products and low in saturated, total fat and dietary cholesterol. The U.S. Dietary Guidelines for Americans endorses DASH as an example of a healthy eating plan, which past NHLBI studies showed to lower blood pressure. A third, control group served had just two 30-minute sessions of advice, at study enrollment and 6 months later, had to follow standard recommendations for blood pressure control, and a third session at the end of the 18-month trial on completion of measurements. The results of the study showed that there were fewer participants with high blood pressure in all three groups. Blood pressure reductions were even more in the intervention groups, and were most prominent in the intervention group that had the DASH eating plan. About 37% of the study participants in all three groups had high blood pressure at the beginning of the study, 22% in the group after DASH and 24% in the intervention group without DASH, and hypertension rate reduced only to 32% in the control group, where participants made fewer lifestyle changes. According to Eva Obarzanek, Ph.D., research nutritionist and a co-author of the study, "This shows that people at risk for heart disease can successfully and simultaneously make multiple changes in lifestyle, for a substantial benefit." Goals for the intervention groups included a 15 lb weight loss (95%of participants were overweight or obese), 3 hours per week of moderate physical activity, daily sodium intakes of no more than 2300 milligrams (1 tsp salt), and limits of one alcoholic drink per day for women, and two per day for men. For the DASH diet, the goals were an increase in the consumption of fruits and vegetables to 9-12 servings per day, consumption of 2-3 servings of low-fat dairy products, and maintaining total fat to no more than 25% of total daily calories. Participants kept food diaries, monitored calories and sodium intakes, and recorded minutes of physical activity to ensure that they are complying with the requirements and making progress toward meeting these goals. Over a third of participants had high blood pressure at the start of the study, of which 62% in the intervention group with DASH, and 60% that without the eating plan, successfully had their blood pressure under control after a year and a half, the readings no longer deemed high, only 37% in the control group. As William M. Vollmer, Ph.D., a study investigator from Kaiser Permanente Center for Health Research noted, "These rates of hypertension control produced by the two interventions are even better than the 50% control rates typically found when single drug therapy is used to control high blood pressure." Compared to the group, there were also significant reductions in the other parameters measured in the study such as weight, and sodium and calorie intake, and increased improvement in fitness, with 25% of intervention group participants meeting the weight loss goal. This study has important implications for the thorny healthcare delivery and costs issues that many countries, particularly in the developed world currently face. According to Cardiovascular Disease Series No. 22, a publication of the Australian Institute of Health and Welfare and the National Heart Foundation of Australia, of 5 May 2004, Heart, stroke, and vascular diseases are responsible for the deaths of more Australians than any other disease group, 50,294 deaths (37.6% of all deaths) in 2002. With heart, stroke, and vascular diseases affecting about 3.67 million Australians, disabling 1.10 million Australians, long-term, the prevalence of these conditions up by 18.2% over the last decade, their total burden expected to increase in the years ahead as the population ages, these diseases commonest in the elderly, they pose important health issues to the country. Coronary heart disease and stroke are the country's first and second causes of deaths, despite the fact that 90% of Australian adults have at least one modifiable risk factor for heart, stroke and vascular diseases and 25% have three or more risk factors, such as overweight (60% or 7.42 million adults), and insufficient physical activity (54% or 7.27 million adults). Others are high blood cholesterol (51% or 6.40 million adults), and high blood pressure (30% or 3.69 million adults), smoking (20% smoke daily or 3.06 million adults), alcohol consumption to harmful extents (10% or 1.54 million adults) and diabetes (8% have diabetes or 945,600 adults.). In fact, some of these risk factors even show unfavorable trends, for example, the prevalence of obesity has doubled over the last two decades, and 10% more individuals were not having sufficient physical activity between 1997 and 2000. However, others are favorable, for example, the 21% and 16% fall in smoking rates for males and females over the last decade, and the 50% fall in the prevalence of high blood pressure since the 1980s, the latter attributable to the rapid rise between 1997 and 2000 in the community use of prescription drugs to reduce blood pressure, among others. A cursory look at these risk factors shows that many are also those that the study mentioned above indicates multiple life style changes could help eliminate. Is it not likely to be more cost-effective to achieve this goal via life style changes than prescription medications, not mention the chances of adverse reactions that could create other help problems with cost implications? Could healthcare ICT not play a significant role in ensuring that the public, and in particular those at high risk for heart and cardiovascular diseases receive and understand the results of this important study? Does this not speak to the value of targeted healthcare ICT-enabled, health information? Would the benefits derivable from implementing the health information technologies required to ensure the dissemination of such important health information not outweigh their costs in the end? Such costs are clearly pecuniary in nature, but could, some would contend even otherwise, for example, the interventions, including legislation, which some would argue are essential to ensuring that society derives these benefits, but which others would deem, constraints, hence costs, for example, in loss of something. Here again, we confront the validity of the arguments for either side of the use of such constraints, regardless of its severity, and in particular in enforceable laws with defined sanctions for their breaches, as for example the imminent Massachusetts law compelling every one of its citizens to purchase health insurance. With legislation banning smoking in effect in many countries, local governments able to pass byelaws and some companies allegedly indirectly assessing levels of physical fitness of applicants, and their weights to determine who to employ, and some calling for legislation on disease prevention, and health promotion, the intercourse of the legal and healthcare dominions seems likely to increase. The success or otherwise of such intercourse however, would continue to depend on its proponents and adversaries able to defend their respective positions, as the case might be, in the courts of law. Some would regard as untenable the position of some in the bioethics zeitgeist linked with an egality rather than equality-based postmodernist, economic utilitarianism that leads to overt consideration of economic cost-efficiency and consumerism. Even if the ultimate goal of population health was a society, where there was no disease and science had succeeded in humankind becoming perfect genetically, and there were no adverse live-events, and relationships issues that created stress and all psychiatric disorders had vanished, and essentially, we lived in a utopia, we are probably light years away from achieving this goal. In the meantime, it is difficult to argue that we should not recognize the disparities among individuals and societies and acknowledge the need for us to incorporate such considerations in our conceptualization of the delivery of healthcare and in every other domain of human endeavor for that matter. In other words, while utopia is a desirable goal that we might just as well achieve at some point in the future, although there are forces both manmade and natural, and in fact, the evolution of some of those hitherto natural forces now make artificial, we need to accept our reality and work with it. Thus, should some able to afford private healthcare even in a publicly funded health system such as Canada be allowed so to do? Yes, says the Supreme Court to Quebec in the landmark Chaoulli-Zeliotis case in 2005. However, and in keeping with our recognition of our reality regardless of whether a country's health system is privately or publicly funded, this should not stop us from continuing to seek ways to improve the health system and make it more accessible and affordable to those that cannot afford to pay for private healthcare. Indeed, could there not be some individuals who opt for such private health services only as a last resort, who would empty their bank accounts to save the life of a loved one to avoid wait lists in a government hospital? In other words, the efforts to make healthcare accessible and affordable should be for all, although some individuals might want to explore other options, including any of a variety of alternative healthcare. Here is the real ethical task. Could we and should we pass laws compelling such individuals to receive healthcare in government hospital, or to regulate the practice of such alternative care? How could we track the evolution of the H5N1 virus and bird flu if we missed significant surveillance biodata because, for example, a large number of people sought health services in alternative medicine practices that either lacked or did not integrate their information systems with a national health information network? Could considerations of the likely adverse consequences of this scenario on overall public health, and on the country's subsequent health spending justify some form of intervention, even legal, streamlining such alternative health practices with mainstream medical practice including the use of healthcare ICT? On the other hand, should individuals be free to choose their preferred healthcare provider, even if outside the mainstream health system, even if from providers whose services have not endured the rigors of scientific scrutiny? Could their choices affect the taxpayer adversely in the end? How could healthcare ICT help in providing individuals the information that they need to make rational choices regarding their healthcare providers? Do we need to restrain individuals who are making choices about their health and health services that are inimical to their interests and that of the larger society with some sort of intervention, even legal? The answers to such questions will determine the extent and nature of the interface of law and healthcare delivery. As the dual objectives of providing qualitative healthcare for all and at the same time ensuring the survival of national economic health, persist, which they inherently would, due to the intricate nature of the link between them, the form and content of this interface would likely continue to feature prominently in contemporary and future healthcare delivery efforts.

References

1. Available at: http://www.cato.org/pubs/pas/pa565.pdf
Accessed on April 05, 2006

2. Carmen DeNavas-Walt, Bernadette Proctor, and Cheryl Hill Lee, Income, Poverty, and Health Insurance Coverage in the United States, 2004, U.S. Census Bureau, August 2005.

3. Available at: http://fermat.nap.edu/books/0309068371/html/index.html
Accessed on April 07, 2006

4. Available at: http://secure.cihi.ca/cihiweb/dispPage.jsp?cw_page=services_omhrs_e
Accessed on April 08, 2006

5. Available at: http://www.nih.gov
Accessed on April 9, 2006

Technical Policy Issues

Software licensing is a major determinant of healthcare ICT costs, and one which management needs to be familiar not just in regard budgetary matters, but also from a technical viewpoint. This is because it would have to formulate usage policies in collaboration with the health organization s IT department in order to ensure that the organization is paying for required licenses, and for those that need them. To understand the difficulty in defining computer software, or simply software, is a step toward appreciating the complex interplay of factors in software licensing. Software is a computer program, a set of instructions, a code in machine-readable form, the entire set of programs, procedures, and routines that make computers work, is readily changeable, and is capable of performing computations, controlling computer hardware, interacting with other software, and with humans to execute sometimes-intricate tasks. Some would consider it simplistic to view software this way, preferring to include all documentations that are relevant to the entire software development process. For them, specification, design, project management, accounting and legal documents, even manuals, would constitute integral parts of software, with copyright implications. The current program/ system conundrum, non-existent in the past when everyone understood the former to mean the code, and the latter a number of programs, further complicates this boundary issue. Indeed, some would consider a multi-tasking software program, as being a system, and these days, a system is often not just the software, but also the hardware, the physical entity it controls to store and execute the program. Indeed, in its modern usage, a system also includes other components that work in tandem to achieve a given task. Then there is the arbitrary, if not confusing distinction between applications software, most familiar to the day-to-day computer user, for example, office suites; system software, such as the operating system (OS) and device drivers that run the hardware; and programming software such as compilers, debuggers, and linkers, which developers use to write software programs. Some even talk about platform software, comprising the basic input/ output system (BIOS), device drivers, OS, and graphical user interface (GUI), all usually bundled with the computers we buy. Considering the foregoing, is it any wonder that software-licensing issues are varied and thorny? Even more importantly for healthcare providers, or for that matter, anyone or organization that uses software, is the cost of software licenses, which can be quite substantial, thousands, even millions of dollars, in some instances. Moreover, software-licensing issues will likely become increasingly prominent with the evolution of electronic health records (EHR), and as the collaborative networks of hospital information systems, physician offices, medical research institutes, and health insurance companies multiply, and software licenses " float " on the networks. That we bought software does not make it ours. Owners of the software, for example, a developer, or vendor, have intellectual property (IP) rights over the product, and often only permit us to use it under certain conditions, which if breached, could result in termination of the permission, even potential liability for infringement. Owners could license their software in many ways, and software users could seek the best license agreement possible, the choices either make expectedly based on factors equally varied. Such factors include the permissions and rights the licensor is willing to grant, and what restrictions to impose, such as who uses the software, how, and for how long, determined by technical, and economic considerations, including the clients and applications/ software, the scope and nature of the sale, and the associated contractual agreements such as for support and maintenance. Software licenses could permit users to use the software for a specific time or forever, hence software could have term or perpetual licenses. For the user, the question would be if the benefit of single payment in the latter case outweighed the costs of upgrades and maintenance support, and in the former, that of regular updates, the costs of license renewal. There are also shrink wrap contracts, license agreements that the user is only able to read and accept/ reject after opening the plastic often wrapped round boxes used to package software. In the U.S., ProCD v. Zeidenburg and Klocek v. Gateway Inc. in the U.S set the precedents for the legality or otherwise, respectively for these types of software licenses, although they continue to show up in software boxes delivered to customers, as are variants such as web-wrap, or click-wrap, for software downloaded over the Internet. Shrink-wrap licenses are often strict, and they give software owners tight control over the product, often at the user' expense. In order to discourage multiple installations, most manufacturers now also have " click-through licenses " to which the end-user must also consent, the goal being to make not only the person that opened the software wrap, but anyone else copying it liable to litigation, and there have been many. In October 2002,

Tube Fab, a Mississauga, Ontario-based manufacturing firm, paid $57,000 settlement for having unlicensed copies of Autodesk and Microsoft software on its computers, and such cases appear in the courts with remarkable frequency, not just in Canada, but also in the U.S, U.K, and many other countries. Indeed, a report released by the Canadian Alliance Against Software Theft (CAAST) and the Business Software Alliance (BSA) noted that software piracy cost Canadian software vendors almost $200 million in lost retail sales of business software applications and the country roughly 12,000 jobs in 2001. With software sales infusing over $6 billion a year into the Canadian economy, concern over software piracy, although not as prevalent as in many other countries, understandably cuts across the country's economic landscape, much as it does in other countries too. Furthermore, with industry-watchdog organizations, such as the Business Software Alliance (BSA) and Software & Information Industry Association (SIIA) ever ready to enforce software licensing, sometimes with a little help from a disgruntled current or ex-employee, the issue is anything but trifle. At $300 per license, a healthcare organization found under licensed for Microsoft Office by 300 licenses is $90,000 under licensed, which it has to pay along with a penalty up to four times that amount, or $360,000, and $25,000 BSA audit fee, a total of $475,000. With the 60-day follow-up audit fee added, another $15,000, the grand total becomes $490,000. What if BSA found other under licensed products, and what does such representation portend for the integrity of the organization and its governance? Original Equipment Manufacturers (OEM) package software, for examples operating system (OS) such as Windows OS, and desktop applications such as Office suites, with the computers we purchase. OEM licenses are common software licenses. Bulk-priced for value added resellers (VAR), they tend to be less expensive than retail packaged software, sometimes significantly so. The flipside is that the licenses always come bundled with hardware, are not transferable, and last only as long as the computer with which they come lasts. There is in general, no other way to buy retail-packaged software, and you pay more, but can reinstall it on another computer, so long as you uninstall it from the previous one. This leaves room for replacing your computer without the need to also upgrade or replace its applications, hence saving costs. Some question the idea of bundling software with hardware insisting that it is a gimmick by manufacturers to sell scaled-down versions of their poor-selling, commercial off-the shelf (COTS) or packaged software, and possibly even to secure marketing mileage with the many software bundled gratis, as many advertise, many of which users do not need. There is also the issue of support, which is much harder to get from second, even third-party manufacturers, as with OEMs, compared to buying your software direct from its manufacturer. Volume licensing is an option larger healthcare organizations should seriously consider. This option has a number of variants, for example, pricing based on the number of computers on which you install the software installation, as is usually the case with desktop applications, or according to some specified metrics, such as the number of processors a server has, as is often the case with server-based applications. Volume licensing saves costs via scale economies. Microsoft, for example, licenses some of its software, for examples, SQL Server, on a per-processor basis, with each processor counting as one, the number of cores (execution resources) and/ or threads (instruction streams) it has nonetheless. This means that your organization only needs four processor licenses, for example, for your four-processor systems, regardless of whether it has single-core, multiple-core, or hyperthreaded processors. It also means that you may upgrade from your current single-core to Intel & AMD's, more-modern (2005) dual-core processors, without incurring additional costs. Some companies, such as Microsoft allow you to reinstall OEM software on multiple computers via rights linked with Volume licensing, including license reassignment, if you have purchased Software Assurance for the OEM, the firm's inclusive cost-saving maintenance program, which enables the purchaser to spread out, defer, and better predict and minimize costs of future upgrades, among other benefits. The company also offers a Windows Server 2003 Client Access License (CAL), required for each user or device (or both) that accesses or uses the server software, namely Windows Device CAL or Windows User CAL, on a Per User/ Per Device mode or Per Server mode, both modes available for either license type. These modes replaced " per seat licenses" given on a named-user basis in past license models. Because costs depend on the number of users or devices accessing the server software, they are more suited to distributed computing milieus, where multiple servers within the health organization serve most devices or users, compared to, for example, its Per Server mode CALs, which suit better, computing milieus with a small number of servers having limited access needs. Indeed, Microsoft has a new CAL suite via volume licensing termed, the Core CAL, which simplifies licensing basic server components across desktop computers, and saves IT staff many woes managing CALs for server software, and not having to worry about the division between manufactures and vendors, many of the latter who balk at these licensing modes, for essentially pecuniary reasons. Indeed, software licensing has always been and remains a complex issue, one that has the potential to create acrimony in an instant, also between vendors and purchasers. Conflict often arises with vendors eager to prevent software piracy and to receive payments for software use, the purchasers often piqued by vendors' reluctance to simplify licensing agreements, and allow more room for tracking software assets to facilitate compliance. Healthcare organizations should be ready to deal with such issues from time to time.

There is also free software license that comes with open-source software (OSS), for example the General Public License (GPL), usually in ubiquitous source code, although not always that free, as software vendors, package and market some, such as Linux (to avoid the GNU/ Linux name controversy), although you do not have to license every installed copy. The problems with such software include a steep learning curve for technology neophytes, limited numbers of compatible desktop applications, and possibly substantial support and maintenance costs over time, although open-source software is gaining increasing attention among technophiles. Furthermore, many common free software licenses, for example, Berkeley Software Distribution (BSD), and Lesser General Public License (LGPL), are GPL-compatible. However, not even free software is free of the controversy that surrounds software licensing, and contracts, which latter are enforceable by contract law, the license, under the terms of copyright law, a distinction that may count depending on your jurisdiction. Some of the protagonists of open source software want it to remain free, but others disagree. However, all agree that even if used for commercial purposes, there should be some regulation guiding its use. You may therefore, not modify, copy, or redistribute, any version without first accepting the terms of the license, under copyright law, and in the case of GPL, may actually demand a fee for your services or resell the software, source-code included, a requirement termed copyleft, a copyright volte-face aimed at the software's redistribution, although changing its text is also prohibited. Issues such as dynamically linking non-GPL software to GPL libraries remain sorely disputed, with some, including the Free Software Foundation (FSF) that owns the GPL copyright, insisting that any executable so dynamically linked is a derivative product, others objecting. Healthcare providers interested in open-source software, and perhaps in linking GPL-based libraries to their own codes may come across vendors distributing, marketing, and licensing such libraries, but should note that they risk the wrath of some in the open source community, who thus far, seem to be succeeding on their terms in the law courts. Incidentally, BSD license seems less restrictive on derived works. Regardless of whatever moral, ethical, or philosophical argument anyone might advance for the unfettered reproduction and redistribution of copyrighted material, including software, any attempt to violate software end user license agreement (EULA) will likely be resisted, perhaps even in court, by its owners, at least for the 70 years copyrights last. Indeed, some laws, for example, the US Uniform Computer Information Transactions Act (UCITA), in force in Maryland and Virginia, allow copyright owners to demand that such violations cease forthwith even without court order, which some argue is giving vendors too much leeway by being able to define material breach and prescribe its remedy. There is also international consensus, and ongoing dialogue, on combating software piracy, and to encourage acceptance of the underlying principles of Intellectual Property rights and compliance with copyright laws, particularly in developing countries, most of which lack the resources to purchase often-costly software licenses, one reason for the enhanced stature of OSS in some, particularly in South and Latin America. Health providers not only need to avoid being embroiled in infringement issues, more importantly, they need to develop appropriate short-term and strategic approaches to software license management. For proprietary software, they need to have unassailable copy prevention and digital rights management policies and programs. For copy prevention or protection, healthcare organizations may use registration keys (usually long, alphanumeric codes), dongles (electronic serial-numbers hardware), or key files (as in the directory where the software is), all required to run the software, or any other effective means. They may also employ digital rights management (DRM) techniques such as content scrambling systems (CSS) and digital watermarking, and invoke DRM protection laws such as the US Digital Millennium Copyright Act (DMCA), if necessary, although DMCA is not fool-proof, as some have exploited its exceptions to allow reverse-engineering for interoperability, encryption research, and security, to perpetrate and flout IP rights. An exception that will likely interest some healthcare organizations, is DMCA Title Two's offer of "safe harbor protection" to Internet Service Providers (ISPs,) protecting them from liability for acting as an information conduit. This protection is crucial these days that many healthcare organizations provide for and run their own Websites, although the law also mandates them to remove material on which a copyright holder is claiming infringement. Also notable is Bill C-60 of 2005, which amended the Copyright Act of Canada, the Bill, among others, allowing for infringement of copyright by circumventing rights management schemes when intended to violate another right. Many healthcare organizations purchase rather than develop their own software. Even those that have proprietary software also often buy software from vendors and other software firms. The costs of the licenses they necessarily purchase in order to install and run the software can add up very quickly. Healthcare organizations therefore also need to seek ways of saving costs on software licenses. They could achieve this goal by using license management solutions that best suit their needs. There are basic license accounting systems on the market that compile inventories of installed software; smart license managers that ensure staffers comply with hospital policies on software license allocations; and license servers able to assign, optimize, and monitor, licenses and their uses across board, including those able to ensure maximal utilization of concurrent licenses during peak usage hours. Healthcare organizations should exploit the opportunities the variety of cost-saving licensing schemes that software vendors and manufacturers currently offer, such as those mentioned earlier. Healthcare organizations should perform baseline software audit, preferably by a third party, if merging with other healthcare providers, and periodic audits, at least annually, even if not doing so. They should centralize all software acquisitions to facilitate tracking of licenses, develop sound purchasing policies, and patronize trustworthy suppliers. They also need to adopt rule-based license management, to prioritize tasks on their networks of workstations and servers, and counter problems with license server management, such as, hoarding licenses by running applications when not needed just so they will always be available for someone's use, which may actually make the organization falsely think it needs more licenses for some applications. Small and medium-sized clinics and physician offices may need no more than basic computer-dedicated, node-locked, and individualized, personal-use licenses, of such organizations. The former license, typically most appropriate for computationally intense software and those used on workstations dedicated to a particular application, user-based licenses best for user-dependent products such as an e-mail product, or any application where user-id lending would conflict with its very nature. Healthcare organizations standardizing on a product would find "site licensing" useful, although agreeing with the vendor on the definition of a site, perhaps testy. Most hospitals will need network licensing, should have a versatile license manager, commercial such as FLEXIm by GLOBETrotter Software (San Jose, California,) the erstwhile industry standard although there is a surfeit of license managers in the market these days, or in-house, and have back-up license servers. Besides open source software are other so-called disruptive innovation such as multitenanted-architecture-based software-as-a-service, and the Web 2.0 movement. The former, essentially piracy-free and with little or no need to maintain older versions, sounds attractive in cost terms, but with patient information shared among healthcare professionals and others, creates no conflict of confidentiality, as would the case with competing businesses with a need to keep business information well away from their competitors. Salesforce.com, among others pioneered the relatively new software delivery model wherein an organization subscribes to software applications hosted remotely by the vendor or installed locally. The model is attractive to smaller organizations with limited IT budgets because there is no need for large up-front license fees, or separate support and maintenance fees, or for installation and integration when hosted. Healthcare providers that decide to explore this option need to pay close attention to and monitor the contract to ensure that it meets their goals, and that they do not overshoot their subscription. Web 2.0 or what prefer to call live Web companies, such as Flickr and MySpace, are gaining patronage, and web 2.0 concepts such as Really Simple Syndication (RSS) and user generated content, which latter has applications for personal health records for example, increasing currency. With the boundaries of the living Web inherently diffuse, facilitated by novel software termed the Web s "connective tissue," this could be a valuable platform for a health community of doctors, nurses, patients, and so forth, operating in individual groups or as one collaborative effort. One way to achieve the goal of targeted health information for example is via RSS, to which individuals could subscribe for information from a Web service. With the immense potential of living Web concept, healthcare organizations and providers also need to consider how they could tap this potential in their value propositions to their clients. Software is a staple of modern-day healthcare delivery, and its licensure, sine qua non to its use. Accordingly, appreciating the issues germane to and effectively managing the latter could facilitate or impede if unattended, the ability of any healthcare organization to achieve its goal of qualitative healthcare delivery in the end, and not doing so could achieve the opposite result. It goes without saying that the more healthcare organizations and providers are able to implement and utilize software and other healthcare ICT, the more we are likely to achieve our goal of making e-health truly work.

As with other organizations, healthcare organizations face unrelenting challenges of network intrusion by malicious persons and groups, the challenges complicated by the increasing vulnerabilities of their systems that progress in mobility, and interoperability between disparate systems and the resulting increase in exploitable communication routes engender. There has been a dramatic increase in the number and types of malware, and we now have spyware, pharming, denial-of-service blackmail threats, frauds, phishing, even spear phishing, and many others, hackers and spammers developing ever more discrete techniques to render systems useless. Indeed, spam and phishing have become the bane of the Internet. Some estimates put the percentage of emails that is spam at up to 90%, financial institutions worldwide losing $400 million or more in 2004 from phishing. Malware attacks are becoming less random, become more focused, target smaller numbers of computers in order to stealthily escape anti-spam techniques that measure email volume. Viruses, worms, and Trojans run into hundreds of thousands and increasing at rates of tens of thousands every month, averagely one-in-thirty and in times of virus outbreaks, one in ten emails, for example, infected with viruses, which means that hospital servers could flood with unsolicited emails in a hours, disrupting, if not grounding services. Worse still, the purveyors of this despicable acts make anti-virus efforts Herculean by "blasting" out numerous novel editions of their malicious logic rapidly to prevent detection or ensure continued effectiveness. There is no doubt about the need of healthcare organizations to pre-empt potentially malicious content from entering their systems. Indeed, it imperative that they do, and in the U.S, for example, certain provisions in the Health Insurance Portability and Accountability Act of 1996 (HIPAA) mandate them to do so. Trojan horses, which do not replicate and must be mass-spammed from, for example, zombie computer networks, hijacked, malware-infected machines, or botnets such as the Zotob worm created in 2005, are becoming commoner but their effect not as devastating as of worms such as Netsky-P, Zafi-D, and Sober-D, and-N, and viruses that are able to proliferate via email systems. Health-related spam, principally regarding drugs their perpetrators claim help improve libido, sleep better, lose weight, even purportedly protect against avian flu, and others such as vitamins, are increasingly common forms of spam. With the increasing threat also from adware and spyware, healthcare organizations will need to focus on integrate antimalware solutions for which they will also have to develop policies to ensure their centralized control. Host Intrusion Prevention Systems are likely to gain increasing currency among healthcare organizations as they offer a mix of security approaches for examples the customary antivirus and firewall protection, as well as application inspection and behavioral containment, although such organizations need to tailor the systems they purchase and implement to their needs rather than buy just any vendors push. Efforts at containing the malicious activities of hackers and spammers are ongoing, involving a variety of different stakeholders, including ex-spammers and hackers. The CAN-SPAM legislation has helped put a number of spammers in the U.S and Canada, out of commission. Internet Service Providers (ISPs) are collaborating and sharing information on the activities of hackers and spammers, helping to preempt them, and launch counter-offensives against their nefarious endeavors. Software companies such as Microsoft have literally declared war on spammers/ hackers. Windows XP SP2 has improved security and protecting individual and corporate computer users. The company issues critical security and other patches routinely, on the average about two such patches monthly, to offer enhanced security to computers. Microsoft now spams any e-mail that does not have a sender s ID, with its adoption of Sender ID technology as a standard to combat spam and phishing. Sender ID combines two earlier security technologies, namely, Caller ID for E-mail, which Microsoft released in February 2004, and Meng Wong's SPF. An e-mail that complies with this technology must have an SPF tag in a Domain Name System (DNS) record to authenticate valid machines that send mail from that domain. With this technology, Sender ID Framework (SIDF), an e-mail-authentication technology protocol, Hotmail and MSN will flag as potential spam any message that does not have the tag to verify its sender. The technology protocol helps tackle the problem of spoofing and phishing by verifying the domain name from whence an e-mail comes, by verifying the IP address of the sender against the supposed owner of the domain that sent it. Sender ID technology thus ensures that e-mail originates from the Internet domain it purportedly came from. The technology relies on Caller ID for E-mail technology and the Sender Policy Framework (SPF), both its SPF-1 and SPF-2 versions that validates sender data, and "from" name, respectively. The technology continues to provoke controversy in the industry, however, some arguing that while its goal is noble, there are concerns regarding the challenges it will create for legitimate e-mail users, and that it is not yet the accepted standard. That it has competition such as Yahoo's DomainKeys, and merged with Cisco System's Internet Identified Mail, the public key cryptography-based DomainKeys Identified Mail (DKIM), and the possible conflicts and standards issues that this might create also concerns some. Nonetheless, many more firms continue to embrace it and launch products and services that support Sender ID, for examples, DoubleClick, Symantec, Tumbleweed, and VeriSign. With Microsoft unbending, the pressure is now on e-mail senders to adopt Sender ID, which requires Internet service providers, firms, and other Internet domain holders to publish so-called SPF (Sender Policy Framework) records to identify their mail servers. Some large e-mail senders already support Sender ID, for example, AOL, and about 30% of e-mails are verifiable by Sender ID. However, only roughly a million domains currently publish SPF records, compared to the almost eighty million registered domains worldwide in 2004, for example, a situation Microsoft wants improved. The company has been pushing this technology on the Internet community for several years now with little success, and decided to go it alone if necessary, apparently, with the of the Internet Engineering Task Force, a standard-setting body, quashed a working group evaluating Sender ID technology as an industry standard for e-mail authentication in September 2004. Some contend that the end-user that will bear the brunt as legitimate e-mails with no Sender ID could get the spam tag when sent to Hotmail users. Besides, critics say the technology fails with e-mail forwarding services. Microsoft must believe that more people would adopt its Hotmail and MSN and more domain holders/e-mail senders publish SPF records, because of its move, criticisms of its technology regardless. Some analysts thought not, and even argued that the move to force the adoption of Sender ID would fail because the notice was too short, that firms already had their annual budget in place and cannot afford the expenses of the changes involved in publishing SPF records, and that Microsoft could not impose its will on sovereign firms. This was in 2005. However, the technology has been gaining increasing acceptance.

Publishing SPF records is not complicated, costs little as it often does not need new hardware or software, and the tasking aspect is compiling an inventory of mail servers and maintaining records afterward, argues Microsoft, which seems determined to have its way this time. Microsoft insists that the growing adoption of SIDF worldwide has resulted in remarkable improvements in the accuracy of its SmartScreen (TM) filtering process, which combined with other technologies, is enable MSN Hotmail to intercept over 3 billion spam messages per day.

As the SIDF case illustrates, one of the most important technical issues that could facilitate or hamper any e-health program is that of the standards to which healthcare ICT must comply for seamless interoperability of disparate information systems. The health sector gulps between 8 and 14 % of Gross National Product in many countries, and because everyone is a potential patient, the concern for the effectiveness of healthcare delivery is catholic. A major hindrance to the achievement of high quality healthcare delivery is the multiplicity of healthcare delivery systems, technologies, concepts, and terms. There is therefore an urgent need for standardization to ease interoperability and facilitate the much-needed information sharing and communication in the healthcare industry. This lack of standards is also a major obstacle to the widespread adoption of electronic health records, but there is progress towards solving this problem. In June 2003, Connecting for Health announced agreement on 10 sets of data standards. Connecting for Health is a consortium of over 100 providers, payers, and others, such as IBM, the American Medical Association, hospitals, and federal agencies. These standards included the National Council of Prescription Drug Plans (NCPDP) SCRIPT prescription-drug information standards, the LOINC vocabulary for laboratory tests, and the Clinical Document Architecture (CDA). They also agreed on a national demonstration project to test that electronic communication utilizing these standards indeed improve the quality of care and prevent medical errors. Most hospitals including in Canada already use one of the standards, the HL7 Clinical Context Management Specification, for administrative and/ or clinical tasks. The consortium hoped the initiative would result in the use of standards being more widespread, and electronic interchange more complete. A pilot study included data from clinical procedures, lab results, prescriptions, and diagnostic summaries. Data on adverse drug events went to the FDA, viral tests, and laboratory results to the CDC for surveillance, and data on quality of care of care, the Centers for Medicare and Medicaid Services (CMS). The U.S. Department of Health and Human Services has endorsed the data standards. Connecting for Health has also been developing and testing electronic personal health records, which, unlike medical records, enable consumers to track their health status, make sound healthcare decisions, gain control over their health, via information obtained from various sources such as from physicians, insurers, hospitals, laboratories, and pharmacies. The organization is also examining certain notable privacy and security practices, in order to describe and publicize feasible solutions presently used. There is even more progress lately, as healthcare IT standards organizations increasingly cooperate with one another. For example, the Accreditation Standards Committee X12 recently signed memorandums of understanding with both Health Level Seven and the National Council for Prescription Drug Programs in the US. HL7 has also recently been signing a series such agreements, including a memorandum with the Institute of Electrical and Electronic Engineers (IEEE), and another with the Engineering in Medicine and Biology Society (EMBS), the goal being to establish guidelines by which organizations will collaborate on future projects and to encourage joint work efforts thereby prevent redundancy in standards developments. It is no doubt in the industry s interests to have memoranda that foster communication among the many standards development organizations within the industry, and that help minimize redundancies in XML development initiatives, foster harmonization of healthcare standards, reduce costs, and facilitate interoperability. ASC X12, accredited by the American National Standards Institute, develops standards for electronic data interchange, for example, NCPDP, standards for prescribing. HL7, which developed messaging standards for use between disparate information systems, and in 2004, signed a separate agreement with NCPDP pledging to collaborate on standards initiatives, is also at the forefront of efforts to define the concept and core features of EHR. The concept of the EHR system is evolving, at least regarding the functionalities that make up a comprehensive clinical system, for which it is often an acronym. Thus an electronic medical records system (EMR) is an aspect of such a system, with scheduling, ordering, care recording, population health, lab information system, decision support and workflow automation, being others. There was no

agreement on EHR definition until recently. In fact, the first published international EHR technical specification ISO/ TS 18308: 2004 Health informatics-
Requirements for an Electronic Health Record Architecture" had seven different definitions with roots in concepts of EHR in the United States, Australia, Europe, and Canada. The HL7 EHR system functional model started life as the Draft Standard for Trial Use (DSTU), expected with experience in usage to graduate to EHR-S Functional Model, for balloting as standard and proposed at the behest of the Centers for Medicare and Medicaid Services (CMS), it recognizes a couple hundred EHR functions. This has created the need to specify what constitutes a minimum set of functions for a specific care setting, for example, hospitals, small physician practices, or nursing homes. The criteria for determining minimal functionally however remain contentious, best available evidence from the literature and expert opinion, among suggestions advanced. Incidentally, CMS was looking for ways to decide which physician practice systems would qualify for differential payment, in an effort to improve healthcare. This is why some have suggested a "fast-track" approach to achieving this goal by concentrating on simple, fast, and minimal requirements for both functions and interoperability such as the six "simple" bundles and processes the Institute for Healthcare Improvement has proposed. These processes require minimal computer use, hence minimal financial outlay, and better chances of widespread adoption. Standards, regardless of whether determined by formal standards bodies or industry consortiums will improve the ability of healthcare providers to share information, enhancing quality of care. With cross-border, even inter continent travel commoner than ever, people need and expect to be able to get high quality healthcare even when they are far away from home. This is more likely to happen if standardized global information networks are in place to facilitate contact between healthcare professionals in different locales or countries. Having international standards will also ensure patients going to other countries for scheduled treatments and surgeries are rest assured their health information will be available to their doctors abroad as and when needed. In Europe, for example, there is a multinational collaboration using telematics for transplantation of bone marrow and other organs currently. The World Wide Web (WWW) is also creating opportunities for cross-national healthcare delivery. Personal health records for example, could be web-based, making access anywhere in the world, theoretically possible, and easy. However, there are significant technical policy issues in

the way of such cross-border access, including those pertaining to standards, which essentially prompted the establishment of the World Wide Web Consortium (W3C,) to guide the Web to its complete potential by developing common protocols that advance its evolution and guarantee its interoperability. W3C is an international industry consortium jointly run by the US-based MIT Computer Science and Artificial Intelligence Laboratory (MIT CSAIL), the France-based European Research Consortium for Informatics and Mathematics (ERCIM), and Keio University in Japan. The over 400-member strong Consortium offers a repository of information on the WWW for developers and users. It also offers a number of prototype and sample applications to show use of new technology. With the increasing importance of the Internet in health service delivery, including the dissemination of targeted health information for disease prevention and health promotion campaigns, healthcare organizations will not only need to be cognizant of developments regarding this valuable technology, but also will have to develop appropriate policies on what to use it for, and how. The Internet is no longer the exclusive preserve of academic departments and research institutes. Since ARPNET, the world's first operational packet switching network first went online in 1968 the Internet has not only ventured into the public domain but also continues to evolve as a versatile communication tool, albeit along a somewhat convoluted path. Among the technical, political, commercial, and other issues that have complicated this evolutionary process, the dispute over Internet governance stands out distinctly. Indeed, this issue is not only stalling the Internet's progress, it threatens its future, even its very survival, which underscores the significance of the World Summits on the Information Society (WSIS), the last held in Tunis, Tunisia, on November 16-18, 2005. This meeting, expected to finalize negotiations on the crucial subject of Internet governance, originated from a 2002 resolution the U.N. General Assembly adopted. The resolution acknowledged the need for world political leaders to "marshal the global consensus and commitment required to promote the urgently needed access of all countries to information, knowledge and communication technologies" in order to fully benefit from the ongoing information and communication technologies (ICT) revolution. The first phase of the UN-sponsored summit held in Geneva in 2003 produced a plan of action to facilitate global ICT diffusion, but consensus over approaches to Internet governance remains elusive and its lack continues to mire ongoing negotiations, although the U.S position seemed to have prevailed. At the core of the dispute is the call by some countries and organizations, including the European Union (EU), for greater governmental control of the Internet via some kind of international agency, akin to the International Telecommunications Union (ITU). The United States takes a contrary stand, insisting that existing systems of technical controls, which the Internet Corporation for Assigned Names and Numbers (ICANN) oversees, constitute the most effective approaches to ensuring the stability and security of the Internet. Indeed, according to Ambassador David A. Gross, The U.S. coordinator for international communication and information policy, the prominence the debate on Internet governance receives might be shifting attention away from other, perhaps more important, issues regarding the Internet. He also has always stressed the need to pursue the Plan of Action adopted at the conclusion of WSIS-Phase 1 in December 2003, which identified clear goals for achieving ICT access and Internet connectivity in rural villages, schools, health care facilities, local governments, libraries, and universities in developing countries. The U.S. is also urging these countries to create a free market environment, which it argues will enhance the diffusion of ICT services as market forces curtail prices, increasing the numbers of subscribers to these services, and creating crucial, yet affordable access to markets and internet-based health services at home and abroad. Evidence shows that per capita income in globalizing developing countries increased 5 percent yearly in the 1990s compared to a 1% decrease in those not doing so in the past decade. The U.S. also plans to continue collaborating with other governments to develop workable strategies for ICT expansion in the developing world, and it is supporting projects aimed at achieving this objective, such as the Digital Freedom Initiative. This joint program of the US Department of Commerce, US Agency for International Development, US Department of State, Peace Corps, US Small Business Administration, and USA Freedom Corps, initiated in Senegal in March 04, 2003, funds projects in Senegal, Indonesia, Jordan, and Peru, with more DFI partner countries billed to join. Over 90 U.S. business, non-governmental organizations, and academic institutions are currently members of the DFI Business Roundtable, working with host countries to expand markets for ICT, and to develop and customize products and services suited to local needs. Further, the U.S. Agency for International Development (USAID) is assisting to expand ICT access and capabilities in about 80 nations, the U.S. government spending about $200 million annually to fund over

500 ICT development activities in its efforts to achieve these objectives. There is no gainsaying that the US funds many other ICT-related projects aimed at promoting economic growth and opportunities for cost-effective health services delivery, in DFI partner-countries, and elsewhere in the developing world. One would therefore be hard-pressed to argue that the U.S. lacks interest in ICT diffusion in developing countries. Why then is it at loggerheads with the EU and others over Internet governance?

Other countries and organizations are also helping to bridge the so-called "digital divide" between developed and developing countries, and there have been significant progress in this regard, for example, the development of the hand-held, Simputer, an acronym for "simple, inexpensive and multilingual people's computer", by the Simputer Trust in India. Also in India, an ICT start-up company called Novatium is offering a stripped-down home computer for about $70 or $75, and in the U.S, MIT Media Lab s "First Mile Solutions" provides remote and rural communities with telecommunications infrastructure. The Open Source movement is providing developing countries with affordable, sometimes even free software, and some countries, such as Brazil, are not just embracing, but are also preaching the Open Source concept. There is indeed, no doubt about the need for a global approach to an essentially all-encompassing Information Society that includes every United Nations member, as agreed to at the first WSIS Geneva meeting in December 2003, where the 50 countries in attendance also agreed to a political Declaration of Principles and a Plan of Action. What remain unresolved are two key issues, namely, Internet governance and the financial mechanisms for bridging the "digital divide". The EU essentially went to Tunis to propose implementing rather than reopening deliberations on agreed principles, and to consolidate progress made in emerging economies by supporting the strategies for expanding Internet access, including the development of creative content and applications, both moves unlikely furor-provoking for anyone. However, it is difficult to say the same thing for its stand on Internet governance, which is to internationalize the management of the Internet's core resources, namely, the domain name system, Internet Protocol (IP) addresses and the root server system. The EU is dissatisfied with the current arrangement wherein the Internet Corporation for Assigned Names and Numbers (ICANN), a private, internationally organized, non-profit corporation, which operates under a Memorandum of Understanding with the US Department of Commerce of 1998, manages these resources. It prefers a new cooperation model involving a medley of stakeholders, including governments, the private sector, civil society and international organizations in Internet governance, a position the U.S flatly rejects. The EU also prefers the simple and efficient financial mechanisms for bridging the "digital divide," using existing UN organizations and government agencies, and promoting public and private sector involvement, with respect to the latter, a reference to the critical role ICT plays in the competitiveness of EU industries in the global economy. Besides being opposed to ICANN controlling the Internet, the EU also favors a stronger emphasis on the public policy interest of all governments, whose role in Internet governance it argues should be on public policy, not routine management of the Internet. In this regard, the EU wants to see reverence for the Internet s architectural principles, including interoperability, and openness. It wants the Internet to be stable, dependable, robust, secure, and to remain "spam free". It does not take much to see why the EU seems particular about these positions. With ICT accounting for 40% of Europe's productivity growth and for 25% of EU GDP growth, experts regard it as the most promising sector of the EU economy. Indeed, the EU adopted an initiative in June 01, 2005, termed "i2010," to promote jobs and growth in the IT and media industries, requesting its member States to define National Information Society Priorities in their National Reform Programs in mid-October 2005 as their contributions to achieving the goals of the initiative. It has even set three policy priorities for i2010, plans it must achieve within three years. They include, developing an open and competitive single market for information society and media services, including supporting technological convergence with "policy convergence" via backing an efficient spectrum management policy, the upgrade of audiovisual media services rules, of the regulatory framework for electronic communications, and of an inclusive and effective Internet security and interoperable digital rights management. The EU acknowledges that it trails countries such as the U.S and Japan, which spends €400 and €350 per head, respectively in ICT research, compared to€ 80 per head by the EU. This perhaps explains the second priority, which is to increase investment in ICT research by 80%, and to reap more benefits from it via such measures as trans-European demonstrator projects, which would validate potentially valuable research findings and encourage the involvement of small and medium sized enterprises in EU research projects. The third priority is to promote an inclusive European information society, and to bridge the social and geographic "digital divide". The EU plans to achieve this goal via such projects as an e-Inclusion initiative, an Action Plan on e-Government for citizen-centered services three "quality of life" ICT key initiatives, namely, technologies for an ageing society, smarter, safer and cleaner intelligent vehicles, and digital libraries to enable global access to multimedia and multilingual European culture. How these different backgrounds to the diametrically opposed stances of the U.S and the E.U. pan out in the end can only be conjectural for now, as is whether the victory the U.S seems to have achieved lasts, either way, with significant implications for Internet policy formulation by healthcare organizations, now and down the road. In its early days, the Internet, based around the ARPANET, was government-funded and mainly used for non-commercial research and military purposes. With its increasing expansion in the 1980s, however, even to some companies such as Hewlett-Packard, it became more difficult to prevent its commercialization, which some passionately detested. Before long, the U.S. Department of Defense stopped funding the core Internet backbone, which led to the shutdown of ARPANET in 1989, the provision of Internet connectivity in the U.S. taken over by the National Science Foundation via its TCP/ IP university network backbone that later became NSFNet, and commercialized in 1995. This kick-started the subsequent exponential growth, and commercialization of the Internet, a term which although widely used to refer to the World Wide Web (WWW), also includes a variety of public, commercial, and educational networks whose numbers keep rising. Besides the ease of creating new Web documents and connecting them to existing documents that the development of the Uniform Resource Locator (URL), and HyperText Markup Language (HTML), web browsers, and the WWW heralded, some also attribute the Internet's phenomenal growth to the lack of central governance, and to the efforts towards non-proprietary Internet protocols. Emphasis on non-proprietary protocols, in particular, fostered vendor interoperability and discouraged any vendor gaining dominance and control over the Internet. On the other hand, as intuitive as it is, that no one organization, country, or firm should control the Internet, it is no less so that the Internet would hardly function without some form of order, which brings the issue of standardization squarely to the fore. From "Requests for Comments" (RFC), started in the late 1960s, with anyone free to suggest ideas for standardizing the Internet, even if only few such ideas or protocols passed the experimental rigor mandatory for attaining official standard (STD)status by the Internet Architecture Boar (IAB), to the International Standards Organization s (ISO), Open Systems Interconnet (OSI) model of the 1980s. From these and to now the TCP/ IP, DNS, POP3, SMTP, URL, HTML, FTP, HTTP, IMAP, and others, the evolution of Internet protocols and standards has been a protracted effort to transition from often-idiosyncratic, vendor/ proprietary protocols, to multi-vendor interoperable network standards. Is the U.S. wary, as some argue, of backtracking to the erstwhile chaotic Internet era, or of crippling bureaucratization, even regulatory curtailment of the freedom of speech and expression, the booming commercial milieu, and the new and outstanding multi-lateral peer agreements and contracts that currently prevail, with an intergovernmental body or agency in control of the Internet? Is the U.S right in insisting that ICANN should have a chance to continue to evolve rather than have it jettisoned? There is little doubt about the various technical, commercial, political, and other issues involved, but could these two key players, the U.S and the EU resolve them, and what would happen if they could not in the end to, for example, the prospects of innovative use of the Internet by healthcare organizations ? What indeed, would healthcare delivery suffer from the ongoing tussle, if unresolved? The U.S maintains its stand that countries aspiring to the "civil society " and ICT diffusion must create and maintain an enabling environment based on democratic principles, the rule of law, and an open market; be committed to content creation and intellectual rights protection; and to Internet security. It supports ICANN, sole-sourced by the Department of Commerce, as the agency for domain name and IP addresses assignment, among its other functions, including essentially policing the Internet, yet there are suggestions that the controversial, not-for-profit organization plans to privatize and to relieve itself of its ties to the U.S government. How much the U.S would budge under pressure from the EU and its allies in the future? The Internet is changing healthcare delivery profoundly as the following examples show. Its numerous services such as the WWW, file sharing, e-mail, instant messaging, mailing lists, Gopher, Usenet, Wide Area Information Servers (WAIS), and real-time webcasts, have been invaluable in facilitating a variety of clinical, research, and administrative tasks crucial to effective and qualitative healthcare delivery. For example, the GÉANT optical fiber network, with speeds of up to 10 Gbit/ s at its core, is the jewel of Europe s research and educational networks, akin to what the consortium, University Corporation for Advanced Internet Access (UCAID) or Internet2, or in this specific context its earlier, relatively-more-public, Abilene Network, means to these endeavors in the U.S. On the clinical front, the Internet is providing health information, is helpful in scheduling clinical appointments, as alerts, for consultations, and is contributing to efforts to reduce wait lists. Surgical wait times in Saskatchewan province, Canada, are down in 2005, 3,200 less than in 2004, according to data recently released by the province s Surgical Care Network, handsome payback for the province s pioneering efforts in publishing its wait lists and other valuable information that helped in reducing the lists, on an Internet website. This information facilitates informed decision-making about treatment and testing options by patients and doctors, hence the optimization of scarce professional work force, and hospital resources. Other provinces for example, Nova Scotia, are following suit. This is not surprising, considering the significance of the issue of wait lists to Canadians, and the questions it raises regarding the effectiveness of the country's health system and indeed, its future, specifically whether it remains publicly funded, or it has a parallel privately funded health system. Indeed, suggestions in some quarters that the emergence of privately funded health system in the entire country is inevitable has been generating heated debate since the recent ruling by Canada s Supreme Court that essentially gives legal backing to operating privately funded health system in Quebec. FedNor, an initiative of the Government of Canada that aims to address the economic development needs of Northern Ontario, announced on October 28, 2005, its plans to give four regional non-profit organizations that will champion the development of broadband services, and Information and Communications Technology (ICT) throughout Northern Ontario, over $1.8M ($1,820,775). This is a major step forward in its April 22, 2005 promise of $10-million to bring broadband access to every community in its jurisdiction via such applications as distance education and videoconferencing, telehealth suites for distant patient consultations, Picture Archiving, and Communications Systems (PACS) online financial networking, and Geographic Information Systems (GIS) for local governments and emergency services. The benefits of Internet applications to healthcare delivery in developed and developing countries alike, albeit in different ways, are legion, as are the implications of changes in Internet governance. There are genuine concerns in the healthcare industry regarding the outcomes of the standoff between the U.S and the E.U. regarding the Internet, particularly in light of recent developments regarding the Internet. Considering that ICANN may be trying to minimize its ties to the U.S. government, how could this affect its relations with the Department of Commerce and the position of the U.S. on Internet governance? A team of Chinese scientists made a shocking revelation in March 2005 of a major flaw in the decade-old, and widely used Secure Hashing Algorithm (SHA-1), an official federal standard embedded in every Web browser and operating system (OS) nowadays, and used to create and to verify e-mail and Web digital signatures, that could make it vulnerable to malicious activities. This security flaw has the potential to compromise the security of patient information, and indeed, any information sharing, or transaction conducted on the Internet. It could mean the development of a new standard, and the need to modify many Internet protocols to support it. Protocols such as Transport Layer Security and Secure Sockets layer (TLS/ SSL,) used by Web browsers for online shopping, and secure banking, Pretty Good Privacy (PGP,) used for encryption and digital signatures, for example in e-mails, and Secure SHell (SSH,)used for remote logins, would need significant reworking and Internet users, mandatory upgrading of their Web browsers, and applications. Do all these not make the U.S position on Internet governance even stronger? Could they convince the EU to acquiesce to U.S demands? The healthcare industry can only hope that events outside its control will not diminish, or perhaps stall progress in efforts, to make e-health work within each country implementing this program, and indeed, worldwide, to improve healthcare delivery using Internet applications and services, and related information and communications technologies.

The foregoing also underscores the importance of standardization in achieving our goals of healthcare ICT diffusion, and the use of implemented technologies to facilitate the delivery of qualitative, and cost-effective healthcare to all. The issue of a multiplicity of standards has plagued the health IT industry for a long time. Indeed, Dr. David Brailer, US national coordinator for healthcare IT, February 2005, stressed the need for coordination of standards initiatives, even suggested that an oversight organization might be necessary otherwise. There is progress lately on the standardization front as healthcare IT standards organizations are increasingly cooperating with one another. The Accreditation

Standards Committee X12 has signed memorandums of understanding with both Health Level Seven and the National Council for Prescription Drug Programs in the US. HL7 has also signed a series such agreements, including a memorandum with the Institute of Electrical and Electronic Engineers (IEEE) Engineering in Medicine and Biology Society (EMBS). These memorandums aimed to establish guidelines by which organizations will work together on future projects and joint work efforts and to prevent redundancy in standards creation and work products. They will also foster communication among the many standards development organizations within the industry. They will also help reduce redundancies in XML development initiatives, foster harmonizing healthcare standards, and by reducing its costs, facilitate achieving interoperability. ASC X12, accredited by the American National Standards Institute, develops standards for electronic data interchange, for example, NCPDP, standards for prescribing. HL7, which developed messaging standards for use between dissimilar information systems, and in 2004, signed a separate agreement with NCPDP pledging to collaborate on standards initiatives, is also at the forefront of efforts to define core features of EHR. On April 07, 2006, Connecting for Health, a public-private collaborative led by the U.S-based, Markle Foundation, released its Common Framework for the policy and technical components required for healthcare information exchange, an approach it had tested in Boston, Indianapolis and Mendocino County, Calif., with 20 million electronic health records from more than 500,000 patients. The framework comprises 16 technical and policy components, among others that Connecting for Health suggests organizations should utilize when developing their system for data exchange. The documents also contain recommended standards and technical specifications, as well as testing interfaces, and contracts and suggested language for healthcare data exchange security and privacy. Here are some of the policy recommendations that Connecting for Health included in its framework: people should be able to control who accesses their information and where it resides, and be informed about the rationale of personal data and health collection, which collection should only be only after due consent by the patient and should be for specified purposes. Others include that the use or availability of personal data should only be for the specified purpose, that people reserve the right to obtain information about those with access to their data, have timely access to the data, which they could challenge and correct, themselves. The organization also recommended that groups controlling personal health data are accountable for the data's security, with legal and financial penalties stipulated for any data breach. The organization also made a number of technology recommendations, including that only a small number of rules and protocols are necessary for widespread health information exchange. It also recommended decentralizing networks, leaving healthcare providers with a direct relationship with the patient to control clinical health data, building networks on legacy technology capacity, and designing them to support all applications, with applications in turn designed to accept data in standard formats. Connecting for Health officials also noted that such a system of data exchange does not need a national patient identifier to match patients to their records accurately, because based, on an algorithm for "probabilistic matching", which the organization tested, the system will not retrieve patient information if it could not match a patient to their record correctly. The organization now plans to center attention on involving patients in health data exchange. Improvements in standardization for examples will facilitate automation of routine tasks, remove delays, and optimize the use labor and other resources, helping lower the costs of health services provision. Standards will make it easier and less expensive for healthcare organizations that prefer to build their IT in-house to buy components. Standards will also increase the market opportunities of vendors, and reduce the cost of equipment and services, including maintenance, to users. Healthcare providers will not have to be stuck with unalike, over-customized systems with limited life spans, worse still are expensive to develop hence to acquire and costly to maintain. Consensus on common requirements will cut the production costs of healthcare information systems, herald market opportunities, and facilitate business intercourse among vendors, and between vendors and healthcare providers. In countries where government pays for at least some of the healthcare, these governments are increasingly demanding compliance with standards in various aspects of healthcare service delivery as a stipulation for remuneration. Indeed, healthcare authorities are also embracing standards because they recognize its benefits in facilitating the collection and collation of data and information for service planning and as a requirement for quality control, hence patient safety. Indeed, mandatory control and certification are becoming pervasive for some forms of healthcare ICT. Healthcare professionals will also benefit from standardization because it will facilitate the use of databases for both patients and for accessing medical information, and for information communication and sharing among professionals. There are concerns in some countries, for example, Canada, as to what use other countries may put personal health information of their citizens, particularly in the wake of global terrorism. These are genuine concerns that need resolution but which, nonetheless, should not create barriers in the way of say, Canadians receiving expedited medical attention abroad and vice versa. These concerns also underscore the need for international cooperation in standardizing relevant aspects of healthcare information technologies. Government agencies are very active in setting ICT standards in Canada but other organizations participate in the exercise. The Provider Registry Pan-Canadian Standards Group, for example, a stakeholder group representing Canadian jurisdictions, health authorities, major health professional colleges and associations, and key vendor associations, aims to obtain pan-Canadian consensus on the interactions and data required to support the registration of Providers. The provider Registry, which is invaluable to the interoperability of EHR in the country, will store identification, demographic data, and professional information on providers. The group hopes the results of its efforts will be the input to the HL7 version 3 technical specifications, which it plans, to submit to Health Level 7 Inc. for approval as an international standard. Indeed, there are several such standard groups including the Client Registry Pan-Canadian Standards Group, Pan-Canadian CeRx (Drug) Standards Group, Provider Registry Pan-Canadian Standards Group, and Diagnostic Imaging and Tele-radiology Pan-Canadian Standards Group. Canada Health Infoway is also devoted to ensuring that the country has a set of standards that will facilitate the interoperability of the EHR systems and technologies in all provinces and territories. It has initiated a pan-Canadian EHR Standards Collaboration Process, including developing certain principles for establishing the EHR standards. It also includes the adoption of the Health Level 7 version 3 messaging standard for all new EHR-related message development, while not dumping but adapting current standards as much as possible. CHI is collaborating with CIHI, HL7 Canada, IHE Canada, and other standards organizations in establishing pan-Canadian EHR standards. The EHR Standards Advisory Committee under CHI aegis promotes the pan-Canadian EHR Standards Collaboration Process including the activities of the previously mentioned groups, the adoption of information standards approved by the EHR Standards Steering Committee, to which it reviews and recommends strategies for the licensing and maintenance of approved information standards. Determining information standards is the first task of the EHR Standards Collaboration Process and these standards follow the definition that the Federal/ Provincial/ Territorial Advisory Committee on Health Infostructure prescribed. Consultation and collaboration are ongoing at various levels of government and its agencies on ensuring that Canada s EHR and other healthcare ICT operate uniform standards in conformity with major international standards. Standards facilitate interoperability of disparate information systems. There are numerous software vendors and hardware manufacturers and they do not all use the same developmental models, architectures, or indeed, identical materials to make their chips, for examples. Different healthcare professionals also do not all purchase their information systems form the same source. It is therefore necessary to ensure that these different systems are able to communicate with one another for us to benefit from the technologies at all. In the U.S. for example, Regional Health Information Organizations, while theoretically supposed to manage specified regions, these organizations, previously termed Local Health Information Infrastructures (LHIIs), and even earlier in the 1980s and 1990s, the Community health Information Networks (CHINs), may even transcend customary boundaries. Furthermore, they will eventually hook up with one another into a nationwide network, a process that compliance with agreed sets of standards will no doubt facilitate, or which the lack thereof will hinder. For examples, there will be need to authenticate transactions and accurately identify patients across projects and regions. The U.S. Health and Human Services Department (HHS) on October 6, 2005, established three partnerships via contracts with private, non-profit entities to tackle issues regarding the certification of EHR and other healthcare ICT products, harmonizing interoperability standards, and differences in privacy and security practices, policies, and laws in different jurisdictions that may hamper health information communication and sharing. The three contracts, on Standards Harmonization Process ($3,300,000), Compliance Certification Process ($2,700,000), and Privacy and Security Solutions ($11,500,000), totaling $17.5 million will assist in speeding up healthcare ICT adoption and in securing portability of health information nationwide. The awardees will form strategic alliances to develop the foundation for meeting the President s objective of widespread diffusion of interoperable electronic health records (EHR) within a decade. The *Framework for Strategic Action: The Decade of Health Information Technology: Delivering Consumer-centric and Information-rich Health Care,* which HHS issued on July 21, 2004, outlines four goals and twelve corresponding strategies for achieving the

President s goal. The awardees will also send reports to the American Health Information Community (the Community), a new federal advisory committee that Secretary Leavitt chairs, and responsible for providing recommendations to HHS on ways to achieve the digitalization and interoperability of health records. An HHS Request for Proposals (RFP), that Secretary Leavitt and Dr. Brailer announced on June 6, 2005, followed its receipt of over 500 public comments via a Nov. 15, 2004 Request for Information (RFI) on the best ways to achieve nationwide interoperability of health information. Based on the RFP, HHS announced on Nov. 10, 2005, it awarded four contracts to develop prototypes for Nationwide Health Information Network (NHIN) architecture. The contract totaled $18.6 million. These contracts, awarded to four consortia, led respectively by Accenture, Computer Science Corporation (CSC), International Business Machines (IBM) and Northrop Grumman, in addition to the previous three mentioned earlier, complete the foundation for an interoperable, standards-based network for secure health information communication and sharing in the country. Each consortium will design and implement a standards-based network prototype in 2006 to test patient identification and information locator services; user authentication, access control and other security and particular network functions. It will also test the achievability of large-scale operation, and make recommendations to "the Community", mentioned earlier. The consortia will collaborate on idea and information sharing regarding architectures and prototypes, and with the public, to facilitate their works. Indeed, the architecture design for each of the networks, once created, will feature in the public domain to motivate others to develop further novel ways to implement healthcare ICT. The NHIN consortia will also collaborate with other HHS partners, for examples the Health Information Technology Standards Panel, which the American National Standards Institute established, the Certification Commission for Health Information Technology, and the Health Information Security and Privacy Collaboration that RTI established, and the National Governor s Association. The four prototype-health information exchange networks will start testing data exchange by the end of 2006, according to Kelly Cronin, director of programs and coordination in the Office of the National Coordinator for Health Information Technology on March 11, 2006. The four awardees will decide on the functional requirements for the networks in June 2006, and by October, detail the revenue and costs models required for networks to become operational, and submit the completed technical design for them in November

2006. Work is also ongoing on the appropriate business model for the regional health information organizations (RHIOs), and recently, government awarded a five-month contract to the American Health Information Management Association (AHIMA) for the development of best practices for state RHIOs regarding governance, structure, financing, and health information exchange policies. The contract on completion would improve our knowledge and understanding of how RHIOs ought to function. The "Community" will in May 2006, recommend on projects to promote information sharing in healthcare, with government by April's end, awarding more contracts to states and private organizations to study privacy and security issues regarding healthcare information sharing.

The need for data and information integration and portability, hence for investments in how best to achieve these goals transcend clinical data and information communication and information, into other areas such as research, the essential ingredient of the innovative medical practices that define the pace of medical progress that we have to expect. Indeed, research into the healthcare delivery and management depends on access to data, most of which, in many countries, resides in 'silos' scattered across disparate and in the main inaccessible data repositories and organizations, except of course to those authorized to gain such access. This no doubt is inimical to progress and needs rectifying, precisely, what researchers are doing at the e-Health Research Centre, in Brisbane, Australia, with a novel Health Data Integration (HDI) tool under development. HDI will provide private and secure access to an integrated virtual data repository. This would facilitate large-scale research and analysis than any "silo" data repository would allow. There is no doubt about the veritable information portal the combined resources in these individual repositories would provide, with potential benefits for unraveling knotty healthcare and other issues for example understanding diseases, their transmission, and treatment better, but the repositories have got to be able to communicate with one another for these to happen. Besides the issues of standards and interoperability inherent in enabling such communication, privacy and confidentiality in fact make it imperative to develop standards that will ensure secure data and information exchange, and help resolve the technical, policy and ethical challenges such endeavors pose. Researchers working on the HDI project are developing privacy preserving linking algorithms to protect identity and personal information in the general milieu, and privacy policies specific to each resource in one, shared. According to the researchers, connecting patient records in different data repositories, simultaneously maintaining patient privacy is core HDI functionality, and data matching achieved utilizes encrypted demographic data, assuring data privacy, with additional safeguards even with same encrypted identifying data presented differently or inaccurately, facilitating secure data networking, including providing a virtual data repository with local control of resources. One could query data repositories and receive results via web services, further underlining the need for not just national but global consensus on standards for Internet technologies, considering the potential cross-domain use of technologies such as HDI for example, from clinical, to administrative, and research organizations and indeed, whenever data access, and control from multiple sources are paramount. A Commonwealth Scientific and Industrial Research Organization (CSIRO) third Science for Breakfast briefing for Parliamentarians in Canberra on 30 November 2005, acknowledged the importance of HDI in contemporary healthcare research and delivery. The briefing, titled "New Approaches to Fighting Cancer", was one of a series The Hon Dr Brendan Nelson MP, Minister for Education, Science, and Training hosted. Professor Richard Head, the Director of CSIRO's Preventative Health Flagship, introduced the Minister and a number of MPs present at the breakfast to the Preventative Health Flagship s collaborative research into colorectal (bowel) cancer. Other researchers also presented findings of multidisciplinary collaborative efforts underlining the value of the role the e-Health Research Centre plays in the multidisciplinary team looking at colorectal cancer by facilitating effective data analysis. Colorectal (bowel) cancer is the second highest cause of cancer-related deaths, after lung cancer in Australia, with one person dying from bowel cancer every two hours, and with 66% to 75% of the condition preventable through a healthy diet and regular exercise, would anyone contest the benefits to research that HDI affords? Should there in fact not more research funds infused into further development of these technologies in order to make them even more versatile tools, and on efforts to standardize them and associated technologies, for example Internet technologies to facilitate their usage? Information exchange is the critical activity that makes healthcare ICT such valuable technologies in contemporary healthcare delivery. Regardless of the technology, it is important that patient information be communicable, hence available for decision-making, which at the point of care (POC) could make the difference between life and death, and many new technologies increasingly have useful applications in healthcare delivery, and some indeed, with legislative backing. For example, on April 11, 2006, U.S. Sen. Sam Brownback, R-Kansas, observed that he will propose legislation to allow Americans to carry their EHR with them "in debit-card fashion," according to a report in Kansas City Business Journal of the same date1. The Senator reportedly made known his proposal for "an independent health care record banking system" at the North Kansas City headquarters of Cerner Corp., whose president, Trace Devanny, noted that importance of federal government efforts to establish standards for the exchange of health care information, for such a proposal to succeed. Senator Brownback's proposed bill will urge HHS Secretary to establish parameters for authorizing corporations, cooperatives and other organizations to become providers of the proposed banking service. With government capping pricing, the bill if passed would enable authorized providers to sell the service, including collecting, storing, and transmitting personal health care data and information, and enable the providers to sell the stored data of consenting healthcare consumers in aggregate form for research and other uses. The data and information remain under the control of the individual that owns them, and with whose consent the provider could sell the information, although they might have to pay more for the latter's services if they refused to allow such sales, according to the Senator. The bill in effect proposes the establishment of a non-geographic version of the regional health information organizations (RHIOs), the health record banking service, expected to reduce costs by preventing the duplication of diagnostic procedures. It would also reduce the rates of adverse drug reactions, by making crucial health information available to the participating patient's care providers when needed, and for sharing with other service providers. With the U.S. likely guzzling about 20% of the country's GDP or $4 trillion annually by 2015, and currently $2.3 trillion, Senator Brownback warned about the health crisis in the country, which no doubt is true, and for which the need for innovative healthcare information technologies, could also not be starker. With these technologies potentially able to not just reduce these spirally healthcare costs, but also simultaneously help provide qualitative healthcare to all, the need to develop standards that would make them interoperable therefore is just as important as investing in and deploying them. The security of patient information is perhaps going to continue to create challenges to future healthcare ICT deployment, and standards would have to be rigidly set in this regard. With the possibility of even a high school nerd able to break into government or company computers, take control of the computers, and make them do whatever he/ she wished, including to manipulate computers on their networks, is it difficult to imaging such hacking into healthcare organizations' computers? The stealth-like spyware or Trojan horses are increasingly the preferred mode for hijacking PCs, the owners of the computers often unsuspecting, and bot networks to which the computers now belong, performing nefarious tasks for their "master" surreptitiously. Experts estimate that almost 200,000 PCs become such zombies daily, the numbers on the rise. That the prevalence of the traditional virus outbreaks are lessening does not mean better security, but in fact worsening security as hackers have transformed form juvenile hobbyists to dangerous professionals engaged in more targeted attacks. Most zombies are computers innocent people used at home with access to the Internet, and telling the millions of affected persons how to configure their computers to repel Trojans or escape a zombie trap is clearly going to be a major endeavor. Health organizations therefore need to have tight security policies and determined IT staff to ferret out malicious logic. Phishing is also on the rise, and increasingly sleek. They should let their staff that even opening a Trojan-laden mail or document could spell trouble, the Trojan subsequently planted on the computer able to monitor and report to its creator every activity on the computer, including Websites visited, bank access and so forth, which is also a good reason to change passwords form time to time. Even cell phones are increasingly vulnerable to attacks, and indeed, some experts estimate cell phone viruses already as many as 200 varieties, thousands of cell phones already infected, Trojan horses and malicious Java software in fact already found. With wireless and mobile devices increasingly used in health services provision, security and standards issue also become critical to address and resolve. Some mobile phone companies have started to develop handsets with built-in antivirus protection, and the recently released Symbian OS v.9 has improved security. Yet, security remain a major issue and potential handicap to healthcare ICT diffusion, some experts extremely concerned that hackers might someday be able to harness their resources to decrypt Internet traffic, essentially crippling all activities on the Internet. There cannot be gainsaying the urgency for the necessary collaboration at all levels and between the public and private sectors to develop the required standards that would make the emergence of the appropriate technologies capable of deterring and stopping the potentially cataclysmic of hackers before it is too late. There are currently a number of different standards both technical and medical, many still under development, consensus on their final state mostly hindering their full development. There coding standards for medical disorders for example, some complementary, other competing, yet others, overlapping, creating ratification problems, which if eventually accomplished does not even guarantee widespread adoption. Much work still needs done on the various issues in order to move healthcare ICT diffusion forward at the pace we should under the present circumstances of ever-increasing healthcare costs, with not even so much to show for it by way of comprehensive, accessible, affordable, and qualitative service provision, in some countries, some would insist. Even if we succeed in securing patient health information as they travel across networks, and the Internet, there is still the problem of authenticating access to the information, not to mention patient identification, and the standards to ensure interoperability of systems with diverse transaction authentication schemes. Vocabulary and terminology also need standardization to avoid the chances of a field clogged with a cacophony of slang, jargon, acronyms, and neologisms. Many healthcare organizations will not be replacing their legacy systems with new ones in one fell swoop. On the other hand, in the main for cost reasons, but also quite rationally, at least presumably, they will likely be upgrading their old systems, which creates the problems of differences in data formats and coding languages, not mention for the large-scale deployment of a national health information network, that of skewed availability of infrastructure nationwide, necessary for networking. Here again, certain basic standards would need establishing upon which more sophisticated ones could emerge over time, lest we totter on indefinitely while our hopes of enjoying the immense opportunities that healthcare ICT diffusion promises remain a pipedream, although the increasing healthcare costs continue apace, as perhaps the deterioration in healthcare quality, and the overall well being of the populace. With countries spending more on healthcare ICT, the U.K's National Health Service for example reportedly indicating in January 2006 that it plans to spend $10.9 billion in a 10-year effort to electronically link NHS healthcare providers into a single national infrastructure, it is imperative to address these and other concerns urgently. For example over patient privacy persist, which a recent survey found 71% of GPs in the country to have. Anew study that the Commonwealth Fund released on April 10, 2006, noted the persistent healthcare ICT disparity between small and large physician practices in the U.S. The study "Adoption of Patient-Centered Care Practices by Physicians: Results from a National Survey", published in the Archives of Internal Medicine, revealed that most primary care physicians want to practice patient-centric care, but find it difficult to do so, 22% of the 1,800 physicians surveyed scored high on implementing patient-centered techniques. Even more of the physicians supported aspects of patient-centered care, with 87% in favor of better teamwork among healthcare professionals, 83%, of patent access to their own health records. The study focused on 11 explicit patient-centered care practices. They include same-day appointments; e-mail with patients; reminder notices for preventive or follow-up care; registries of patients with chronic conditions; patient medication lists; electronic medical records; and information from referral physicians promptly available. Others are medical records/ test results readily available when needed; patient survey data fed back to practice; and patient ratings of care affect compensation; information on quality of care of referral physicians available. The central problem standing in the way of many of these physicians, concluded the researchers is the lack of healthcare ICT, which underscores the need to promote the more widespread use of these technologies. There is little doubt that a practice that has implemented an electronic medical record system (EMR) and other information technology for example, would likely be better able to track its patients with high blood pressure or asthma, including determining how many of them have these conditions, hence adopt the necessary measures to improve care delivery for them. The study also revealed the barriers to healthcare ICT adoption, for example, lack of training and knowledge and costs, 63% and 84%, respectively. On a positive noted, the authors observed that the Certification Commission for Healthcare Information Technology; the HIT standards panel, e-Health Initiative's Working Group on Practice Transformation; and the technical assistance professional associations and Quality Improvement Organizations, among others are making significant impact on small practices regarding healthcare ICT implementation. We could still do much however, to improve on the just 16% of primary care physicians that the study found communicate with patients via e-mail, and the only 12% with the intent to do so in the next year, despite the efficient and inexpensive communication avenue e-mail is. We also need to improve on the 23% of the doctors that use EMR, and less that 48% that send patient reminder notices. As Karen Davis, president of the Commonwealth Fund observed, "Patient-centered care practices are not just about having a good bedside manner, "adding, "Practices such as good physician-patient communication and publicly available quality information are necessary to provide healthcare that is well-coordinated, efficient, and effective." Without widespread healthcare ICT adoption, we are unlikely to achieve these goals, and sufficiently to make any remarkable to the overall health of the populace. This is even more considering the paradigm shift in healthcare delivery toward population health in many countries in recent times, with increasing emphasis on primary, ambulatory, and domiciliary care. General practitioners, family doctors, and the smaller healthcare providers are at the forefront of these services. That they therefore need to implement healthcare ICT in order to be part of the national health information network is not in doubt. In the U.K for example, Tony Blair, the country's prime Minister on April 04, 2006, indicated his government's intention to press on with health service reforms despite stiff opposition, job losses, 7,000 recently, and financial deficits, about £800 million over the last fiscal year (FY), in the NHS. Mr. Blair made his intention known while speaking at a Downing Street summit to address the financial crisis in the NHS, with Health Secretary, Patricia Hewitt, and 16 senior managers from health authorities and trusts in England in attendance. The Government also wants to cut the number of strategic health authorities in England from 28 to 10, and require Primary care trusts "to cost 15% less" in management and administration in a "service reconfiguration" bid. Halfway through the present Labor government s 10-year NHS plan, it is unlikely to embark on wholesale hospital closures or mergers, as did the Conservative government's plans to close or merge a number of hospitals in London, for example, in the early 1990s or is it likely? What is certain is its shift in emphasis toward community-based treatment, as in a White Paper published in January 2006 that set out government's plans to transfer a significant portion of current acute hospital work to more local services for examples, GPs, clinics and community hospitals, is not in question. Furthermore, NHS patients GPs refer for most non-emergency treatment and diagnosis procedures since Jan 1, 2006, have had the option of at least four hospitals, some run by the independent sector, in the hope of stimulating competition and improving standards of care. Indeed, government seems determined to press ahead with plans for the private sector to carry out up to 15% of elective surgery, professional and union opposition notwithstanding. Coupled with the new payment by results approach with effect from April 2006, hospitals will also have to ensure their survival under an unforgiving tariff system, and matters would actually worsen when they have to comply with EU working time directive limiting junior doctors to a 48-hour week by 2009. This combination of factors not only places the future of hospitals in jeopardy, but also underscores the need for widespread healthcare information technologies to facilitate the efficient and effective delivery of health services in the community, and indeed, in the hospitals, which in the case of the latter, could in fact help ensure their cost-effectiveness. The more efficient and cost-effective a hospital operates, the less likely it would have to close or merge with another, at least in theory. No doubt, several other factors determine the need or otherwise for hospitals, but costs feature prominently since resources are in essence limited, which in fact is why the issue of hospital closures is gaining increasing prominence in the U.K. healthcare scene, some speculating the imminent closure of several NHS hospitals, others compelled to cut costs significantly. These are measures are apparently inevitable, as government revamps funding approaches to NHS trusts, and attempts to arrest the loss of thousands of jobs as hospitals run millions of pounds in losses. With such dire warnings in some quarters, that another possibly 13,000 more jobs could go over the next six months, this widespread "reconfiguration" of the health service, a Whitehall way of describing hospital closures, cuts in services and further job losses, some way, is indeed inevitable, and part of the drive towards ambulatory and domiciliary care. This shift in orientation to healthcare delivery may indeed turn out to signal the demise of the hospital, as we know it today, because as the demand for hospital beds declines, many of them will have no choice but to scale back their services or in fact eventually close. Indeed, government is moving along a three-phase process namely, expose the scale of the deficits, accept job cuts as essential to improving the hospitals' efficiency, and close hospitals if necessary. There is no doubt about the need for investments in healthcare ICT to smoothen this transition to community-based services, and with the NHS billed to receive over £90 billion a year by 2008, a three-fold increase in ten years, such investments will hopefully occur. Some, including professional associations such as the British Medical Association insist that Labor's reforms were responsible for the present quagmire of the NHS, in particular the new payment by results system wherein hospitals received reimbursement based on the number of operations they performed. Nonetheless, no one seems in doubt that some hospitals will have to close sooner than later. The question is if the adequacy of

Government's preparation for the crucial role that healthcare ICT would play in the success of the shift in healthcare delivery model to community-based services. This question becomes pertinent considering concerns that over twenty key academics in computer-related sciences raised for an independent audit of the technical feasibility of the NHS national program for IT (NPfIT), to which the Department of Health responded, reassuring the public of the appropriateness of the scheme s technical architecture, and the transparency of its conduct. As it is for any IT project to succeed, NPfIT also needs end-user acceptance, including attention to cultural, organizational and change management matters, which some claim the scheme sorely lacks. This is apart from other problems such as project intricacy, developmental delays, inconsistent leadership, and policy changes that have bogged the project and in part led to concerns in a number of different quarters. These are not only issues that could escalate overall project costs but also create unnecessary bottlenecks that could derail the entirety of Government's health reform plans, hence need urgent attention. It is no doubt daunting to implement a national care records service, including an integrated health information system for communicating and sharing EHR on 50 million people, but nonetheless doable with proper planning and the engagement of qualified professional staff handling both the technical ands management aspects of the project. In fact, the project should be bottom-up, akin to the concept of the five "cluster" areas in England, with local health networks, which themselves would have different components, lab and pharmacy information systems for example, that may be evolving at different rates, coalescing into a national health records system. Such an incremental approach to development would make it easier to make specification changes when necessary without incurring excessive costs, offer realistic project timescales, hence minimize completion delays, and make a hugely complex project estimated costs of NPfIT by some, in the neighborhood of £20bn, roughly thrice the estimated procurement cost by NPfIT £6.2bn, easier to manage, among other advantages. The estimated total costs are not surprising as implementation costs of IT projects are typically thrice to five times their procurement costs. There is no doubt about the importance of addressing the policy and other issues that may hinder progress in achieving the desired goals of the government to automate its health service delivery. The benefits derivable from so doing must however outweigh its cost in pecuniary terms as well as the improvement in the quality of healthcare delivery necessarily would. Indeed, efforts to ensure the latter would more than likely guarantee the latter, or compromise it otherwise. By further plunging the NHS into financial doldrums, an ill-planned and executed healthcare ICT scheme would make it even more difficult to deliver needed services to the people by the cash strapped health organization. This could on the aggregate result in a decline of the overall health of the populace, with further worsening of healthcare costs besides the increased burden on the ill and their families, and before we know it, we are in a vicious cycle spiraling down whereto is anyone's guess. The example of the NHS applies of course to other countries developing an e-Health scheme and intent on making it work. There is no gainsaying the importance of a determined effort to resolve the important technical policy issues that could make or break such a well-meaning intention, and urgently too, were such countries to achieve their goals.

References

1. Available at:

http://www.bizjournals.com/kansascity/stories/2006/04/10/daily18.html
Accessed on April 17, 2006

Human Issues in Healthcare ICT Diffusion

Some have argued that health information technologies will soon become utilities much like electricity and water supply. The reasoning is that they will soon become ubiquitous as prices fall. The argument goes further that because every healthcare provider has them, they no longer confer competitive advantage on any. Finally, because they do not give any organization competitive edge over another, they deserve no strategic consideration. As logical as this argument sounds, it is indeed not necessarily true. To underscore this assertion, consider the case of knowledge acquisition. There was a time that only a privileged few had access to higher or indeed any form of education in even the most developed countries of the world. In fact, this continues to be the case in many poor countries. Going by the argument that the more widespread the adoption of health information technology, the less competitive advantage it offers, the more people acquire higher education or any kind of knowledge, the less competitive advantage there is for the acquirer. Nothing, of course can be further from the truth. Clearly, it is possible to derive competitive advantage from knowledge, no matter how ubiquitous, depending on what you do with it. Everyone knew that apples fell from the tree but it took the genius of Isaac Newton to give us the laws of gravity, on which Albert Einstein built to give us the special and general theories of relativity. No matter how ubiquitous its use, health information technologies, like knowledge, could still confer competitive advantage depending on the ideas driving their adoption and the purpose of their implementation. There is therefore a need to have clear ideas of the purpose health information technologies would serve for a particular health organization. Put differently, to tailor the implementation of health information systems to the organization's needs. The organization's strategic objectives should, of course feature along considerations of those needs, which will manifest in operational goals. It is true that management of healthcare providers must work with limited capital budget for which other demands compete in our contemporary world, but healthcare ICT can be a valuable resource to foster the delivery of qualitative, accessible, and affordable patient care. The adoption of health information systems can be not only strategic but also will likely yield ample returns on investments in progressively reducing healthcare costs on the one hand, and even more importantly, improving the health of the populace, hence creating an enabling environment for a nation s sustainable economic development.. A recent U.S national survey revealed that just 3% of U.S. adults eat a healthy diet, exercise regularly, maintain a healthy weight, and do not smoke, all of which are important lifestyles that prevent heart disease, and lack of which could in addition to increasing the risk for heart disease, could make existing heart disease worse. Heart disease is the number one killer of both men and women in the U.S. and contributes significantly to healthcare costs. Yet, heart diseases are preventable, and for those that already have heart disease, embracing these healthy lifestyles could improve their heart and prolong their lives. Many already know about the benefits of these lifestyles, and many perhaps do not. In any case, would it not probably make a difference even to those that already do to reinforce the message to them about the immense benefits of these simple measures to their health and well-being? Could such reinforcement help reduce the prevalence rate of heart diseases and by extension, reduce healthcare spending on these conditions, in addition to making the populace healthier and more productive? The question then is how people receive the message, which is where healthcare ICT plays a crucial role, because of the many opportunities that these technologies offer to disseminate health information efficiently and cost-effectively, which underscores their strategic significance for contemporary healthcare delivery. Would it not be cheaper and faster, for example to deliver important health information via electronic than via snail mail, and considering the pace of progress in Medicine, hence the rate at which it might be necessary to disseminate such information? For those at risk of developing or that already have heart disease, would it not be necessary to deliver targeted health information with updates on evidence-based prevention and issues, and would such efforts not yield returns on investments in tangible and intangible terms ultimately? Many people would undoubtedly benefit from tips regarding choosing health foods, commencing and sustaining an exercise program, and quitting smoking habit. Many others would benefit from information on the latest research findings on the health benefits of vitamin supplements, on losing weight and on overweight/ obesity, different foods in an effort to restrict saturated fat, trans fat and cholesterol, and on gender variations in the symptoms and signs of heart diseases. Is it not important for the public, particularly those at high risk for cardiovascular diseases to have this information, delivered to them, in a concise form, analyzed and explained? Would this not more likely increase the number of individuals practicing healthy lifestyles than expecting them to seek this information themselves via Internet search engines for example? No one would dispute the fact that there is already a surfeit of information out there on the World Wide Web, so much that it would boggle even healthcare professionals trying to keep up. What is more, most of this information is stale, and some even slanted to suit the marketing needs of its purveyor. This combination of factors certainly does not serve the interest of the public, and indeed, compromises it. People not only need current and accurate information, they need it now, and in a form contextualized to their tastes, and delivered in the manner most suited to them. Such targeted health information would not just be more useful in helping individuals understand their health and whatever ailments they have, it would keep the public informed in a way that is more likely to result in attitudinal changes for the better. With the increasing versatility of health information technologies is it not time that we leveraged their immense potential to promote health and prevent diseases, and even more, to assist in delivering novel treatment options, and would investing in these technologies not make sense particularly in the current dispensation in many countries with staggering healthcare bills? The U.S. for example spent $1.9 trillion on health in 2004, 16% of its gross Domestic Product (GDP), 7.9% more than in 2003[1], much more than any other developed country[2], and rising. Private companies and other payers are also reeling under heavy healthcare costs, some for example, Ford Motors Corp., retrenching staff en masse, to stay profitable, if not afloat. Many are placing their hopes of curtailing their healthcare costs on emerging new healthcare delivery models, such as the consumer-driven health-financing model, which because it offers healthcare consumers more control and, because they pay part of the bill, make them more active and discerning in their choice of healthcare providers, and treatment plans. This would reduce healthcare costs by fostering competition among healthcare providers thus bringing down prices, among others. By building moral hazard into health information, proponents of this model argue, healthcare consumers would also have to take necessary measures to embrace healthy lifestyles, and make cost-effective choices regarding health services utilization. Although some contest the moral hazard case[3], there is no disputing the increasing currency of the consumer-

driven healthcare delivery model, up to 25% of large employers on board, with more planning to offer some form or another of a consumer-driven health plan down the road, according to some experts. Given this rising profile of the model, certain important questions arise, were it to achieve its intended results, of which the most fundamental is how we expect healthcare consumers to make rational choices without the necessary information to assist them in so doing. This again, highlights the equally increasingly important role that healthcare ICT will play in healthcare delivery in the days ahead. Considering the afore-mentioned and the immense benefits of healthcare ICT to our health and well-being, why is the adoption of these technologies in the health industry so slow? With the industry one of the most information-intensive, why is widespread ICT diffusion in the industry lagging behind that in similar industries, according to some estimates by as much as a decade? There is no simple answer to this question. In fact, the reasons for this state of affairs are legion, one of which is resistance to healthcare ICT adoption and usage by individuals and organizations. Let us explore this particular reason a little deeper.

An April 12, 2006 New York Times editorial, for example notes that the U.S Centers

for Medicare and Medicaid Services (CMS) has important provider quality and pricing information in its database that could assist companies and employees in their choice of the doctors that provide the best service at the most sensible cost. However, the agency reportedly denied a request from Business Roundtable, comprising CEOs from 160 major U.S. firms that provide health insurance to over 25 million employees, to disclose information on the cost and quality of care that individual physicians provide to Medicare beneficiaries. The agency reportedly denied the request because a 1979 federal district court decision prevents it from disclosing data on Medicare reimbursements to individual physicians under the Privacy Act. The information that Business Roundtable requested would assist it in guiding workers, retirees and their dependents to the best doctors and with the best value propositions, insurance plans and employers on the choice of doctors to include in their networks, and patients their choice of physicians, the paper argues, suggesting that Congress amends the law if necessary. There is no doubt that the paper's position is sound, and that the flow of crucial information to the right person or location at the right time, is sine qua non to the success of any healthcare delivery model, let alone, one that purports to place the healthcare consumer at the center of the healthcare delivery universe, literally. The above, this time legal constraints, exemplifies one of the many issues standing in the way of healthcare ICT diffusion and utilization, but there are many more, with just as many diverse origins. Indeed, some view these issues with enough seriousness to hold that the healthcare industry is under threat from three main sources, namely: the slow adoption of IT, the ever-increasing medical costs, and the cost of technology. There is little doubt that clinical IT systems, for examples bedside decision-support tools, electronic health records and E-prescribing, can save costs by improving hospital business processes and minimizing medical errors, but many healthcare systems lack the funds to implement healthcare ICT projects. Resistance to healthcare ICT cuts across the healthcare spectrum, including in the pharmaceutical industry, and their effects could be far-reaching, including compromising patient safety, and worsening the already heavy financial and human burden of disease. It could also create significant ethico-legal issues with possible equally significant economic consequences for a variety of healthcare players, as the recent Appeals Court ruling in the U.K. reveals. On April 12, 2006, a London appeals court declared that a local health service had acted illegally in preventing a woman with breast cancer from obtaining a potentially lifesaving medication. This decision overturns an earlier lower court ruling, and compels health authorities in Swindon, where the woman lives, and where there are at least twenty other such patients, to provide her with the medication, Herceptin. Many believe that the decision has potentially wide implications for breast cancer treatment and healthcare costs in the National Health Service (NHS). It also has implications for regulations regarding experimental drugs, and those still on testing to determine their efficacy and adverse reactions. Treating a patient with Herceptin for one year can cost up to $50,000. Despite her doctor s prescription, Swindon Primary Care Trust, refused to treat the woman s breast cancer with Herceptin, a Roche product, licensed for use in late-stage breast cancer, but which some studies also showed is effective to treat HER2 early-stage breast cancer, such as the woman has. The Health Department had ordered local health services not to withhold its use exclusively on costs grounds, its high costs blamed on research costs and social benefits, and some would argue, delay in approval for use by the relevant authorities. A government-appointed board is currently evaluating Herceptin. The ruling by the Appeal Court of London will likely end the so-called postcode lottery, in which treatments are available in some postal zones, but not others, making treatment available to anyone prescribed the medication, wherever he/ she lives. Swindon health service will not only give the woman the medication, but will also pay her legal bills, about $520,000. It will also have to provide Herceptin to other patients as the ruling's language implies that it is illegal to provide some clinically eligible patients and not others the medication. Some caution about the wider implications of the ruling for the ability of local health services to make their own judgments in their bid to spend taxpayers' money most cost-effectively, an equally legitimate concern, and which raises the question relevant to this discussion, namely, the need to provide qualitative healthcare services within limited resources. This issue is relevant here because one of the ways by which we could achieve these dual goals, the widespread deployment of healthcare ICT itself has numerous constraints, some of which the case of the woman mentioned above exemplifies. One of the reasons for delays in drug approvals by organizations responsible for doing so, such as the U.S. Food and Drug Administration (FDA), is precisely the lack of or inefficient use of healthcare ICT. For example, it should surprise no one that many of the results of scientific experiments on these medications and other important documentation that these organizations need to make decisions on the medication approval are still in sheaves of paper rather than in electronic formats, faxed, or sent by snail mail. Some of these documents might in fact be sitting in manila folders on someone's in-tray for weeks, if not months. As with all paper-based documentation, when they finally leave the office, they may be incomplete or contain inaccuracies, or even sent to the wrong places by accident. These series of events limit the ability to make decisions, and delay the approval process, hiking the costs of development, which the pharmaceutical companies invariably later pass on to the healthcare consumer. Could speeding up the evaluation process by the government-appointed board, which determines which drugs are used and for which illnesses, help reduce the costs of Herceptin, hence reduce the financial burden on the health Trusts, and make it easier for them to provide patients with needed medications? Should this not apply to other such approval boards and organizations elsewhere in the world? What role could healthcare ICT play in this process? Even where the electronic technologies are available, some scientists are reluctant to communicate and share results of investigations with their colleagues, for a variety of reasons, including lack of confidence in the confidentiality of such electronic transmission. Resistance to healthcare ICT could therefore occur, even with the technologies, in place, which further highlights the complexity of the human issues involved in healthcare diffusion, and which need addressing to ensure that this diffusion, not only happens, but that end-users use the technologies, as they are essentially useless without decisions emanating from their use. Consider another recent development4. In the U.S., the House Ways and Means Health Subcommittee recently

heard on April 12, 2006, the urge by some, public, and lawmakers alike for the House to act on a bill (HR4157) that would support the adoption of health information technology, similar to that, S1418, the Senate already passed. However, the bill is pending in the House partly due to concerns from privacy advocates of inadequate safeguards. Several members of the House spoke favorably about the value of healthcare ICT to healthcare delivery. Rep. Nancy Johnson (R-Conn.), chair of the subcommittee and sponsor of the House bill, for example, noted that the health care ICT could help improve safety and quality of care and reduce wasteful health spending. Indeed, Rep. Pete Stark (D-Calif.) suggested increasing Medicare payments, making healthcare ICT adoption a requirement for participation in Medicare, and expanding the use of the electronic health records (EHR) system created for the Department of Veterans Affairs, which according to Kenneth Kizer, a former VA official, should be used across the U.S. The bipartisan House support for healthcare ICT implementation speaks to the appreciation of its benefits, yet privacy issues dog its implementation. The concern of the 26 privacy advocacy groups that called for increased privacy safeguards in the proposed House bill, reflects the pervasive public concern about this issue, and one that is likely to inhibit not just individuals, but other healthcare ICT end-users for example doctors, wary of litigation, in adopting and using healthcare ICT. In other words, addressing these privacy issues is a necessary endeavor by all governments, organizations, and other stakeholders, keen to see healthcare ICT more widely used in the health industry. There are a number of dimensions to this issue. The primary concern is digitalized patient health information communicated and shared among healthcare professionals and others that have access to them, falling into the wrong hands. There are also a number of ways through which this could happen, some due to technical-related, policy-related, and others human related issues. It is necessary to tackle the problem at its various sources in order to resolve it successfully. Some of these issues may overlap, for example human related overlapping with technical, and/ or policy issues, which underscores the need for a thorough understanding and analysis of these issues.

Let us consider some of the technical related issues. One of the chief concerns regarding electronic health records (EHR) is ensuring the privacy and confidentiality of patient information. Add this to the threat of malicious logic, often termed viruses, including worms, Trojan horses, trap doors, and denial of service and the future of EHR will likely look anything but bright. It is inconceivable that we will all continue to lack the high quality service provision in healthcare that we take for granted in less critical domains of our lives simply because of worms. Yet, medical information systems (MIS), including hospital information systems (HIS), laboratory information systems (LIS), picture archiving systems (PACS), and other clinical-related information systems, are prime targets for hackers on the prowl for exploitable software and end-user logical or physical access vulnerabilities, among others. Hackers are increasingly developing hybrid programs for multi-pronged attacks, making counter-offensives against them exceedingly more tasking. It is imperative for healthcare organizations whether they are large hospitals or solo physician practices, to secure the integrity and confidentiality of patients' information in their care, and so is it for MIS vendors to support them in doing so. The need to keep patient information from falling into the wrong hands is even more compelling in these days of rampant identity theft. Patients health information now moves freer and faster among healthcare professionals and facilities, some in different cities, even countries. Such information available in real time at the point of care (POC) is potentially life saving. On the other hand, its corruption by malicious software can result in data damage or loss, or can degrade the system to the point of compromising service delivery, even putting patients in jeopardy. Viruses and other malicious programs not only damage software they can also destroy hardware, for example by switching a disk drive off but not parking the read-heads. Identity theft, when unauthorized persons using malicious logic pose as authorized recipients of data, can result in a breach of confidentiality. Denial of service attacks, which may exploit system vulnerability, or overload it with malicious data, can result in system malfunction, or shutdown. A worm can target the hospital's email system, disrupting sometimes-critical information flow. The manner notwithstanding, the result of an attack by viruses and other malicious software on MIS can be catastrophic for the patient. Preventing viruses from gaining access into MIS is crucial to securing the systems' integrity. The question remains, however, how much risk a system is still at, even with its software built in-house, in a sterile milieu, and it is stand-alone and service-free, with flawless access control. This perfect scenario hardly exists in real life. Someone somewhere in the hospital is more likely to access the system with a data-laden floppy disk or CD, which data may also have a Trojan horse masquerading as an authentic program only to effuse its malicious content on deployment. Further, via its connection to the Internet, or any external network, the ports and modems of MIS can create easy entry portals for harmless and unauthorized data alike. There are several other ways malicious programs may attack MIS, which is inherently risk-prone to a certain degree. This is why healthcare organizations need to take the matter seriously and mitigate the risk to the best possible extent, with the active collaboration of their vendors. How can the healthcare organization protect its MIS? Systems not connected to any other are less vulnerable although they still face possible internal attacks and need protection. The corollary is also true: the more the systems connected in MIS, particularly the more those sharing the same port, or software platforms, the more vulnerable they are, as hackers striving to achieve maximum damage often seek such systems, which will therefore attract more hackers, further increasing the system s vulnerability. It is useful to perform enterprise risk and threat analysis to ensure rational and optimal resource deployment prior to adopting any preventive measure. The healthcare organization should also conduct risk analysis and plan approaches to mitigation. It should establish security policies and procedures and have disaster preparedness and damage control. It should also train its staff on its security protocols, among other similar issues and should consider using key-locked cabinets, and in general make physical and logical access to the systems strict. It should configure its network routers and other devices for antivirus protection and implement a multi-layered defense system including the use of firewalls, virus scan, intrusion detection system, privacy service, and activity logging and analysis, among others. Healthcare organizations should require vendors deploying MIS to ensure the system is secure via a number measures. The vendor should also start with use risk and threat analysis. Among other measures, it should compute, compare, digitally sign checksums, and conduct systems profiles. It should scan the systems throughout its entire life cycle with properly configured and maintained, including updated with the latest definitions, virus scanning software, and build buffer overflow prevention, detection, and removal into the system's design. It should conduct software inspection and audit, and ensure knowledge of and access to updates of security patches, which it should develop and make available to the client. Collaboration between vendors and health organizations is important for these measures to succeed, which no doubt will help enhance system integrity and reduce its vulnerabilities to malicious attacks. These are just a few of the measures healthcare organizations and others handling patient health information could take that would help reassure the public about the safety, privacy, and confidentiality of their health information, hence encourage them to embrace healthcare ICT. These measures are also crucial for those that share the information for use in decision to be able to use this information confidently, and without fear of litigation. In short, these and other measures that provide technical security for patient health information constitute important focal areas in our efforts to promote more widespread healthcare ICT implementation. As noted earlier technical and policy issues may overlap and both may interweave with human issues and contemporary information systems continue to face a variety of security threats. The perpetrators of these malicious activities tend to target organizations just as much, if not even more than they do the public. Hackers write viruses, worms, Trojans, and other malicious programs for a variety of reasons, for examples to seek attention, show-off among peers, pecuniary gain, outright malice, and as some claim, to expose the vulnerability of some institutions, for example, banks, and major software companies. Whatever are the reasons hackers do what they do, the consequences of their actions are legion and often serious. Many of the issues concerning the security of patient information remain unresolved, and recrudesce with every computer security breach that comes to public attention and understandably so. It is fair to say that such security issues are in part responsible for the slow pace of electronic health record (EHR) adoption. With so much efforts, and investments that have gone into implementing EHR infrastructure and systems over the years, should a handful of malevolent individuals be able to derail the process of improving healthcare delivery, and in effect, the quality of life of the majority of people, thereby compromising their abilities to be happy and productive citizens? Such questions have prompted some to stress the important role government plays in promoting and ensuring ICT security, be it in the health industry or elsewhere. Security measures including encryption, privacy, anti-spam, firewall, and antivirus software, 3DES (data encryption standard), an assortment of authentication, authorization, and administration models, biometrics, even quantum cryptography, protect against intrusion detection, and improve access-control, and security management, or do they? It is easy to blame Internet Explorer vulnerabilities for buffer overruns, and the network administrator for leaving NetBIOS (Network basic input/ output system) gaping, but who is supposed to answer to whom at the other end, some would query? After all, there would not be any issue were someone not trying to exploit these vulnerabilities. No doubt, hackers have spent time behind bars, albeit some, only to return to hacking with Olympian zeal. Indeed, some have changed their ways, now vigorously and unabashedly deploying their hacking skills in counter-offensives against their erstwhile kin, among the reasons advocates of more measured government intervention in computer security issues give to back their position. An appropriate public policy framework can doubtless buoy ICT security, but indiscriminate applications of government regulations can stifle the freedom and creativity crucial to staying one step ahead of hackers, who have the capacity for example to release five variants of a "worm" within a few hours of the original version "hitting the stands." There should be a balance between regulatory and non-regulatory approaches to ICT security. Policy makers will find it helpful in striking this balance to appreciate the peculiar nature of the Internet, essentially a decentralized, ephemeral entity with no physical boundaries, and freely accessible, rather than simply imposing stringent regulations on its technical design and development domains. Indeed, private organizations are key players in the ICT arena, owning and controlling a significant proportion not just of the networks but also of the industries that they serve. The public expects these private organizations to ensure the security of the networks, a demand that government often feels bound to endorse. The public also expects government to secure the personal records of persons in its custody, for example, health information, records incidentally within networks and computer systems often built, run, and controlled by private organizations. It is obvious why government needs to tread softly in dealing with ICT security issues by fiat. Yet, it cannot standby and let private organizations do as they please or only act when hacking bites legislators, as for example, when California State legislators finally passed a law mandating firms to let the public know whenever there is a security breach in their clients' personal records, for example credit card information. Both government and the private sector thus owe it to the public to work together on solving ICT security problems. One could argue that private, for-profit organizations have more compelling reasons to keep hackers at bay, and government is responsible for supporting them in this regard by ensuring that relevant legal sanctions exist for those who are intent on causing chaos in cyberspace. However, what justification would government have to institute regulatory measures when its own ICT remains vulnerable? Government has first to deal with that, and develop and implement benchmark security policies in its various agencies. It is also increasingly clear that while it is okay to have laws to deter would-be and punish offending hackers, implementing laws that promote ICT security, protect networks, and stipulate legal responsibility, is equally important. Also important are improving public awareness and understanding of ICT security issues, fostering research and creativity, and addressing related issues on the World Wide Web such as on-line business dealings and consumer security. Indeed, government needs to develop appropriate ICT security strategies, and implement measures not only for "critical infrastructures" for examples, the central bank, water, and electricity supplies, defense and security, and emergency services, but also for effective communication of knowledge on security flaws and solutions between them. By securing its own networks, it would be much easier for government to reassure the public not just of the safety and security of information in its care and to ensure that the private sector follows suit, but also that of government business in general.

Human issues hampering healthcare ICT diffusion come in various forms. Some end-users simply do not want to use any technologies, either because they are uninterested in learning to use them, consider they are incapable of so doing, are simply technophobic, or feel threatened that the technologies would result in their losing status, or even their jobs. This is why it is crucial to buy end-users in with any efforts to implement healthcare ICT, and right from the start. Several studies have demonstrated the importance of such end-user buy-in for the successful implementation of healthcare ICT, for example, a recent study set out to examine users' attitudes to electronic medical record system deployment in Kaiser Permanente Hawaii. This study, carried out by four primary healthcare teams in an equal number of clinics, and specialty departments in one hospital, on Oahu, Hawaii, involved 26 clinicians, managers, and project team members. Kaiser Permanente discontinued implementing an earlier system in favor of a competing one, shortly before the interviews for the study. Published vol 331 of the British Medical Journal in 2005, the study revealed users dissatisfaction with the decision to adopt the EMR, and that software design problems led to increased end-user resistance to its use. The study also showed that the system reduced physician productivity, especially earlier on in the implementation phase, and led to even more end-user resistance. The researchers recommended ensuring early proper project perception, and system selection, testing, and adaptation, as well as strong leadership to increase the chances of end-user acceptance of implemented healthcare ICT. Canadian Health Minister Ujjal Dosanjh at the time, on May 25, 2005, announced the launching of a searchable online database containing all drug-related adverse reactions from the Canadian Adverse Drug Reaction Information System (CADRIS). Health Canada's Canadian Adverse Drug Reaction Monitoring Program (CADRMP) developed the database. Consumers, physicians, nurses, and drug companies report the suspected adverse events with all data updated four times per year. Anyone connected to the Internet can now look for adverse drug reactions that reported since 1965 on this Web site. This is clearly a positive move for the public empowerment and for transparency in the drug industry. Patients no longer have a lengthy wait to obtain such information, as was previously the case. The database, which enables queries by product, active ingredient, date of report, patient age and gender (name excluded), and outcome of adverse reaction, facilitates continuous monitoring of drugs to ensure their benefits outweigh their risks. It also aids Health Canada in updating product labeling and information. According to Health Canada, reactions may occur within minutes or years after using the product and could be minor reactions such as a skin rash or life-threatening events such as a blood disorders or liver damage. Incidentally, the database has been online at cbc.ca/ news since early 2004 when CBC (Canadian Broadcasting Corporation) acquired it using the federal Access to Information Act. Several thousand visitors accessed the database at CBC since February 2004. The site contains information on prescription and non-prescription drugs, natural health products, biological products (including vaccines), and a variety of other pharmaceuticals. However, CADRIS database does not cover all adverse reaction reporting programs of Health Canada, which maintains separate reporting systems for immunization schedule vaccines, pesticides, medical devices, cosmetics, other consumer products, medication incidents, medical errors, transfusion-transmitted injuries, among others. A collaborative Cross-Branch Working Group that shares best practices in monitoring activities links these disparate systems. The Web site cautions visitors that the adverse events are suspected and possibly incomplete. Furthermore, it warns that an underlying disease process or another coincidental factor might cause an observed reaction rather than the drug taken. Patients should therefore, consult with their doctors before taking any decisions about medications. There is no doubt that such public disclosure of vital health information would also help to reassure the public of efforts undertaken regarding patient safety. However, in a broader sense, they constitute critical aspects of the sort of confidence building that is essential to user-buy-in across user domains. There is no gainsaying the need for such cross-domain end-user acceptance of healthcare ICT for us to achieve such widespread diffusion and usage of these technologies to make any significant impact on the health of peoples and on the overall health of the economies of nations. In the developed world, people are living longer, shifting the demographics of these countries, often termed the graying of the population. Many and quite rightly believe that there is need for active participation of seniors in society, something that could not only help keep them mentally and physically healthier, but will no doubt improve their quality of life (QOL.) Indeed, there is an active ageing debate afoot in Europe currently to find ways to achieve this objective, including the role that information and communication technologies (ICTs) could play in active ageing in work, employment, and in other areas. The IST program's eInclusion@EU project, which supports the idea that every citizen should have the opportunity to participate in and benefit from the information society, aims to find such ways. This project, which ends in December 2006, aims to spot novel policy approaches and measures to facilitate the achievement of this goal, on an even keel, hence e-inclusion. Such measures will also include addressing the challenges people with disabilities and seniors in accessing the information society's tools and services, that is, e-accessibility. Cross-domain buy-in efforts will ensure the success of these measures, and might even spurn new ideas that would further facilitate the achievement of the set goals. According to Michal Arend, Swiss sociologist and leader of the part of the project involved in ICT-supported access to work and employment ICTs have considerable potential for facilitating active ageing in work and employment." He added," However, the general awareness about pertinent ICTs potential is still low and many active ageing experts and promoters are unaware or skeptical about the possible contribution of ICTs and other modern technologies". This clearly attests to the importance of end-user buy-in. ICT promotion policies could enhance the prospects of people at risk of exclusion from the labor market getting jobs. ICT could also increase flexibility in offices and workplaces, and offer opportunities for inventive arrangements that better suit personal options, duties, and limitations, for examples, those age-related. Furthermore, experience with ICT use acquired at work could help with use in other areas such as seeking and receiving health information that could also be important life quality boosters. Scandinavian countries, especially Finland have long recognized the concept of active ageing and related ones such as e-inclusion and e-accessibility, but they are catching on in other European countries, although some would argue not fast enough in many European Union (EU) member States, particularly those that have a lower life expectancy and higher unemployment rates. Nonetheless, and in particular with most EU member States initiating measures to increase retirement age, albeit slowly, the need to appreciate the potential value of ICT in achieving not just more age-friendly work processes and working milieus, but also by extension improving the mental and physical well being and the quality of life of its peoples is becoming increasingly clear. Even this appreciation needs translating into action, and experts believe the lack of this latter is also holding back the implementation of the necessary active ageing programs. The lack of action itself ascribed to the institutional fragmentation of duties, and non-cooperation among the peoples in these organizations, in sharing ideas and policies, might again have roots in inadequate buy-in of these individuals from the start. This perhaps prompted at least in part the IST-sponsored workshop on ICTs' potential role in active ageing in work and employment, held in October 2005. Indeed, according to Arend, "The workshop was just one step in launching a dialogue and bringing together people who could help to develop more comprehensive and better coordinated future research and policy strategies at the European and national level. There is no doubt that such measures could help move many valuable healthcare ICT-backed initiatives forward in not only European countries, but in others across the globe. This example also illustrates the interconnection mentioned above between technical, human and policy issues in making e-health work. Policymakers and employers for example need to collaborate in facilitating actionable programs to expedite the convergence of active ageing and e-inclusion policies. Thus, emphasis on issues such as funding e-skills of working seniors, designing ICTs aimed at age-related acuity, agility, and cognition changes, and devising ICT-related work to suit the needs of older workers should feature prominently in such intersectoral initiatives. There is also the issue of healthcare ICT adoption by physicians. Despite its promise, the large-scale deployment of health information technology sometimes seems unlikely to happen anytime soon. This is largely due to the skepticism of the people that will use the technology, that is, the clinicians. Clinicians and hospital administrators just do not appear trust the IT industry to deliver safe results. This has made it almost impossible for the industry to get independent medical practitioners and small physician groups in particular to embrace electronic medical records. Without the participation of small medical practices, the concept of a healthcare network becomes essentially meaningless, despite the spirited efforts of the Canadian, American and other governments in the developed world to encourage its widespread deployment. Should we blame doctors for the problem? Some doctors may also have a phobia for technology but the problem goes far deeper. In the past, solutions were too costly for sole practitioners and small group practices. The solutions were also very unreliable. This combination essentially priced the very people expected to use the technology out of the market. Perhaps the industry needs to rethink its pricing policies for EMRs and other HIT. On the other hand, governments should continue to pursue their goals of making the use electronic medical records standard practice. It should continue to support efforts by the private sector to develop certification standards for ambulatory EMRs, possibly fund some pilot programs in different parts of the country, and realign its payment structures to address the role of IT in improved outcomes. Vendors are making strenuous efforts to cut down prices and set industry-wide standards and should continue to do so. Doctors should recognize the potential value of EMRs and other healthcare IT to high-quality healthcare delivery and not see IT as having a negative business value. One way to avoid IT having a negative impact on their practices finances is for doctors to engage in the strategic planning of IT investments to meet the mission and goals they set out to achieve in their practices. There is no doubt that the widespread adoption of healthcare information technology remains low and speeding it up requires the concerted efforts of all the stakeholders involved as the following U.S. study by Center for Studying Health System Change (HSC) showed. The HSC's Community Tracking Study Physician Survey interviewed 12,400 physicians in

2001. The physicians answered questions on the use of computers or other types of IT in their practice to support five clinical functions namely: obtaining treatment guidelines, exchanging clinical data with other physicians, accessing notes on individual patients, generating treatment reminders for the physician's use, and writing prescriptions. The results showed that most of the physicians did not and that the larger the practice, the higher the chances it would use IT. Seventy percent of physicians in one-person practices, group practices with less than fifty physicians, and hospital-owned practices, were unlikely to IT. A quarter of the physicians did not use computers or any other forms of IT whatsoever for any of the functions in question. A quarter used some form of IT for one of the functions, and only a tenth had practices with IT support for four or five functions. Physicians most often used IT to acquire information on treatment guidelines (53%). Few physicians (11%) had e-prescribing in their offices. Physicians in larger practices (over fifty physicians, in teaching hospitals, and in staff or group model HMOs, used IT more than other physicians did. Primary care physicians used IT mostly to as treatment reminders and prescribe electronically, while specialists, for access to and exchange of clinical data and patient information. Older physicians, those 55 years and older, did not use IT as much as younger physicians did for all clinical functions safe for treatment reminders. Studies that are more recent indicate physicians are increasingly deploying healthcare ICT but the rates across all spectrums of doctors are still relatively low, compared to other industries such as the banks and financial institutions that are equally information-intensive as the health industry. The Institute of Medicine and others studies have clearly highlighted the prevalence of medical errors and many other studies have clearly shown the value of IT in preventing them. Indeed, nobody seems averse to calls for patient safety, for ensuring qualitative healthcare delivery, and for the security and confidentiality of patient information, by concerned advocacy groups such as The Leapfrog Group, Washington, D.C-based not-for profit healthcare purchasers' organization. The significant role ICT will play in the future of healthcare delivery seems clear. What remains wooly though, is how it is going to play this role if the people that will use it refused to embrace it. It is doubtful that many healthcare organizations realize how serious this problem is. Would one not be hard-pressed to argue that the healthcare industry lacked awareness of goings-on in the technology industry? Would one be, to assume that there were change-related issues involved in the seeming non-involvement of the healthcare industry in the widespread ICT adoption evident in related and other industries? If this assumption were true, one would hardly be wrong to conjecture that it is time that industry leaders took a fresh look at change management. Change is an inevitable aspect of human existence. Witness the child growing up into an adult, and the adult into senescence. The changes we undergo permeate all aspects of our lives. We cherish some of these changes, others, not that much, and when we have grown accustomed to a particular situation, or way of doing things, we may resent change outright. In particular, if people could not see the justification for change, if they considered that their previous ways of doing things worked well for them, why should they want them to change? The healthcare industry needs to direct and manage change in implementing healthcare ICT. The reasons for change in a healthcare organization can be internal, for examples, management, or organizational change, problems with workflow, changes in work scope, or reduction in staff strength. Change could also follow emergence of valuable new technologies, pressures from advocacy groups, changes in government policies and regulations, or increasing competition. Common to both the internal and external change drivers, however, is that the status quo no longer meets desired objectives, and requires revamping. This should be an important justification for change that a healthcare organization should emphasize in any initiative to implement ICT. This is because it will be easier for end-users to see the rationale for implementing the new technology, and be more open to using it. There should be end-user buy-in from the start, with the other benefits of the new technologies, both tangible and intangible, explained to all staff members that will use them. However, it is important to be realistic about expectations change will bring, and this applies to management and end-users alike. In particular, management should be wary of pressures from some quarters that may result in a misjudgment of the real benefits derivable from the new technologies, and in under-or over-expectations of their capabilities. In planning for change, it is necessary to determine the dimensions, goals, and scope of change the healthcare organization wants to pursue. Implementing new technology is, in this instance, the primary dimension, but it should not be the only dimension since the impact of such implementation will reverberate on other aspects of the organization's operations. For examples, it may require certain changes to management practices, increase the organization s capabilities, require modifications to the organizational charts as new staffs come on board, and job descriptions change, possibly even as offices undergo structural changes. The organization should have an organized yet flexible plan that it monitors and evaluates periodically in order to ensure the chances that the changes implemented will last. That an organization s culture, politics, and opposition to the proposed technologies by formal or informal groups within it can result in failure of the change process, with possible financial losses for the organization, underscores the importance of the human aspect of technology implementation. Change management will likely succeed if management is not bearing down on staffers, if there were across-board participation from the start, if change occurred incrementally rather than in one fell swoop, and perhaps most importantly, if management appreciated the dynamics of the political and cultural milieu in which the planned change would occur. There has also been immense progress in the developing innovative information and communications technologies for improving healthcare delivery. As noted earlier, the medical profession is one of the most information-intensive, most of the information also rapidly changing and most useful at the point of care (POC). ICT adoption, and diffusion, could help leverage these valuable technologies for quality healthcare delivery in the clinic and emergency room, the ambulance, the operating theater, and the nursing home. Every stakeholder involved should help make these things happen. I   mplementing change is not easy, and if implemented, difficult to sustain, the old status creeping back, sometimes, surreptitiously. The complexity and inflexibility of the change process, emphasis on a management-driven approach to change, insufficient user buy-in, end-user resistance to change, inadequate post-change evaluation and monitoring, are some of the problems blamed for change being so enigmatic. Yet, implementing healthcare ICT often involves changing what people do and how, including learning new tasks, discarding entrenched attitudes, modifying work culture, perhaps even thinking entirely differently about their organizations, no mean tasks for many of us. There is consensus on the need for healthcare ICT diffusion. Healthcare providers and organizations are starting to invest substantially on ICT. There is much talk about implementing electronic health records (EHR) nationwide in many developed countries, and physicians are even receiving government largesse to support their office automation efforts.

The private sector is also playing its part in different ways to support and facilitate healthcare ICT diffusion, and in the process helping to achieve the delivery of qualitative healthcare at affordable costs, both key goals that healthcare stakeholders expect healthcare ICT implementation to facilitate. The following example clearly illustrates these points. Dell, the PC manufacturing industry leader is embarking on an initiative aimed at curtailing employees medical bills. With this initiative, announced on April 10, 2006, the company becomes the largest U.S. employer to offer workers EHR capable of tracking their insurance claims and drug prescriptions. The company believes that this initiative is a major step toward allowing its 26,000 employees coordinate their own healthcare in an effort to improve patient safety and control costs. Indeed, the company offered some level of EHR to its employees since 2004, but the upgrade expected on Apr. 20, 2006 will enable the system to capture new information about treatments and test results automatically as opposed to employees entering the data manually. By improving the efficiency of healthcare processes, this will free resources to focus on patient care rather than administration, hence improve the quality of the service delivery. In particular, the company envisages that EHR will help it improve preventive care, including sending automated alerts based on added information to employees personal health records, about changes in health status, and in care needed, accordingly. Thus, someone recently diagnosed with high blood pressure might receive information about how to monitor blood pressure, and on necessary dietary changes such as restriction in salt intake, and the need for, type, and extent of physical activity and on what to do in case certain symptoms such as severe headaches emerge that might signal potentially catastrophic developments. The new system is an addition to the company's existing effort to promote the use of data-mining software to seek patterns in an employee s medical care by its benefits providers in an effort to help those employees with known health problems or health risk factors seek needed help, including company-offered coaching programs. There is inherent respect for patient privacy in these initiatives, with the company blind identified employees, even as it receives these vital health data and information. The company s new initiative is the latest in recent corporate moves to utilize healthcare ICT to manage corporate health care, and is in consonance the U.S government's national health-information network (NHIN) goals, which essentially would comprise electronic health data on every resident, facilitate information communication, and sharing among healthcare providers, thereby improving healthcare delivery. Such databases also offer veritable information portals for excavating cryptic patterns that could yield potentially valuable information for disease prevention, and drug safety, and public health management. Indeed, according to David Brailer, the national coordinator for health-information technology at the Dept. of Health & Human Services, healthcare ICT could add $140 billion annually to the $2 trillion health care industry productivity. It could do this in a number of ways including cutting down on medical errors and duplication of lab tests due to lack of or defective access to patients health records. Almost major U.S companies now see the need for and value of some sort of employee-directed online health-management tool. Dell s EHR system, the technology for which WebMD Health provides, is voluntary, although the company hopes many of its employees would join in, again, underlining the need for end-user buy-in. In fact, some contend that besides the initial involvement of its employees in the initiative from the start, the company needs to establish such additional confidence-building measures. Such measures include giving its employees access to online services such as Subimo, based in Chicago, which rate the quality of care of different hospitals and physicians offices and comparing the prices that they charge for specific services. There is no doubt that such measures would likely increase the number of its employees that sign on to the EHR program. This is particularly important to ensure the success of the program, and other such programs, which essentially promote healthcare cost sharing. Workers would certainly be shrewder in the choices they make regarding their healthcare, which paying part of whose costs they are likely to want to be, if they had the necessary information to make those choices. The companies moving in this direction of cost sharing also have an important stake in ensuring that it works since it would save them in some cases significant healthcare costs. With the crucial role that healthcare ICT could play in not just facilitating the provision of such information, but in differentiating healthcare providers regarding the quality and sophistication of service offerings, companies are likely to be doubly interested to encourage healthcare ICT diffusion across board. While Dell has not yet done so, other major U.S. firms including Cisco Systems and General Electric have embraced pay-for-performance healthcare delivery, with its untrammeled emphasis on quality, which healthcare ICT no doubt could play a major role in achieving. It is hardly surprising that companies are seeking ways to reduce skyrocketing healthcare costs including making workers pay some of their healthcare costs, with benefit costs several times higher than inflation rates in recent times. This accounts for the increasing currency among U.S. companies of restricted benefits plans for example health-savings accounts (HSA) among whose features are higher deductibles and other out-of-pocket expenses, but lower premiums. Whichever approach companies adopt, the need for healthcare consumer to have current, necessary, and adequate information is paramount and healthcare ICT, and in particular the EHR, has a major role to play in the efficient and effective dissemination of such information in the current dispensation. Indeed, it also has a crucial role to play in streamlining and improving work processes in the administration of healthcare, which is another important fund guzzler in the U.S health system, as it is indeed, in those of other developed and other countriess. Thus, Saskatchewan as with other provinces and

territories in Canada recently initiated plans to improve the scheduling of healthcare providers in the province with the collaboration of Saskatchewan Health and the Saskatchewan Association of Health Organizations (SAHO) to implement an electronic staff scheduling system over the next two years. The province anticipates that the new staff scheduling system will optimize resource utilization, including the deployment of health professionals and reduce administration and paperwork, freeing up time for use in patient care, and better manage overtime and seniority. Managers will no longer have to spend time scheduling employees, but instead use it for staff leadership endeavors, to support colleagues at work, and to improve and ensure the delivery of qualitative healthcare. According to Health Minister, Len Taylor, "The software will make more efficient use of the employees currently in the system," adding "The staff scheduling software is another measure Saskatchewan Health is pursuing to help manage staff challenges in regional health authorities." Indeed, the province already currently uses a number of staff scheduling tools, from manual entry systems to computer software tools. With over 65% of its health sector employees (24,600 staff) on shift work, many in more than one health care facility, and wages and benefits comprising over 70% of health care budgets, there is little doubt about the staff scheduler will yield returns on the $3 million invested in it. This money is from the $66 million the federal government promised at the 2004 First Ministers meeting, which itself underscores the commitment at all levels of government to ensuring that the country s e-health program succeeds. There is evidence for increasing government healthcare ICT spending in not only Canada, but also in the U.S., the U.K., and many other countries. In the U.S. for example, a recent Forrester Research survey released at the end of March 2006 indicates an expected rise in healthcare ICT budgets at large U.S. hospitals to about 3.1 percent in 2006, most on clinical software upgrades. However, some contend that the findings may apply more to spending patterns in the large healthcare institutions, and not to the smaller ones with limited financial resources. Significantly, the survey shows increased investment in data storage systems, including on picture archiving and communications systems (PACS), and on disaster recovery systems, not surprising considering the adverse experiences after hurricane Katrina in New Orleans and adjacent states, and on systems integration. Other factors that will determine how much more healthcare providers spend on health information systems include those peculiar to and that drive the healthcare industry including the costs of prescription drugs, health reforms, changing disease patterns and prevalence, demographics, and government regulations and policies, among others. One key development that will also drive healthcare ICT spending in the coming years is the shift in healthcare delivery models, in particular, in its financing, for example, the pay for performance model. The idea of pay-for-performance program has been around in the US for sometime now and it is only now gaining increasing acceptance. The initiative aims to reward doctors with bonuses for meeting certain standards of care. The bonuses, which range from $50 to $160 per patient per year, could add up to significant amounts in some practices. One of the hindrances to the adoption of IT by physicians is the perception that health plans, insurers and patients, not the doctors benefit from these IT investments. However, the pay-for-performance program seems to be a win-win situation as patients receive higher quality care, doctors make money, and health plans that have often invested millions of dollars on healthcare IT finally get doctors to adopt IT and integrate it with the health plans systems. What s more, participating health plans save money through reduced hospital visits and unnecessary testing, bonuses regardless. The program has its critics though, who posit that some doctors might refuse to take on seriously ill patients because they do not want to compromise their scores. Nonetheless, the large firms, determined to reduce healthcare costs, fully back the program. Indeed, an alliance of employers, payers, and providers launched the non-profit Bridges to Excellence in 2003, launching the program in Ohio, Kentucky, and Massachusetts, with measures in three areas, namely: diabetes care, cardiovascular care, and patient-care management systems. As more health plans embrace the program, its organizers are adding on new care standards in cancer care, asthma and pain management. A number of physician organizations, including the American Academy of Family Physicians and the Medical Group Management Association support the program. In late March, 2005, the program attracted a new participant, CareFirst BlueCross BlueShield, which said that it would pay doctors up to $20,000 to install electronic patient records systems as part of its record-keeping bonus plan. The health plan s program would span 10 states and cover over 2 million individuals. Regardless of healthcare delivery model, however, there is hardly any contention regarding the value of healthcare ICT in improving healthcare delivery and the need for all, healthcare providers and consumers alike, and in fact, all else that use communicated and shared health information in decision making and process improvement, to implement and use these technologies. Would it not help the public for example, and in particular, individuals at high risk for developing prostate cancer and high blood cholesterol levels to be aware of recent research findings connecting the two, and could such knowledge not help reduce the prevalence of these conditions, and the associated morbidities, mortalities, and healthcare costs? Scientists now have evidence linking high cholesterol levels to an increased risk of prostate cancer, although the Italian scientists that analyzed data on 2,745 men noted the need for further research to consolidate their findings. Significantly, this study published in the Annals of Oncology, points to cholesterol use by the body to produce male hormones previously linked to prostate cancer, and suggests that people can do something themselves to reduce their risks of developing prostate cancer, one of the main killers of men, and U.K's commonest male cancer, for example. Despite its shortcomings, to which the researchers admitted, for example, relying on patients reporting details of their own medical conditions, the apparent link between high cholesterol and prostate cancer seemed to be authentic, and the researchers found no such link between prostate cancer and ten other medical conditions. The data that the scientists examined, on 1,294 men with prostate cancer, and 1,451 men admitted to hospital with non-cancerous disorders, showed that men with prostate cancer were about 50% likelier to have had high cholesterol levels, the link even stronger among men diagnosed with prostate cancer before 50 years, and after 65 years. In these groups, the chances of reporting high blood cholesterol levels were 80% more than by men free from cancer. The researchers also found prostate cancer patients were 26% likelier to have had gallstones, with leaner men seemingly more at risk. According to one of the researchers, Dr Cristina Bosetti "Androgens, hormones that have a role in prostate tissue and cancer, are synthesized from cholesterol, suggesting a possible biological relationship between high cholesterol and prostate cancer." Because of the link between gallstones, which often contain cholesterol, and high cholesterol levels, that found between gallstones and prostate cancer is not surprising, and suggests a similar biological mechanism. This also implies that some cholesterol-lowering statin drugs might be able to protect men against prostate cancer, although this is yet to have scientific backing. According to Professor Nick James, a University of Birmingham cancer expert, the link between cholesterol and prostate cancer is "entirely plausible' adding, "There is a lot of circumstantial evidence suggesting that diet is a factor in developing prostate cancer. For instance, the disease is more common in northern European countries, where consumption of animal fats is relatively high", although unconvinced that male hormones were important in the disease's pathology, rather he thinks that some of the chemicals the breakdown of cholesterol produces are carcinogens. Should men not reduce their intake of fatty foods and red and processed meat, and eat oily fish and a high fiber diet with porridge oats, and a lot of fresh fruits, and vegetables on a daily basis? How many of them would know the result of the findings of this research were there no determined effort at targeted health information, which would deliver this and other crucial and current health information, possibly analyzed and contextualized to them, perhaps into their email boxes? Could healthcare ICT not play a key efficient and cost-effective role in this regard? How would it do that if we did not make prior effort to ensure that healthcare ICT implementation becomes more widespread, including ensuring that all end-users embrace and use these technologies? Consider another important recent finding on prostate cancer. Scientists have also found that a diet rich in a fat found in oily fish and some seeds may protect men with prostate cancer from the disease becoming more aggressive, metastasizing, or migrating to and invading other tissues and organs such as the bone marrow, and becoming deadlier, which lab tests found omega-3 oil, present in fish like salmon, prevented. The study, conducted at Manchester's Christie Hospital, and published in the British Journal of Cancer has sparked keen interests among physicians, and the public ought to know about it, particularly men with the disease, that simply eating a diet with the right balance of omega-3 and omega-6 fats may prevent prostate cancer from spreading, and seriously threatening their survival. This would improve monitoring, and facilitate surgical or radio therapeutic treatments. Earlier research has suggested omega-3 fats, also found in some plant sources such as pumpkin seeds, may help reduce cancer risk and in fact the risk of developing other health problems for example heart disease. Omega-6 fats, abundant in vegetable oils, nuts and seeds, are also important to us being healthy. Interestingly, omega-6 fats increases the spread of prostate cancer cells into bone marrow, which omega-3 fats blocks. According to researcher Dr Mick Brown, "It is possible to have a healthy balance of these two types of fat, we only need about half as much omega-3 as omega-6 - that will still stop cancer cells from spreading." Researchers believe that the tumor cells might be utilizing omega-6 fats for energy production that they use to grow and to migrate, a process that omega-3 fats seem to block, somehow.

U.K s Food Standards Agency recommends men consume up to four portions of oily

fish a week. Is it not imperative that we send this sort of information out to men rather than wait for them to seek it? Should it be difficult to do that in these days that they could receive such information even on the go, with wireless and mobile devices now used for an increasingly larger number of medical diagnosis, monitoring, alerting, treatment, and other applications both within and outside hospitals? With increasing confidence building that the emergence of cutting-edge security technologies engender, more healthcare professionals and in fact the public are becoming more comfortable using today's multipurpose mobile and wireless technologies. This is another example of the benefits of such confidence building exercises and the multifaceted approaches toward achieving them, including via technological improvements, or change management brainstorming and training sessions. There are increasing opportunities for mobile access these days with even electric utility companies providing broadband access over conventional power lines. It is interesting that many of these mobile access technologies are wireless. Experts predict the options are increasing and that we will have an even wider variety of wireless access within the next couple of years. 3G cellular data technologies will offer great opportunities for healthcare applications. The data speed of the 1xEV-DO Rev A and HSDPA versions of 3G promise increased speed compared to

300 Kbps of the 1xEV-DO and UMTS networks, for example. There is also progress on the wireless broadband front. There are already mobile wireless broadband technologies for examples UMTS TDD and FLASH-OFDM, Mobile WiMax promising even more opportunities than its fixed version. There seems to be stalling of the hitherto rapid spread of Wi-Fi hotspots because of the rather obscure roaming contracts vendors offer consumers, although a number of cities are already implementing the so-called Wi-Fi clouds, simply Wi-Fi covering the entire city. Stratellites, stratosphere-based, balloons are also coming with some experts convinced that they will be more cost-effective ways to provide broadband access over wide areas than current technologies. There might be various permutations of these different technologies in the future, with a blurring of the domains of wireless ISPs, cellular operators, voice-over-IP vendors, and other industry operators, driven by customer needs and market trends. The healthcare industry needs to be in the loop regarding these developments, which continues apace, as this would facilitate decision making on the most appropriate data access technology for an establishment, which would in turn determine which hardware and peripherals to purchase. Indeed, most hospitals still abhor the use of cell phones near their electronic equipments, for example, in an intensive care unit (ICU), to reduce the chances of interference hence equipment malfunction, which could put someone's life in jeopardy, but cell phone use is becoming ubiquitous in other parts of many hospitals. With wide area networks (WAN), healthcare professionals no longer have to be in the hospital premises to access their patients health data and information, including lab results that could provide information that would determine for example, antibiotic use, which they could text message to their patients, for faster prescription pick-up, or at designated pharmacies. Would this not reduce wait times for treatment of sometimes life-threatening infections, or one that could result in chronic sequalae with devastating consequences for example permanent fallopian tube blockage with resulting infertility? So-called peel-and-stick band-aids now exist, handsets that could measure blood sugar, and pressure or alcohol levels and act as a wireless pacemaker. Radiofrequency identification devices (RFID) are wireless means for monitoring patient movements, tracking equipments around the hospital, and medical and pharmaceutical shipments prior to and while in hospital, including shelf-space utilization, and product integrity in the warehouse or hospital stores. Wireless and mobile devices are

also gaining increasing currency in ambulatory and domiciliary care, areas in which their usage is likely to increase even more. This is considering the shift toward caring for an increasingly graying population as with many developed countries, in the community, in the comfort of their homes, and among their loved ones, which no doubt enhances their quality of life. CardioNet, a U.S firm has developed wireless technology for outpatient cardiac monitoring, continuous ECG via a wearable sensor able to transmit information via Bluetooth to a monitor that the individual carries, then onto CardioNet's service center, which an onsite technician analyzes and immediately passes via electronic alerts to the physicians, who could also read it online. Philips Medical has developed "Smart Wireless Band-Aid" technology, an RFID-based adhesive patch able to monitor heart rate continuously and transmit the data to a handset, for onward transmission over a cellular network to a doctor's office. Korea's LG Electronics' cell phone can measure and display blood glucose, track the results and transmit them to the person's doctor. Some companies have developed sensor technology able to measure ambulatory patient's heart rates, blood pressure and blood oxygen levels, and again, transmit the results via handsets to healthcare providers. For the equally many at risk for heart attacks and similar potentially fatal heart diseases, there is now a wireless pacemaker able to detect abnormal heart rhythms and alert one's doctor, and wireless technologies that could monitor an implantable cardiac defibrillator to ensure its proper functioning. Is it not important for people to know about these technologies and the benefits to their health that they offer? Would such knowledge delivered to them not help reduce morbidities and mortalities, and healthcare costs ultimately? Furthermore, although they tend to be costly initially, would more-widespread use of these technologies not bring their prices and make them more affordable to even more people? With cell phones, becoming increasingly multifunctional, more healthcare providers will find uses for them. Doctors, physiotherapists, dieticians, and other healthcare professionals can now make visual evaluations of their patients' conditions via pictures transmitted to them by the patients via cell phones. This could help in determining the need or otherwise for immediate consultation, treatment review, further counseling, and other management activities that could save the expense of physical contact with the healthcare provider while delivering effective care. The cell phone, which incidentally is even more commonly used in some developing countries than land phones and computers, could therefore, be versatile tools for cost-effective healthcare service delivery even in these countries with minimal telecommunications infrastructures. Do all these not point to the need for people to be aware of the potential of healthcare ICT in improving their health and reducing their pain and suffering even when they suffer from a disease? Would it not save significant healthcare costs in the end to invest in the technologies and make efforts to use them? Should we not therefore be encouraging all those that need to use them to purchase and implement them? The discussion thus far clearly underscores not just the value of healthcare ICT in healthcare delivery but also the need for all healthcare stake stakeholders to embrace and use these technologies. It is not enough for governments and healthcare organizations to appreciate the value of these technologies. They also need to invest in them, and having infused their oft-scarce financial resources into doing that, to ensure that the end-user utilizes them accordingly. These are the only ways we could derive the expected benefits that these technologies promise. Health spending now averages about 9% of total national spending among OECD countries, twice its 1970 share, 14% in the United States even as far back as 2001, now more and still the highest among these countries, and rising in all expectedly with their population ageing, and demand for health services increasing. With up to three-quarters of health spending coming from the public treasury in many OECD countries, it is hardly surprising the concern in these countries about increasing health spending. This is even more so with the percentage of the population in its working years falling, with corresponding decreases in government tax revenues, yet its health spending likely to increase. Should these countries therefore reduce benefits or increase taxes? Even in the U.S., with healthcare considered essentially private-funded, public spending on health is higher than the OECD average, although along with Mexico and Korea, its public sector spending is less than half of total health expenditures, whereas the OECD average is more than 70%. Incidentally, health outcomes do not always tally with more health spending, hence the need for rational and effective disbursement of scarce financial and other resources on health, which the appropriate deployment of healthcare ICT could help ensure. For instance, New Zealand and the United States have infant mortality rates twice those Japan, the variation across countries in life expectancy at age 65 is over ten years even among OECD countries, variations that could also occur within the countries, among others due to disparities in access to care, which again, healthcare ICT could help correct. These technologies for example offer immense opportunities for effective yet inexpensive targeted health information dissemination and for health promotion, and disease prevention campaigns. Such efforts might be able to help us roll back the increasing health menace of overweight and obesity that is threatening to become if it has not already become an epidemic in many countries, developed and developing around the world. Considering that these conditions often cause chronic health problems that create substantial health and financial burdens, should wee not tackle them head-on by investing in the required technologies that could help in preventing them, or monitoring the diseases they cause hence reducing their costs? Even if we did, should also not be ensuring that people purchase, implement, and use these technologies? Does this not speak to the need for the sort of buy-in and the variety of confidence-building efforts mentioned earlier, and others? Even in developed countries such as those in the OECD, staid shortcomings in the quality of health service delivery cause pointless deaths, disability, and compromise health and well-being. All of these contribute to escalating healthcare costs. Many of these countries have therefore begun evaluating and tracking healthcare quality and to institute other measures to improve performance, using a variety of healthcare-ICT backed techniques. Desirable as these measures are, they will likely fail without the individuals running the systems earmarked for quality improvement evaluation knowing what the exercise is all about, and not for example thinking it is a witch-hunt. This again emphasizes the key role of involving the end-user in every aspect of healthcare ICT implementation, maintenance and quality evaluation, in short throughout every stage of the technology's life cycle. Such involvement improves the likelihood of the end-user understanding what he/ she needs to about the technologies, which is important in reassuring him/ her about the potential benefits of the implemented technologies, and in some cases, allaying fears of the technologies rendering them redundant, and posing a threat to their livelihoods. In these days of consumer-centered health services, we must continue to improve our service offerings and yet be flexible enough to meet the specific requirements of certain patients, for example the elderly, and those with disabilities. Healthcare ICT could help in achieving these goals, and we need to inform these groups of the opportunities that health information technologies offer them, for example wearable wireless devices that could assess an elderly s potential to fall and alert him/ her and raise alarm or alert designated services such as a doctor or 911 in case they fall. Such technologies are useful in particular for seniors living alone, and could reduce the prevalence of fractures due to such falls, reducing pain and suffering, and costs of surgery and related care that these fall incur. Despite their usefulness, would seniors be able to purchase and use them not aware that these and other valuable technologies even exist? Many experts recognize that in the end, increasing efficiency is perhaps the best option to reconcile increasing demands for healthcare services that an increasingly aging population demands with the public financing limitations many of these countries have. In other words, we need to continue to seek to spend these limited resources more judiciously and not simply cut healthcare costs wholesale. This way, we are more likely to achieve better value for the money so spent. Health reforms ought to examine closely the role of healthcare ICT in achieving this goal, including in instituting the necessary structural reform to our health systems required for the changes in health services administrative and delivery processes that these technologies could help improve. There is no doubt that healthcare ICT could help achieve the improved efficiency, equity, and effectiveness of the health services, which often constitute the goals of such health reforms. Healthcare ICT could also help contain rising hospitalization and prescription medication costs, and put the push toward ambulatory and domiciliary care on a firm footing.

Decentralization, privatization, or something akin to it, implementation of effective health-sector management systems, setting priorities, and increasing financial options are typical market-oriented health reform measures that many countries embark on in recent times6. While details vary among different countries, health sector reforms in Canada and the U.S. for examples essentially focused on decentralization and social security systems reforms, while the U.K., and other European countries focused on new fiscal and health care delivery measures, and yet other countries in Europe, for examples Hungary, on Soviet-style health care systems. The types of health reforms regardless, these reforms profoundly affect peoples lives, including their access to and their ability to afford qualitative health services and here is where healthcare ICT could help. Regardless of the reform model, the ultimate goal of healthcare delivery should be to deliver qualitative healthcare to all cost-effectively. Healthcare ICT, implemented widely across healthcare stakeholder spectrums, could no doubt create the opportunities for the health systems process improvement necessary to achieve these goals. As noted earlier however, many countries, even those that have invested significantly in healthcare ICT, are still a long way to such widespread healthcare ICT diffusion. In the U.S. for example, The Agency for Healthcare Research and Quality (AHRQ) released a report on April 11, 2006, conceding that while the fact that healthcare ICT helps to improve quality of care for patients is not in doubt, most health care providers need more information on implementing these technologies successfully, a process AHRQ is helping to rectify. It is doing so using findings from over 100 projects across the U.S., projects that constitute the agency s multimillion-dollar health ICT initiative7, 8. The report, Costs and Benefits of Health Information Technology, which AHRQ s Southern California Evidence-based Practice Center-RAND Corporation prepared, examines a number of studies on the effect of healthcare ICT on the quality and safety of care and on the costs and organizational changes required to implement these technologies. According to the report, "HIT has the potential to enable a dramatic transformation in the delivery of health care, making it safer, more effective, and more efficient. However, widespread implementation of HIT has been limited by a lack of generalizable knowledge about what types of HIT and implementation methods will improve care and manage costs for specific health organizations". As we have been emphasizing in this discussion, this report shows that healthcare ICT deployment results in significant improvements in the quality of healthcare delivery, hence the need for more widespread diffusion of these technologies. The report also shows that these benefits of healthcare ICT have occurred principally within large health care systems that invested in, substantially, and developed their own health information systems. AHRQ s initiative is collating data required on approaches to facilitating widespread healthcare ICT diffusion, in particular in the ubiquitous physicians' offices and smaller hospitals. More physicians and smaller healthcare providers that operate with limited budgets would likely consider implementing healthcare ICT if they had a clear idea of the effect of such implementation on their practices. This report shows that many might not have had such information. "Health care providers need reliable information that tells them what they can expect when they implement health IT systems," noted AHRQ Director Carolyn M. Clancy, M.D. "Leading institutions in health IT have shown that these systems can produce improved quality and patient safety. But smaller practices and hospitals need to know how these improvements can be achieved in settings like theirs, using the kinds of commercial systems, they are likely to employ.

AHRQ's health IT initiative is designed to generate and share the kind of information providers need. The $166 million initiative, launched in September 2004, with most projects having 3-year duration, focuses on the effects of health information systems implementation in community-based health care settings, using nonproprietary systems. There is no doubt that this initiative would help promote healthcare ICT adoption by financially challenged healthcare providers. Considering a the result of a 2005 RAND study that estimated that widespread adoption of electronic medical records and other health IT could save over $81 billion yearly and improve the quality of care, this initiative, and others by interested healthcare stakeholders are certainly worth the effort. Such efforts make it even more feasible for the U.S. and indeed, other countries to achieve the dual objectives of providing all their citizens with qualitative healthcare without necessarily crippling their overall economy in the process. Health will continue to be the most important attribute anyone should have, as it underlies life itself, at the individual level, and is crucial to our abilities to be fulfill our responsibilities to ourselves, our families, and to society. Each person therefore has the duty to be healthy and stay so. However, we all are collectively responsible for the survival of our society and of humankind, a duty those before us duly performed, which is why we are here in the first place. In ensuring the continuity of humanity, we must therefore help our fellow humans in becoming healthy and sustaining it. Such commitment recent developments in world health, including the effects of global warming and the possibilities of an avian flu pandemic, among others, inform us need not be restricted to our respective shores. Despite this need for us to appreciate and work towards societal and indeed, global health and well-being, to which the increasing interests worldwide in population health attests, we must also recognize our limitations in achieving these lofty goals. No nation has inexhaustible funds, or for that matter, enough healthcare workforces, to meet current not to mention ever-increasing healthcare needs, for example. We must therefore seek ways to achieve the dual objectives of providing comprehensive and qualitative healthcare as cost-effectively as possible. Every country would need to do this in the context of its overall strategic direction and intent. This means that healthcare provision will continue to have a variety of financing tints for example. Regardless of the approach to healthcare delivery however, the dual objectives would remain constant. What will also remain constant is the important role that widespread healthcare ICT adoption will play in achieving the dual objectives.

References

1. Smith C, Cowan C. Heffler S, Catlin A, the National Health Accounts Team. National health spending in 2004: recent slowdown led by prescription drug spending. Health Affairs. January/February 2006:186-196.

2. Hussey PS, Anderson GF, Osborn R, Feek C, McLaughlin V, Millar J, Epstein A. How does the quality of care compare in five countries? Health Affairs, May/June 2004:89-99.

3. Gladwell M. The moral-hazard myth. The New Yorker. Aug. 29, 2005.

4. Available at: http://www.medicalnewstoday.com/medicalnews.php?newsid=41377
Accessed on April 12, 2006

5. Available at:
http://www.businessweek.com/print/technology/content/apr2006/tc20060407_825324.htm
Accessed on April 14, 2006

6. Cassels A. Health sector reform: key issues in less developed countries. Geneva, World Health Organization, 1995.

7. Available at:
http://www.ahrq.gov/downloads/pub/evidence/pdf/hitsyscosts/hitsys.pdf
Accessed on April 15, 2006

8. Available at: http://healthit.ahrq.gov/tools/rand
Accessed on April 15, 2006

Healthcare ICT Management Issues

Information or "content" is the fundamental element that binds all information systems.

This is even more so in the health industry, where the communication and sharing of patient information are the critical tasks of these systems that confer on them the immense benefits that health information systems offer. Intelligent content management is therefore one of the most important management issues that could determine the success or other wise of an e-Health program. In other words, it is not enough to have content. In fact, the health industry has an information glut, and at the rate at which it generates new data and information, both in clinical and research areas, and indeed, in others such as administration and finance, for examples, it could only become more awash with content. Without this mass of data and information collated, stored, and organized in ways that would facilitate their access and usage, they are, essentially, useless. This why the report in "IST Results" on Jan 19, 2006, regarding the development of a smart, easy to use, Web-based, knowledge and multimedia content and workflow management platform, with quick access time is welcome news. According to Witold Staniszkis of Rodan Systems, Poland and coordinator of the IST program-funded ICONS project that built the platform "The platform supports uniform, knowledge-based access to distributed information resources available in the form of Web pages, existing heterogeneous databases [formatted, text and multimedia], business process specifications and operational information, as well as legacy information processing systems". The ICONS platform is able to tackle the most crucial problems of staffers in knowledge intensive organizations, such as healthcare organizations. These include, information idleness and lack of relevant information; a deluge of unclassified documents; defective integration with external sources of important information; and the dearth of uniform, user-friendly, and personalized interfaces. The technology will also help facilitate smooth communication between individuals and among groups in the healthcare organizations, and overcome the problems an often-overwhelming user learning curve poses. The content that a healthcare organization may need to manage do not necessarily reside in the same physical location, or used by the same set of staffers. Thus, some of the information resides in hospital settings, others in community health centers and living divisions, and yet others in the offices of family doctors, chiropractors, optometrists, psychologists and counselors, physiotherapists, and other healthcare professionals affiliated with the organization. The technology also helps with the systems integration and interoperability such situations demand, and depending on the scope of the project, sequential and incremental deployment of the ICONS platform, for example, over time, might be easier and more cost-effective. Its sophisticated knowledge management features, for examples, automatic text classification, intelligent, rule-based workflow management, graphic user-friendly browsing interfaces and a Topic Map standard compliant concept glossary are now in the OfficeObjects Workflow™, proprietary content and workflow management software that Rodan Systems developed and markets. Experts note the value of this platform in developing generalized, process-based applications solutions, not surprising considering its declarative knowledge-based, flexible business process management milieu, with concepts and definitions in the platform easily sharable, besides described in its glossary. There are other aspects of content management that will be increasingly important in healthcare organizations, and among all healthcare stakeholders and the could facilitate or hinder the progress any e-Health program, and just as with the role that ICT could play in meeting the challenges of content management as the above example illustrates, it could itself be the problem. Consider the case of the e-mail, a versatile communication medium in all establishments, including in healthcare organizations, these days, where in the latter it serves both clinical and administrative purposes, among others. Efforts to make it more secure to send and receive information via e-mail have led to the emergence in recent times of such technologies as Sender ID, Sender Policy Framework (SPF), and DomainKeys Internet Identified Mail (DKIM), the major underlying task of all of which is to authenticate e-mail as correctly as possible. However, experts now warn that incorrect e-mail authentication could create a new set of problems of its own that could destroy essentially, any organization's email system. Technology has moved beyond merely reworking Simple Mail Transfer Protocol (STMP), the fundamental email technology to authenticating e-mails. No doubt, e-mail authentication is necessary to protect the integrity of the information it contains, and to combat the increasingly common nuisances of spamming and phishing, among others, which could render an organization's e-mail system just as worthless. By helping strengthen mail filters, such technologies make it more difficult to forge e-mail addresses, and flush them with unsolicited mails. Indeed, many organizations now send authenticated mails, which Microsoft, the chief protagonist of e-mail authentication, is conscientiously promoting. Experts are however concerned that not only is it difficult for an organization to adopt and implement sender authentication, upwards of four to eight months in some firms, but it could just as problematic to manage it. For large healthcare organizations, these issues could pose significant management challenges. DKIM attaches a digital signature to outgoing e-mail, enabling recipients to verify that the message is from its purported source. Sender ID is even more advanced, requiring Internet service providers (ISPs), firms, and other Internet domain holders to publish SPF (Sender Policy Framework) records in order to identify their mail servers, which some large healthcare organizations may need to do. While this does not involve spending money on some new hardware or software, the necessary task of compiling and maintaining an inventory of all the mail servers that it demands could be Herculean, and expensive. With the operations of some healthcare providers, health plans, and other healthcare organizations now interstate, and even international, and with equally numerous and disparate email gateways, it might not at all be easy to know all the mail servers via which staffers send emails in the organization s name. With the prospects of an arm of the organization, setting up a host for sending email but did not register the hosts with SPF records, go that of e-mail service providers deleting all e-mails failing an authentication check, a situation whose consequence some managers would rather just imagine. It is therefore important for management to ensure accurate compilation of these mail servers if it were to avoid these possible devastating consequences. With many companies, publishing incomplete SPF records, or not informing recipients to expect no mils form other servers, junk and spoofed emails, and those from other malicious sources will continue to evade filters. Consider for example a patient receiving an email from ˙a hospital˙ requesting certain private information from the patient, the patient unaware that he/ she is responding to a fake, who is now in possession of this information. This is a situation that healthcare organizations cannot afford, considering the many laws, for example, certain aspects of the Health Insurance Portability and Accountability Acts (HIPAA) of 1996, in the U.S., protecting the privacy of patient information. This is besides the chances of litigation by the patient, which could deplete the hospital ́s purse and dent its image significantly. Healthcare organizations will therefore need to consider adopting email authentication technologies and to establish the necessary policies for their implementation and operations. They will also need to consider additional measures to make emails more secure, as authentication by itself may be insufficient to eliminate the menace of email spamming and other unsolicited emails. Besides, filtering authenticated emails could result in false positives, with some erroneously deemed as spam, which is why some antispam technology vendors actually recommend that organizations do not do any filtering on SPF. Some email security firms for example, CipherTrust, now examine the email sending patterns of a particular domain, say, kkhealth.ca, which contributes to a decision whether emails from that domain are junks or not. Termed e-mail accreditation and reputation services, this seems to be the future direction of e-mail security, with such firms able to assign " reputations" to computers and Internet domains from whence e-mails come, assigning negative ratings to spam senders, and positive ones to those that do not. CipherTrust, which developed IronMail Gateway 6.0 and IronMail Edge, now shares some of its reputation data with the public via the TrustedSource Web site, the latter essentially a reference tool that anyone could use by simply entering a domain name, which produces a list of the Internet Protocol (IP) addresses of computers that send e-mail for the said domain. On drilling down and clicking on each sending address, it would be possible for the user to tell whether a specific computer has been sending junk or genuine mails. This way the individual could decide on whether to block the address or not, as could for example, a healthcare organization, which latter could also find out the systems on their networks sending out e-mails other than the designated e-mail servers, in other words, if for example, the networks had zombie computers. Zombies are machines that hackers and other cyber crooks have hijacked and are using for spamming and other nefarious activities. TrustedSource also provides information on the adoption of novel authentication-technologies and catalogs Internet domains that send e-mail using DKIM and Sender ID. Healthcare organizations might want to implement e-mail scanners such Cipher Trust's IronMail Gateway 6.0, and IronMail Edge, which actually can scan e-mail at the periphery the healthcare organization's networks keeping malicious traffic at bay, and preserving precious bandwidth. The foregoing illustrates how important it is to manage a variety of aspects of the technologies that e-Health relies on for its success, besides simply implementing them. It also shows the complexity of content management in general, and points to the varieties of problems that could emerge and that would of even especial significance in the health industry, specifically those pertaining to the privacy and confidentiality of patient information.

W ith the patient or healthcare consumer, increasingly the focus of healthcare delivery,

such issues could pose major management challenges not just from the perspective of the patient, but also that of the healthcare organization, both with a real chance of derailing any e-Health development program. With regard to the patient for example, should anyone expect patients to consent to the sharing of their records among even healthcare professionals if they had no guarantee of its security? How could we expect an e-Health program to take off, let alone succeed without the confidence of those whose private information we want to share? Would patients not in fact likely sue any healthcare organization responsible for letting such information fall into the hands of hackers, for example, or identity thieves? Would the consequence of a zombie computer in healthcare provider s network serving as conduit for say pornographic solicitation, not be ballyhoo, or indeed, eventually attrition and demise, in the new patient-centered healthcare-delivery dispensation? What could such developments portend for an e-Health program for hackers to extol their success publicly in hacking into the database of a large healthcare organization or a key health plan? Healthcare organizations will also face challenges that insider threats pose. They must therefore also implement the necessary security technologies and establish the required policies to detect and stop unauthorized outbound transmission of patient information and other crucial data and information. In other words, a crucial aspect of content management is to prevent leaks of private and confidential data and information proactively by blocking the outward movement of materials from its systems that violate corporate the established corporate policies among others. Besides preventing the internal and external threats to its contents, other management issues that healthcare organizations regarding content include managing the technologies required for information collection, collation, storage, and dissemination. In particular, healthcare organizations need to know what to do with its often-rich content store and databases lest they miss the opportunity to extract valuable and actionable knowledge from them, and content is not necessarily restricted to text, with cutting-edge technologies emerging for searching and organizing medical images in large databases more efficiently. A Danish-led research project, Deep Structure, Singularities, and Computer Vision (DSSCV), has made significant strides on using advanced mathematics such as scale space theory, singularity theory and algorithmics, as the basis of a better approach to index and search medical images in the large digital databases of hospitals and healthcare organizations. The E.U's IST-sponsored project, 36-month, EUR 1.500.000 project, commenced on October 01, 2002, ended in November 2005, its long-term goal, to contribute to software tools that would enable doctors and hospital technicians to speedily search and match X-rays, magnetic resonance images and computed 3D tomography scans, especially of the craniofacial region. The researchers envisage the start of the development of even more sophisticated algorithms for image understanding that could improve healthcare delivery immensely. According Professor Mads Nielson, of the IT University of Copenhagen, "Let's say a doctor has a new patient with a broken bone, he remembers seeing a similar fracture and wants to recall how he treated that patient, but doesn't remember the case number. By inputting the X-ray of the new patient, this computer system would allow finding the relevant, digitally stored image of that kind of fracture," adding, "Anybody that needs to compare or search images for specific features could use the technology," although its widespread practical applications will need at least another five years of development. This is not surprising, considering the complexities of describing shapes mathematically, and as the professor explained, "To efficiently compare shapes, you need something that doesn't compare every feature··· An analogy would be a stadium full of 20,000 spectators, and you want to find your brother", he says. "You are not going to look at every wrinkle, eyebrow, and strand of hair. You eliminate the details that are irrelevant in order to zoom in on your brother." The researchers are using advanced mathematical theories to achieve this sort of delineation, and although computer vision is still exploratory, standardization of its approaches are starting to crystallize, which would facilitate its widespread utilization in healthcare delivery in the near future. There is little doubt that such projects would benefit from international collaboration in other to speed up its progress and its diffusion in solving, practical healthcare delivery problems, and as Professor Nielson indeed said, "We've done the deep mathematics. Now we'd like to do another project with other partners more involved in the practical issues, such as doctors and hospitals. The above example shows the various dimensions of content management that are crucial to making any e-Health program work. Furthermore, the point made about the need for international collaboration in sponsoring such research efforts is an important aspect of the management issues that confront organizations both, in the public and private sectors, governments, and even regional and international bodies such as the E.U. Such collaborations would be important aspects of the concerted efforts by all healthcare stakeholders to contribute to improving healthcare delivery via health information and other technologies, not to mention the economic benefits that could accrue from them at the local, national, or international, level as the following recent research findings show. The U.S. National Institute of Health (NIH) on April 20, 2006 released a report indicating the findings of a comprehensive review of all phase III clinical trials a Federal agency supported. The National Institutes of Health's National Institute of Neurological Disorders and Stroke (NINDS) sponsored the clinical trials between 1977 and 2000 at a total cost of $335 million. The findings show that conservative estimates of the economic benefit in the U.S. from just eight of these trials were in excess of $15 billion over a ten-year period. The study, published in the April 22, 2006, issue of" The Lancet , also noted that an estimated extra 470,000 healthy years of life were attributable to new discoveries from the trials. This study is pioneering in methodically analyzing the effect of a publicly funded research program on medical care, public health, and health care costs. The 10-year return on the investment (ROI) in clinical trials research funding, according to the study, 4600%, the projected benefits of the trials over the same period, over $50 billion, significantly more than NINDS total budget of $29.5 billion in that period. What's more, the ROI via health benefits occurred within 1.2 years post trial funding, which justifies the comments by Dr. Elias A. Zerhouni, Director of the NIH that 'The results of this analysis demonstrate the return of the public investment in NIH research for the American people not only in economic terms, but in additional healthy years of life." Indeed, according to the Director, ' We are transforming the practice of medicine by moving into an era when treatment will increasingly become more predictive, personalized, and preemptive". It would hardly if at all be presumptuous to add that healthcare ICT would be playing a crucial role in the transition to this era with the immense benefits that these technologies offer in not just facilitating treatment and improving the quality of healthcare delivery, but also in creating efficient and effective options for disease prevention campaigns. The eight trials the study evaluated for example include a trial of tissue Plasminogen Activator (t-PA) for ischemic stroke, which showed that t-PA, could prevent brain damage if used within the first three hours of the start of a stroke. Would it surprise anyone for example how many lives we could save implementing a telehealth service in a hospital in a remote area with experts in another, able to walk the ER doctor through the management of patients with a stroke in the former? This is not to mention preventing the healthcare costs that the sequalae of improperly treated strokes typically engender, and the burden of a chronic, debilitating, disease on patients, and their relatives. This is also true for another of the trials, namely a Randomized Indomethacin Germinal Matrix/ Intraventricular Hemorrhage Prevention Trial, which revealed that using indomethacin in premature babies could prevent brain hemorrhage. The estimated net benefits of each of these trials were over $6 billion over a decade. Besides these direct benefits, the trials might also others with just as profound potential economic and health impact, for example, methodological progress and novel scientific discoveries that could they could generate. The e-Health program needs to continue to benefit from such ongoing research efforts hence must have in-built flexibility to adapt to changes in medical knowledge and to exploit opportunities emerging technologies offer in improving its processes and workflows. However, these opportunities will elude the program without an appreciation of the need for the types of collaborative efforts in initiating and funding researches mentioned above. Thus, part of making an e-Health program is managing its content efficiently, which includes updating it, hence the need to support research activities that produce the new information for such updates. In fact, it is doubtless that database management will be of utmost importance in many respects at the levels of both the healthcare provider and indeed, the public health level. Patterns, cryptic and otherwise could emerge for example, using sophisticated data mining technologies that could reveal hitherto unknown natural history of diseases that could inform policy formulation on resource allocation and utilization. Such patterns could help in disaster preparedness, and response management. No doubt, patient information, communicated and shared among healthcare professionals could make the difference between life and death to patients if available accurately, promptly, and readily in real time at the point of care, for example. However, the health industry is so awash with information from a variety of sources, including with clinical, financial, administrative, and research data, among others that healthcare organizations should readily exploit in sound decision-making, which underscores the point earlier made about the need for intelligent management by healthcare organizations of its veritable content sources. With governments, even at local levels investing in efforts to understand the healthcare needs of its peoples, a necessary prelude to appropriate health services provision for them, the need for such smart data usage is not in doubt. An example of such efforts at healthcare delivery improvement is the recent announcement by the New York State health department to create six regional demonstration projects at a total cost of $6.5 million in grant awards to assist in tackling the multifaceted health care needs of Medicaid enrollees at risk of, or that have chronic illnesses. The chronic illnesses for which the aims of the demonstrations include the promotion of novel, effective approaches to their management include mental illnesses, and heart and kidney diseases, among others. An important objective of the projects would be to promote is to promote the doctor-patient relationship in the entire health service provision-process. This goal is in keeping with the prevalent view in the healthcare and related industries of the central importance of the patient in contemporary healthcare delivery, that of empowering the patient by creating the enabling milieu for them to have a better understanding of their illnesses, the treatment options, lab investigations, and other aspects of their conditions. This way, they become more active in decisions regarding their health matters, and not just passive recipients of their doctors decisions and instructions. The State Health Department will assess each program to determine its efficiency and effectiveness in providing healthcare to patients. There is no doubt that healthcare ICT would play an important role in initiating the sort of novel approaches to healthcare delivery that the State department will be looking for in these demonstrations. Part of the likelihood that these technologies would play such roles would involve their appropriate deployment in content intelligent content management by these demonstration projects. Such content as providing the patients with current, accurate, targeted, and contextualized health information on their conditions for example would be a crucial aspect of promoting better understanding of their illnesses. There is a wide array of health information technologies capable of facilitating this process cost-effectively. These technologies could also help provide those at risk for these conditions the necessary information to help them avoid eventually developing the diseases as much as possible, which is feasible with many of the chronic illnesses, for example, diabetes, via relatively simple, yet effective lifestyle changes. With governments in many countries reaffirming their commitments to improving healthcare delivery, despite many of them experiencing unprecedented increases in their healthcare spending, which clearly are unsustainable, would investing in technologies capable of enabling these governments to achieve their dual goals of delivering qualitative healthcare to their peoples while simultaneously reducing healthcare spending not be strategic?

Indeed, that this is so is evident in the substantial IT investments in a variety of health

initiatives by many of these countries, and their continued commitments to do even more in this regard as the following shows. According to the country's new Health Minister, Tony Clement, in a speech on March 30, 2006, to a gathering of doctors, the new federal government in Canada for example, intends to realize its goal of reducing the wait-time problems confronting the country s health system. The government in fact not only acknowledges the wait-list problem as one Canadians rate highest on the government's priority lists, but also intends to use, among five action items, to gauge its success. According to the Minister, the federal government would base its approach to wait-time reductions on four pillars, namely, research, technology, interagency and intersectoral collaboration, and tackling human resources issues. By investing in research, as the above NIH example illustrates, the government hopes this could generate new knowledge that would help with its disease prevention efforts, at the primary, secondary, and even tertiary levels, thereby reducing the need for the utilization of hospital services, hence wait times. Indeed, this would also likely result in significant costs savings, thus helping achieving the dual healthcare delivery objectives mentioned earlier. What s more, in tandem with the government s second pillar, namely investments in technology, and as it plans to do, specifically in domains such as shared patient information and on cutting-edge digital imaging technologies, achieving these goals would be easier much easier. Besides freeing physicians time that he/ she could turn over to patient care, these technologies would make decision making on patient management more efficient and evidence-based, reducing the chances medical errors, and ensuring patient safety, while at the same time affording the patient the opportunity to receive qualitative healthcare. The overall effects of these would be to reduce morbidities and mortalities, hence the burden of disease in human and material terms. Even the ubiquitous telephone offers ingenious and cost-effective low-technology approaches to healthcare delivery as in telephone-based cognitive behavior therapy (t-CBT), whose effectiveness in treating depression several studies have shown. Recently, Yale School of Medicine started an NIH-sponsored study to determine the prospects of telephone monitoring of symptoms and weight could reduce hospitalization rates in heart failure patients. Termed Tele-HF, it is a four-year randomized controlled trial (RCT) that the National Heart, Lung and Blood Institute in U.S funds. The trial will enroll more than 1,600 heart failure patients throughout the U.S., nationwide, and assess the effectiveness of a remote monitoring system on patients from 15 community-based cardiology practices. Because the health of patients with heart failure typically deteriorates over a couple of weeks leading to their hospitalization, such monitoring could alert their doctors to intervene earlier to prevent further deterioration in their health. This would likely reduce hospitalization rates, and according to the trial´s principal researcher and Professor of Medicine, Dr. Harlan Krumholz, "This study will provide a remarkable opportunity to determine if a low technology intervention can help heart failure patients. This intervention will engage patients in their care and improve communication with their physicians." The telemonitoring system works this way: The patient phones an automated system to answer questions regarding symptoms and then enter his/her daily weight, responses and information that clinicians at each practice could then access via a secure Internet site, review, and take appropriate actions. This system not only improves the patient s access to specialist cardiology care, he/ she becomes an active participant in the management of their conditions. Expectedly, the study will confirm the hypothesis that patients monitored would fare better and have less frequent hospitalizations, which would further confirm the cost-effectiveness of even low-levels healthcare ICT in improving healthcare delivery, and the need for more of such research efforts to enhance our understanding of the value of these technologies. Previous studies have attested to the health and economic benefits of healthcare ICT implementation, for example a September of 2005-RAND study that showed how widespread adoption and appropriate implementation of healthcare ICT could save the American health care system over $162 billion yearly. As mentioned above, the need for intersectoral, and interagency collaboration, among different levels of government for instance will minimize jurisdictional wrangling, which would foster not only such research efforts, but also the sort of free-floating data and information exchange necessary for rational decision making, one of the key requirements or the success of any e-health system. This also underlines the need for recognizing and acting accordingly on the crucial roles of human beings in any system, and the required issues to ensure that they not only embrace the system, but also are committed to making it work. According to the Minister, restating the government s commitment to the pledge of a health care guarantee that the ruling Conservative party made during the election campaign, offering a guarantee without having a foundation in place to deliver it would be essentially untenable, describing the pillars as a sense of what that foundation is. It is therefore clear that management at any level ought to be looking at issues such as those mentioned above as the bedrock of any viable e-Health system. Such a system, no doubt is sine qua non to any government or any country achieving the dual goals of providing qualitative health services to its peoples without necessarily wrecking its economy in the process. Indeed, the above assertion holds true regardless of the funding system of the country s health services, for the simple fact that the patient remains the center of health services delivery, after all we are delivering healthcare to none other the patient, or in general, the public, so human beings remain the center of the health services universe, so to speak. This might have informed the statement to the media by the president of Canadian medical Association, CMA, Dr. Ruth Collins-Nakai, after the Minister s speech that the CMA has proposed the machinery to make the government guarantee possible. According to Dr Collins-Nakai, the association proposed a $2-billion health access fund, with costs split evenly between the federal and provincial governments. This fund would give patients the option to seek healthcare somewhere else after waiting longer than the established wait time for medically necessary healthcare in their own domain, a sort of safety valve to secure the guarantee that the federal government promised. In a related development, the provincial government in Alberta appears to have backed away from two of the most contentious aspects of its so-called Third Way, Medicare-reform plan, some say, at least for now. On April 20, 2006, Health Minister Iris Evans attributed this to public reaction to the government's private health care plans. According to the Minister, We are not prepared to proceed with private insurance at this time We are not recommending that doctors working in both (public and private) systems be part of the policy framework. This latest decision puts to rest at least for the time being, the government s hitherto plans to allow doctors to operate in both systems concurrently, and Albertans to buy their way to the top of wait lists for surgeries such as joint replacements, risking a breach of the Canada Health Act, which reports indicate the federal government strictly frowns upon. The government plans to focus now on improving on training programs and on recruiting healthcare professionals to ensure that its peoples have adequate numbers of health-care workers in the future to cover the health services. According to Mr. Clement, "You can do a heck of a lot of innovating within the confines of the Canada Health Act," noting that an Alberta pilot project significantly reduced wait times for hip and knee replacements in Calgary, and that, "There's lots of ways the private sector can be involved within the rules of the Canada Health Act." There is indeed, sufficient room to innovate healthcare services implementing healthcare ICT, the funding system of the health services notwithstanding. A publicly or privately funded health system could afford neither to spend increasingly more on health services, nor to deliver poor quality healthcare, indefinitely. Even if there were no public outcry in both cases, poor quality healthcare would result increasing morbidities and deaths, further increasing healthcare costs, eventually plunging the system into bankruptcy. It is imperative therefore, for both systems to deliver affordable and cost-effective, qualitative health services, which healthcare ICT could help achieve. Many for example believe that taking B vitamin supplements could help prevent Alzheimer's disease (AD), and Parkinson's disease, or make their effects less severe. However, a recent Agency for Healthcare Research and Quality (AHRQ) report released on April 21, 2006, found no conclusive evidence to support this popular belief. There is also no conclusive evidence regarding whether the presence or severity of these disorders depends on if someone had a B vitamin deficiency. The only study of berry consumption in humans also found no association with Parkinson's disease. To be sure, the report notes that vitamin B1 and folate deficiencies in animal studies in general result in neurological dysfunction and B6, B12, or folate supplements may perk up neurocognitive functioning, and that folate and B12 protect indeed, ward off genetic deficiencies for modeling AD. They also note that thiamine and folate influence neurovascular function and health, but the benefits of these vitamins in humans do not seem that clear, evidence for the possible benefits of B1 and parenteral B12 in AD, only tenuous, and those of B6 and folate even fuzzier. The report stressed the need for further studies to identify possible mechanisms by which B vitamins could act to prevent specific brain disorders, particularly Parkinson's disease, and to identify the exact parts of berries that might be medicinally useful. Are these findings not important for people to know, particularly in the present dispensation, with the increasing expectation of patients to be active participants in their health matters? This is just one instance of the need for current, accurate, analyzed, contextualized, and targeted health information delivered to the healthcare consumer, and for which healthcare organizations and stakeholders at different levels would need to establish appropriate policies for its execution. Such targeted health information could serve a variety of purposes, for example, health promotion, and disease prevention, and the provision of the latest information on disease conditions, including their treatments. Would the healthcare consumer armed with such information not be better able to make rational decisions about his/ her health and regarding the choice of healthcare provider, and treatment options? Would the ability to be this discerning not empower patients, enable them receive the best care, and at reasonable and affordable costs? Would this not reduce morbidities on the aggregate and healthcare costs with fewer hospitalizations and less use of expensive lab investigations, and prescription medications? Would all these not be achievable by the relevant healthcare stakeholders investing in the appropriate healthcare ICT for the dissemination of such targeted health information? Could there not be the involvement of the different elements mentioned earlier, for example, interagency collaboration in organizing and implementing an even wider health education campaign for example, using some novel technology an earlier international public-private sector, research-collaboration venture helped develop? There is no doubt about the enhancement of the chances of success of any e-Health program with the healthcare stakeholders involved in its implementation and utilization embracing such a flexible, multidimensional management orientation to the tasks involved in achieving this goal. Health information communication and sharing among healthcare professionals is just as important as information dissemination to the healthcare consumer. The announcement by the U.S. Food and Drug Administration (FDA) on April 22, 2006 that it is adopting the Systematized Nomenclature of Medicine (SNOMED), specifically, its "Problem List" Subset, as the standard computerized medical vocabulary system for use to code electronically, important terms in the Highlights section of prescription drug labeling, will no doubt facilitate the sharing of drug information. This move also no doubt underscores the increasing recognition by healthcare stakeholders of the need for health information dissemination, communication, and sharing. It also exemplifies the point about interagency cooperation in moving e-Health implementation forward, as it certainly does for the efforts of the other U.S. agencies involved in advancing the federal government's efforts to implement EHR for Americans within the next decade. The move in fact also demonstrates the significance of management formulating and adopting the necessary standards policies that would also help speed up the widespread adoption and utilization of electronic health records and other e-Health technologies, all of these inferences further underlining the need for a multidimensional management orientation mentioned earlier. The move by the FDA would enable healthcare professionals throughout the country to access and share critical health and treatment information electronically, hence easier, faster, in real time, and more efficiently. As Dr. Andrew C. von Eschenbach, the Acting Commissioner of the FDA notes, "Today's action moves us closer to our goal of establishing electronic medical records for most Americans within 10 years. With the increasing use of electronic medical records and other computerized methods for managing healthcare data, the issues around electronic data standards and standardized terminologies will become increasingly important." The Acting Director further adds,

"Once we have implemented a national e-health record, health professionals will have quick, reliable, and secure access to patient information that can be cross-referenced with critical treatment information, including the information in the Highlights section of drug labeling." The College of American Pathologists (CAP) developed SNOMED (Systematized Nomenclature of Medicine) and it is one of the terminologies for the healthcare ICT infrastructure for clinical language, the U.S. chose. The Problem List Subset of SNOMED, which a Department of Veterans Affairs (VA)/ Kaiser Permanente alliance produced, is able to code certain terms in the Highlights data elements of the new format for prescription drug information electronically the format mandatory with effect from June 30, 2006, for recently approved, those in the past 5 years, and newly approved drug products. This would enhance the product information sharing in FDA-approved package inserts. The SNOMED system provides coding for clinical terminology to facilitate cross-system computer readability. So rather than referring to a heart attack as such as in often the case, or as a myocardial infarction, infarct, or an MI, SNOMED gives it one code for use in medication product labeling. This will certainly facilitate the interoperability of electronic systems that exchange FDA approved labeling information hence will improve patient safety and overall healthcare delivery. In May 2005, the Department of Health and Human Services (HHS) announced that federal agencies would use SNOMED CT for the exchange of clinical information across the federal government for laboratory result contents, non-laboratory interventions and procedures, anatomy, diagnoses and problems, and nursing. FDA s decision to adopt the standards is therefore not surprising, and indeed, the agency continues to collaborate with the federal Health IT Standards Panel. A licensing contract with the CAP that the National Library of Medicine (NLM), a part of the National Institutes of Health (NIH), administers will facilitate ready adoption of the standards and interoperability of the information systems of U.S. healthcare professionals, hospitals, insurance firms, and other relevant healthcare stakeholders, incorporating this uniform terminology. Offer of the Problem List Subset of codes for labeling use is gratis via the National Cancer Institute (NCI) Web site. These developments augur well for the future of healthcare delivery in the U.S., particularly as it transitions into the e-Health age. Dr. von Eschenbach also stressed this point when he says, "We have today announced an important step toward creating an electronic environment for drug information exchange that can provide American patients and healthcare professionals with critical information at the point of care." He also adds, "The use of SNOMED in this way opens the door to establishing another key element in building a unified electronic health information infrastructure in the United States. We likewise are committed to electronic exchange of safety information on prescription drug products globally, and we will continue to support our ICH agreements in this regard." As if to underscore further the point, Dr. Bob Dolin of Kaiser Permanente also says, 'The FDA's adoption of SNOMED codes to encode the highlights section of drug labeling is one of the most significant advances in patient care since the introduction of automated drug-drug and drug-allergy checking software." With patient safety a major issue in contemporary healthcare delivery, there is no overstating the significance of these developments. However, efforts need to continue towards unifying the somewhat crowded structure product labeling (SPL) arena, with other terminologies for examples, LOINC, the NCI Thesaurus, NDF-RT, and others that patients and their doctors have to grapple with in addition to the Problem List Subset of SNOMED in the new physician labeling design of January 2006 also in current use. Each prescription information update in the new format goes to the DailyMed, an NLM-sponsored, interagency Internet health information clearinghouse that thus offers current medication information on FDA-regulated products on the house to healthcare consumers, doctors, nurses, and other healthcare stakeholders. Anyone could in fact look up comprehensive, current, and accurate information on any medication or FDA-regulated product at the Website, which also has extra features including forms for voluntary and mandatory reporting of adverse drug reactions to the FDA by patients and healthcare professionals alike. Other developed countries have similar Internet portals albeit with slightly different foci. Canada launched on May 25, 2005, its searchable online database containing all drug-related adverse reactions from the Canadian Adverse Drug Reaction Information System (CADRIS). Health Canada's Canadian Adverse Drug Reaction Monitoring Program (CADRMP) developed the database. The public, physicians, nurses, and drug companies could report the suspected adverse events with all data updated four times per year. Anyone connected to the Internet could also now look for adverse drug reactions that reported since 1965 on this Web site. DailyMed also offers opportunities for updates notification via Really Simple Syndication (RSS) feeds, whéreby DailyMed delivers notification of updates and additions to Drug Label information shown on its site to anyone with an RSS Reader interested in such updates, an example of the sort of targeted health information delivery whose use would likely become more widespread in healthcare service delivery. There is also likely to be increasing collaboration among healthcare stakeholders in the efforts to provide the healthcare consumer and their doctors, among others with this sort of targeted health information, and current health data and information in general. Michael J. Lincoln, MD, Chief Terminologist, Department of Veterans Affairs Office of Information attests to this when he says, ̀VA will use the FDA DailyMed messages to increase the quality of its pharmacy terminology, used to deliver over 110 million outpatient prescriptions per year to our nation s Veterans. SPL and DailyMed will also support VA s electronic Problem List and related administrative applications. VA is excited to be collaborating with Kaiser, FDA, and others to provide up- to- date medical information that improves patient safety and care quality." Healthcare organizations will need to determine in which areas of healthcare ICT implementation they will need to collaborate with organizations in the health and other industries in other to facilitate the achievement of the objectives of their value propositions. The realization of these goals is in some instances, for example in a private health system, crucial to the effectiveness of the service profit chain of healthcare providers, and ultimately their survival. Even in a public health system, the delivery of qualitative health services under budget restraints implies close attention to how to deliver these services most cost-effectively. In both cases therefore, management's collaborative initiatives on healthcare ICT projects that could assist in achieving these dual objectives could be anything but an exercise in frivolity. This is in addition to such efforts constituting these organizations contributions to the widespread diffusion and utilization of healthcare ICT, and in helping to ensure the country's shift toward e-Health works.

Even in a utopian world, where funds are abundant and readily available, it is still prudent to utilize the funds efficiently, after all today's surplus may be what will be available to fund future projects when funds start to dry up or are no longer so easily obtained. The reality in fact is that funds are not so copious and free flowing. Many organizations, including those in healthcare operate with limited budgets and often under financial constraints. With the costs of healthcare provision escalating for a variety of reasons, including the heavier disease burden of chronic illnesses, changing demographics, and costs of medications, among others, many healthcare executives struggle to show the value of projects they implement in order to justify making funds available for the projects. This is even more so with regard to healthcare ICT whose promise of cost saving and better outcomes have often failed to materialize despite substantial investments in a variety of information systems by healthcare organizations. To be sure, it was relatively easy to calculate the costs of and the expected savings in implementing the transactional systems used in the financial departments of healthcare providers two or so decades ago. Studies such as those conducted at the acute care unit at El Camino Hospital and the ambulatory care unit at Harvard Community Health Plan in the 1970s robustly confirmed the cost saving and quality enhancing values of these transactional systems, which incidentally only a few sophisticated healthcare organizations deployed. Times have since changed. Applications have become more complex, as have the environments and circumstances under which they operate and needed to support them. These are the days of the Internet, with its potential to broaden the scope and functionalities of applications, and spawn a set of security, privacy, and other issues. There is the explosion of applications with potential to enhance productivity yet equally to create standardization and integration problems that could compromise the utility and by extension the value of some or even all of the applications a healthcare organization implemented. There is also the information glut that is making ever trying to use our innate cognitive capacities to sort out seem ridiculous yet perhaps more meaningful when IT simply dumps it before us. How does one know the value of the applications so much money went into implementing given these complexities? Some say this is near impossibility, yet the hospital board wants to know on what parameters to base its investment decisions, or indeed, why it should not cut the hospital's operating and capital budget in the next fiscal year. Every healthcare organization needs to have business goals in line with its stated vision, mission, and value propositions, and be committed to strict financial discipline. It needs to ensure that its healthcare ICT investments support these business goals. The requirements, costs, and benefits of the proposed healthcare ICT are important focal points in making a case for investment but so are the business plans and performance objectives of the healthcare organization. The planned healthcare ICT must have a viable business case. The healthcare organization must deploy healthcare ICT to solve stated business problems. It will be easier for the organization to achieve return on investment (ROI) if it could make a strong business case for its healthcare ICT investments, for example the achievement of specific objectives relevant to certain measurable health indicators, recognize and accomplish critical success factors salient to value, and ensure the achievement of this value ultimately. Coupled with skyrocketing expenses, it is little wonder that hospital management boards have been struggling to raise funds for capital and other projects, making it ever more difficult to find the resources to fund healthcare ICT projects. This is clearly a management challenge that is ongoing and which solving would require adroit management in the years ago for a variety of reasons, in particular government efforts and those of other payers to trim healthcare spending. One of the major efforts of contemporary hospital managers will therefore be finding ways to control healthcare ICT costs. There is no question about the poor showing of the Medicare finances of acute-care hospitals in recent times. Not with hospital costs per case increasing on the average by

31% between FFY 2000 and 2004, but Medicare reimbursements per case increasing only by 14%, during the same period, and by 7% and 4%, respectively between FFY 2003 and 2004, for the top 10 diagnosis-related groups (DRG), for examples. Hospital CEOs should be interested in these figures, and in what their utilization review or quality control committees are saying about other such clinical parameters as average length of stay, readmission rates, specific DRG costs, clinical path variances, and nosocomial infections. The unfavorable rates of these service quality measures are no doubt contributory to the increasing difficulty healthcare organizations have raising funds, capital, or operating, which puts them in a quagmire considering that they actually need more money nowadays to meet increasing needs for service provision including for seniors, and managing chronic non-communicable diseases. They also need more money to build more inpatient facilities, and to upgrade old and implement new technologies. With hospital CEOs and physicians recognizing the need for collaboration to overcome a common challenge, that of controlling the costs of service delivery, they will be able to work toward this goal knowing that it is in their respective interests to do so. ICT can help improve the ratings for the aforementioned parameters hence the quality of service delivery while simultaneously cutting costs. One way healthcare providers are controlling costs is by implementing clinical resource management systems although there are varieties of other ICT that can help minimize costs by improving clinical, administrative, and financial processes. The technologies that a hospital decides to implement notwithstanding, no CEO would want ICT costs to end up worsening the hospital's financial burden and making the whole idea of trying to cut costs seem meaningless. Hospital CEOs should therefore, be keen to control health ICT costs while making the technologies work for their hospitals to reduce overall costs and improve financial performance. In any case, health information technologies do not have to be expensive to help deliver qualitative healthcare as the following study shows. Primary care patients with depression and anxiety often prefer psychotherapy to medication. However, access to psychotherapy is limited due to the small numbers of therapists trained in evidence-based treatments. In a study of the clinical efficacy and cost-effectiveness of computerized cognitive-behavior therapy (CBT) for depression and anxiety (Br. J Psychiatry 2004 Jul; 185:46-54), British researchers randomized 274 patients to 9 weeks of computerized CBT or conventional primary care that may include psychotherapy referrals. The patients' diagnoses included depression, anxiety disorders (panic, social, or specific phobias) or mixed anxiety/ depression. Primary care physicians had the option of prescribing medications to all the patients. A third of eligible patients declined to participate in the protocol and 27% of the patients that received CBT dropped out by the first post-treatment review. The study showed that computerized CBT produced sustained and significant improvements on depression, work, and social functioning. The level of patient satisfaction was also significantly high. The effects of computerized CBT were significant only for severe illness regarding anxiety measures. With regard to cost-effectiveness, the CBT patients had higher service costs but lower costs from lost employment. Computerized CBT had a higher probability (81%) of being cost-effective. These studies showed significant benefits of computerized CBT in typical primary care patients suffering from depression and anxiety. The exclusive reliance of the studies on patient self-reports for outcome, the lack of blinding of the treatments, and the high attrition and refusal rates limit the findings of the study and raise doubts about the acceptability of computerized CBT, which latter could become more widely accepted with the tailoring of interventions to the needs of the individual patient. Nonetheless, the study demonstrates the versatility of even so-called low technologies in delivering cost-effective and qualitative health services. Of all the components of information systems, software stands out as one capable of introducing the most variance into projected estimates of health ICT implementation costs. It is not that we should discard caution in purchasing hardware and peripherals. On the contrary, by subjecting the process to competitive bidding and due diligence, we often have a chance to choose excellent products at competitive prices. With software, however, the story is quite different, which underscores the need for those responsible for funding software projects to be aware of a variety of preventive cost-cutting measures to avoid the sometimes-grave financial repercussions of flawed software. Many health organizations have their in-house IT department. Others rely on vendors to advise and supply them with required software to meet their needs. Yet, others combine their in-house resources with those of outside software firms either in a collaborative effort to build software or in a new model of outsourcing that does not render in-house IT staff essentially redundant. The approach regardless, costs considerations are vital. Furthermore, it is still all about software development and many of the same problems inherent and accidental in software production and the basic principles of controlling costs apply. That testing for example should be done in tandem throughout each life cycle phase is crucial to saving costs with any software development process. In other words, the organization contemplating customized software development should insist on this approach, including product testing by a software quality assurance (SQA) team, rather than wait until post-integration acceptance testing, when it will be too late to prevent the huge financial losses that often result. Even if buying shrink-wrapped software, the organization might want to be involved in the software s a-and b testing to be sure it is not fault-laden, and can work with the organizations' hardware. Healthcare organizations will also be able to control costs by insisting on efforts to improve the software process by both in-house and external IT organizations. Healthcare organizations should insist that IT organizations they deal with be certified by any of a number of national and international initiatives on software process improvement such as the Software Engineering Institute's (SEI) Capability maturity Models (CMM), the International Standards Organization's ISO 9000-series, and the software improvement capability determination (SPICE,) an over 40-country strong international initiative. Since 1997, SPICE has become ISO/ IEC 15504 or simply 15504, reflecting its takeover by the ISO and the International Electrotechnical Commission (IEC.) These initiatives are measures of software quality with particular emphasis on management of the software process, which if sound, will naturally result in improvement in techniques, and tools, with eventual improvement in product quality. Many organizations have saved millions of dollars implementing software improvement process in their in-house IT departments and insisting on IT firms they deal with having superior process improvement certifications. The basic idea behind process improvement initiatives such as CMM is that the efficient management of the software development process will complement and enhance technical expertise, improve tools and techniques, and by extension, improve product quality. Improved software process management has resulted on the human resources side, in improved creativity and software development techniques, higher morale, reduced overtime and off-sick hours, fewer turnovers of technical personnel, and fostered healthy working relationships. On the technical and business sides, it has led to reduction in time to market and post-release default rates, and increased productivity. Developments in the computer industry are also broadening the opportunities for healthcare ICT applications, and the scope of the understanding of technical issues that the management of healthcare organizations needs to have in order to establish appropriate healthcare ICT acquisition, maintenance, licensing, and other policies. There is little doubt for example about the increasing significance of the portability of healthcare information, developments in the mobile and wireless industries converging with those in the computer industry to actualize these prospects. Mid-year 2005 for example saw Samsung becoming the first laptop manufacturer to embed chips in laptops, expanding their range of Wi-Fi access, and speeding up their performance. Samsung has an arrangement to embed chips from start-up Airgo Networks, which uses multiple-input multiple-output MIMO) technology, to boost bandwidth, and to increase the speed and distance range of wireless networks. Airgo is putting MIMO s capacity to increase data rates at 45mbps, although the technology could transmit data faster, up to 100mbps, and broaden signal range to roughly 600 to 900 feet. Compared with the current the range of current 802.11-based wireless networks of 150-300 feet, and an optimal transfer rate of 54mbps, or in practice averagely 25 mbps, this is a remarkable development in the industry, particularly for consumers, who have had to contend with narrow range and dawdling data transfer rates. Wireless routers and network interface cards using MIMO are already on the market, sold by firms such as Belkin and Linksys, but now, MIMO lies embedded directly within the laptop. Industry pundits agree that this is a bold move by Samsung, and that customers will benefit from being now able to get more speed and bandwidth than they ever had. Considering MIMO operates on 802.11g and 802.11b standards, what then is new? The uniqueness of MIMO is in allowing the transmission of two or more discrete signals over the same 802.11 radio channel simultaneously without interference, making it possible to transmit more data over the on hand radio spectrum than hitherto possible. Many laptops are currently wireless-enabled, and use Intel's Centrino chips that transmit and receive radio signals using single radios compared to the Samsung's Airgo chips that utilize two radios. Using two radios increase the transmissible data, and the reliability and efficiency of transmission. The double-radio approach also eliminates interference by "echo" radio signals that springing back off walls, depreciating data transmission speed, and compromising connectivity. This is because, and unlike the single-radio, MIMO-enabled radio listens to the echoes and channels radio traffic to a single, dominant path. Furthermore, with MIMO technology, because it uses more than one radio, it is possible for Wi-Fi signals to travel round bends and other physical obstacles, something that was previously impossible. MIMO technology is blazing the trail for the next-generation wireless standard called 802.11n, the Institute of Electrical and Electronic Engineers is still working on. These laptops, which would improve access to patient information by healthcare professionals on the go, are likely to gain wide acceptance among healthcare professionals, particularly with portable computers becoming handy enough to fit into doctors clinical coats these days. The emergence of dual-mode handsets also typifies the new league of devices capable of a seamless convergence of wireless and cellular technologies. There are already cellular smart phones, such as the Nokia Communicator 9500 and the Siemens SX66, which support 802.11 on the market but these devices pale in significance when compared to these devices, capable of carrying voice calls over wireless. These devices, whose projected annual sales worldwide experts put at well over $100 million by 2010 are variously termed voice over Wi-Fi(VoWi-Fi), or voice over wireless LAN(VoWLAN), among others, are capable of roaming from the home or office wireless networks to cellular carriers, for example, Verizon Wireless. Experts believe that the rush to this pre-standard arena has to do with the crucial need for cost-effective, real time voice and data services, hence not surprisingly healthcare organizations chief among them. Some vendors for example, utilize a cross fiber/ coaxial backbone to transmit voice and data services to itinerant users, signals from the cellular WAN and the Wi-Fi LAN transmitted on this infrastructure to broadband antennas capable of simultaneous multiservice delivery via minimal numbers of multi-antenna, access points. Dual-mode devices enable seamless transition from one platform to another at minimal costs to consumers, although they are unlikely to be widely available for some to come. There are commercially available dual-mode handsets in the US, for example, Motorola's CN620, and in Japan, for example, NTT DoCoMo's N900iL FOMA handsets. It may indeed, be possible that the wireless carriers are not in any hurry to see these devices on the market because there is a lack of consensus on the convergence as opposed to the seamless side of the technologies. This lack of standardization has roots in the varied special interests of industry players in these technologies. The UMA (Unlicensed Mobile Access) group for example, comprising among others, British Telecom, Cingular, Alcatel, Motorola, Ericsson, Motorola, Rogers Wireless, Nokia, Siemens, and Nortel Networks, proposes a cellular-centric solution. This means a dual-mode handset user could call and take calls across any wireless LAN and IP network only via the UMA network controller s gateway to the mobile network hub. The ideas of this group, perhaps, and as some would no doubt insist, the most influential of the lot, contrast with those of the SCCAN (Seamless Converged Communication Across Network) group, comprising Avaya, Proxim, Chantry Networks, 2Wire, and others, which essentially is an enterprise-based solution, and prefers to mobile telephony an extension of the PBX functionality seen in enterprises. MobileIGNITE (Mobile Integrated Go-to-Market Network IP Telephony Experience), on the other hand is a vendor-initiated venture, actually by BridgePort Networks, and is an exclusive wireless firms club (Kyocera, Verisign, Taproot, IBM, as it has no mobile carriers. The solution, which is SIP-based, is a coalition program of a number of pre-tested technologies, whereas the Wireless Wireline Convergence Working Group of the International Packet Communications Consortium, with many soft switch vendors in its fold, has Cisco, Alcatel, NexTel, Time Warner Telecom, among its membership. The group aims to develop a suitable platform for providing transparent and seamless mobility that it could map to IMS, across wireline and wireless networks. IEEE 802.2, on the other hand wants to support handover between 802 networks, wired or wireless, and between 802 and non-802 networks. IEEE, a strict, standards-based organization will likely be the final arbiter. It will be interesting to see which of these groups gains the upper hand in not only regarding standardization, but also market share, in the end, although some industry watchers would argue that the Avaya/ Motorola convergence solution appears to be ahead. On January 2003, Motorola Inc. (NYSE: MOT), Avaya Inc. (NYSE: AV), and Proxim Corporation (NASD: PROX) announced their intention to collaborate on the creation and deployment of converged cellular, Wireless Local Area Networking (WLAN), and Internet Protocol (IP) Telephony solutions capable of delivering enhanced communications mobility and network connectivity. They planned to achieve these goals via a number of products, including Motorola s Wi-Fi/ cellular dual-system phone, Avaya s Session Initiation Protocol (SIP)-enabled IP Telephony software from Avaya, Proxim s voice enabled WLAN infrastructure. With WiMAX-based 802.16e handsets, Skype-on- smart phone devices, and 3-G enabled, PocketPC-based smart phones, and other novel technologies all potential competitors in the emerging convergence market, resolution to outstanding standardization and platform issues might have to come sooner than later. As noted earlier, one of the main benefits of these convergent technologies concerns cost savings, in particular via less network management expenses, reduced usage charges, and the optimization of devices. Healthcare professionals for example will be able to access valuable patient information and their hospital's network applications from within and some distance away from the hospital, improving patient care and overall efficiency. These technologies also improve communications via such features as on-demand conference calling and vocalizations access to important hospital's network applications, for example email service, directories, and calendars. The question for management would be deciding if these technologies offer their establishments solutions in keeping with their needs, and their budgets, and that would foster the achievements of their strategic aspirations.

Besides these considerations, however, management also needs to be able to account for

their decisions for healthcare ICT acquisition, and implementation and institute appropriate mechanisms to evaluate and audit them. Some argue that part of the slow adoption of ICT in the health industry has to do with the earlier experiences implementing these technologies, specifically regarding project delays, budget overruns, and perennially unreliable products that gobble up scarce funds in relentless maintenance and other costs. These developments indeed, prompted some to levy accusations of a lack of accountability on the part of the management and boards of the healthcare organizations involved. In these days of spiraling healthcare costs, there is unlikely to be much tolerance for such spending spree on valueless technologies as witnessed in those earlier days. Indeed, President Bush signed the Public Company Accounting Reform and Investor Protection Act of 2002, aka the Sarbanes-Oxley Act, into law on 30 July 2002. Hailed as a major change to federal securities laws in the US in a long time, it was no surprise that the two US Congressional bodies sanctioned the Act unanimously with corporate scandals in the air prior to its enactment. The act aimed to review archaic legislative audit requirements to ensure more reliable accounting practices and corporate disclosures. By mandating management to use risk management techniques such as Committee of Sponsoring Organizations of the Treadway Commission (COSO), among others, the Act aims to assure the protection of investors. COSO, extensively used internal control benchmarks for IT auditing prescribes appropriate control milieu assessments, determination of control goals, performing risk assessments, and identifying controls. These are ideals no one would dispute could foster high quality ICT governance. The problem is that they seem to be slowing down and increasing the costs of ICT projects, the reason being that project teams must now carry out more detailed and thorough quality-assurance assessments and testing throughout project life cycles for documentation of IT controls. Project managers are complaining that the need for additional sign-offs during different phases of projects along with other mandatory controls-related checklists are retarding the pace of their projects, and the longer the project takes, the more they cost, which financiers are unhappy about. Concerned ICT industry stakeholders are scrambling for measures to take that would prevent the requirements of the Act from having a negative influence on ICT project costs and cycle times. These measures, such as holding back software upgrades to ensure they do not affect end of year financial closure, and that controls requirements related to the Act including quality assurance testing and necessary documentation feature in project planning right from the start. Healthcare ICT governance will certainly benefit from compliance with the Act. Management could reduce the pains of compliance by taking necessary proactive measures that would ensure project life cycles and costs remain within projected limits. Management would need to institute the necessary measures to streamline, standardize, and consolidate their processes and technology assets. Management should formulate the appropriate policies for example, that the hospital's IT department does not indulge in recommending and/ or acquiring unnecessary applications, each for example, each of the multiplicity of hardware with its unique configuration. It should also endeavor to rationalize healthcare ICT use, and avoid excess capacity and wastage, thereby reducing costs, and freeing resources for other valuable projects that could enhance its hospital's ability to achieve its overall e-health goals. Management via its establishment s IT department should establish firm control over its client servers and We-based architectures, for example, among other IT assets, not least, security-related issues, which are crucial to maintaining the integrity of the hospital s networks and other computer systems. IT infrastructure management is a major management issue in the quest to make e-Health the future of healthcare delivery in many countries already reeling in overwhelming healthcare spending, and some would insist, with yet visible cracks in the healthcare delivery services. Some healthcare organizations might want to consider embracing standardized application platforms and software development language, and to ensure that the software, hardware, and other IT that they purchase meets specific needs. They may also want to lower costs by their choices of storage devices, servers, PCs, Notebooks, and other technologies, and to ensure that their technologies are scalable, and reliable, with as little downtime as possible considering the costs in human and material terms in a healthcare milieu for example. Open-source applications might even be viable options for healthcare organizations in some countries. These various measures to ensure rational healthcare ICT investing however needs to evolve in the context of the healthcare organization's set goals, which their service offerings reflect, and because such goals need set in turn based on the needs of its clientele, and the overall direction of health services delivery in the milieu in which the healthcare organization operates. Thus a healthcare organization serving a community of predominantly elderly healthcare consumers in a healthcare system moving increasingly toward e-Health would probably need to give serious consideration to having the necessary IT infrastructures in place to exploit the opportunities for service provision such new technologies as described below offer. The EU-IST is funding a project developing a mobile device that provides emergency assistance to people at risk. The MobilAlarm project₃ has developed a mobile

device about the size of a cell phone and less than 100mg that enables users to place an emergency call to a service center, for example, a hospital, satellite positioning via GPS able to give accurate information on where they are to 50 meters or less. The device has four plainly visible user-friendly, buttons, compared to the many features of regular cell phones including small buttons and prints, which seniors often find mind-boggling, essentially limiting their use in emergencies, when speed and ease of use are paramount for any device to be valuable in this population. This is more so considering that some of these elderly people have age-related vision restriction or even health problems that impair their motor skills. According to Stefan Lilischkis, the MobilAlarm project manager, "The handset has two large buttons on the side that when pressed simultaneously initiate a call to the service centre. For people with diseases such as Parkinson's this is an important feature, because it allows a user to make an emergency call by simply gripping the device, rather than having to find and press a button." A different button makes the call to a pre-programmed telephone number, for examples, of a friend, relative or neighbor, the devices enhanced audio features enabling communication without the senior holding it up to his/ her ear. A third button serves call termination. "When an emergency call is placed to a service centre the operator who takes the call automatically receives the user's file on their computer, and, if necessary, can use the GPS tracking to obtain information about the location of the person on an electronic map", stresses Lilischkis. He adds, "This is particularly important if emergency services are to find them quickly, especially if the person does not know where they are or are having difficulty speaking". This new device is superior to current mobile devices able to tell where a person is, most of which transmit GPS data via an SMS message. The MobilAlarm system on the other hand, utilizes the Care Phone Protocol, which one of the project partners, Attendo Systems developed. This protocol is able to transmit data via a voice channel, enabling instant information arrival, unlike an SMS message that could take minutes if not hours to do so as network traffic permits. This system's GSM even makes connectivity for emergency calls possible in some places where cell phones cannot. Tested among seniors in the U.K, Spain, and Germany in 2005, the response was overwhelming favorable. Noted Lothar Jennrich-Gügel, the founder of the German Parkinson Self Help Group, involved in the trials, "Parkinson patients could be very mobile but abhor going out because of the risk of facing a life-threatening situation. Based on this a mobile alarm system is urgently required." There is no doubt that this device will gain increasing currency in many developed countries with an aging population as it has the potential to improve the quality of life (QOL), of these seniors, and of those with chronic illnesses and physical disabilities. Others at risk of domestic violence for example or other forms of aggression or in hazardous occupations will also likely embrace a versatile device such as this that could potentially save their lives. Interestingly, the development of many more of such valuable yet not threatening healthcare information technologies could help thaw the resistance among many regarding the adoption of these technologies. Indeed, changing this resistance is one other major management task in the efforts to foster the widespread implementation of healthcare ICT, required for ensuring the move toward e-Health continues unabated. Such attitudinal change is not limited to the public. In fact, as the reception, the seniors gave the MobileAlarm system during its trial mentioned above shows, and the recent evidence of many in the personal health records (PHR) systems also indicate, the public is increasingly open to the use of healthcare information technologies.

It is in fact healthcare providers and others in the health industry that some would insist seem to be recalcitrant to change when it comes to the adoption and usage of these technologies. Healthcare organizations therefore need to do more regarding change management among its cadres. Healthcare organizations, just any other service endeavor, must provide value-added transformations for its clients. A healthcare organization's services are both internal and external, the former, activities required for its operations, including human resources, finance, administration, IT, and estate services, and the latter, its products and service offerings to its clients. Regardless of its funding type, every healthcare organization needs to ensure the efficient and effective running of both its internal and external services. Indeed, it has to keep devising innovative approaches to meet the requirements of changing times, for example, new legal constraints for administrative accountability, or changing disease patterns, or emerging novel healthcare-delivery paradigms. On this score, the flexibility that Canada's Health Minister, Tony Clement expressed in dealing with the issue of wait times in the country is hardly surprising. According to reports in the National Post on April 22, 2006, the Minister offered the province some leeway on tackling the patient wait times issue albeit with a proviso; whatever the province does has to be within the confines of the Canada Health Act. The Minister noted that after all, Alberta's pilot project on hip and knee replacements succeeded in reducing the wait time from 47 weeks to 4.7 weeks, without contravening the provisions of the Canada Health Act. A few days earlier, Ottawa threatened to stop $1.75 billion in federal transfer payments to Alberta if it forged ahead with its 'Third Way 'health reform including allowing private insurance and doctors to work in both the public and private health systems. Alberta backed down, but with the Health Minister's offer, that each province and territory should seek its own innovative ways to tackle the wait lists problem, the province's next moves remain unclear. What is certain though is that healthcare ICT could help in significantly reducing wait times in several ways, including streamlining appointments scheduling/ referral system right from the family doctor's level all the way to the specialist at the secondary tier of health services delivery, and indeed, up to the third, in university teaching hospitals, and other specialized-care healthcare facilities. This is besides the indirect effect on hospital utilization rates that could result from intensive healthcare ICT-backed health promotion and disease prevention projects. These measures require the efficient running of the health system s internal systems. In other words, the health system's internal services such as administration, human resources, and finance have to be running smoothly and efficiently for its offerings to the public to work equally efficiently. Because as we have just noted, the system is intercalated, with the patient waiting for hip and knee, or cataracts surgery, or those waiting to the heart specialist or for chemotherapy with a cancer expert, coming from the lower rungs of the healthcare delivery ladder, this efficiency and effectiveness necessarily must be pervasive. Thus, it is not enough for the hospitals to be efficient, but the family doctor s practice also has to be for the entire system to work. Given that implementing the appropriate health information technologies could help improve the efficiency of the workflows and processes of these internal services, the need for ensuring their acceptance and utilization by the end-users in these establishments becomes quite pertinent. Healthcare organizations must indeed, pay attention to change management, as change is inevitable in not just their ability to provide the services for which they exist, but for their very survival in the first place, considering the ever-increasing healthcare costs that are becoming just as increasingly unsustainable in most countries. Consider the implementation of new technologies. This in itself is an indication for change. The healthcare organization s employees are going to have to change their work practices, some even their job descriptions, and location, removed form their erstwhile colleagues and friends, and thrust in new environments, under different managers, perhaps. These changes could be traumatic for some people, and others could resist them for a variety of other reasons, including the threat of losing their jobs to these new "machines". Whatever the reason for resistance, management on its own or via the services of consultant needs to involve their employees in planned ICT projects from the start, albeit via representative dialogues, and brainstorming. This would facilitate a sense of ownership among all employees and allay looming fears. It is important to recognize the establishment's culture and work with it to modify if gradually and methodically to suit the new dispensation. This would make tackling resistance less arduous although efforts must continue to build and sustain the change momentum in particular by reviewing progress regularly and making the necessary adjustments to consolidate gains. As difficult as this exercise could sometimes be as the slow pace of ICT adoption in the health industry in part indicates, change management is simply imperative were any healthcare organization to achieve its goals of delivery qualitative health services with the limited budgets that most have. To further buttress the point, even healthcare ICT implementation, and acceptance by staffers do not signal the end of the story. Software is an important component of any healthcare information system for example. Yet, software notoriously cannot be entirely bug-free. The language, the set of nominal and relational terms and the grammatical structure or architecture of software, the coding in the software, is an essential aspect of its design, yet not the only one. In fact, we can regress software design into a first step, its linguistic logic, the language use to express its grammatical structure or architecture, and a second, or meta-logic, the language we construct to express linguistic logic, the suppositions and limits of the architecture. In other words, software design involves the design of software language, logic, and meta-logic, and matters could get complicated depending on the sophistication of the application, as one would expect for mission-critical applications commonly used in healthcare delivery, some with millions of lines of code. The more sophisticated the software and the less skilful the programmers, among other reasons, the likelier the chances of the software having bugs or failing to run as it ought to do. Bugs may are also relatively common in novel software, with less experience understanding it in its entirety even by IT personnel, and end-users misuse, due such misunderstanding. For these and other reasons inherent in software in general, and in its software development, healthcare organizations must live with the issue of bugs, ensuring the inclusion of the appropriate clauses in their software licensing contracts that mandates vendors to upgrade the software to newer versions periodically. Now, this is where the imperativeness of change management mentioned earlier comes in. Because of these periodic version upgrades, the end user may also need reappraisal of his/ her training on the use of the newer versions of the software, and sometimes the newer versions could amount to major changes in the work processes of some end users. In other words, the healthcare organization that implements healthcare ICT would need to accept the need for ongoing change management, lest it invests in technologies non-usage renders redundant. Healthcare ICT implementation at the healthcare organization level could be quite daunting, yet necessary for the entire e-Health program of any country to work. Some larger organizations might even need a full complement of implementation staff including managers in order for the successful implementation of large healthcare ICT projects. Some would say for examples that such major projects ought to have an implementation team to ensure the achievement of deliverable milestones when due.

Such a team would include a custom support manager, who provides on-and off-site system end-user support upon completion of system deployment. This manager and his/ team receive and act upon user reports on problems post-implementation. The team is crucial to sustaining the end-user support post initial training and other change management measures, by maintaining adequate communication with users, and offering contingencies to ensure continuity of system usage and minimize user frustration. The product development manager oversees the completion of the project as scheduled, and that the product meets functional requirements, quality assurance standards, for examples stress, and routine/ exception handling tests, in collaboration with the quality assurance team. The product development manager also assesses system request changes including code reuse to avoid duplication and save costs. The quality assurance manager carries out stress tests in conjunction with its product development counterpart as earlier noted. The manager also works with the custom support manager in testing new requirements for enhancements based on end-user experience, and issues the deployment manager raised, to ensure the new changes work in real life. The product manager works on justifying needed process improvement and product features, and the functional requirements to translate them into software. There are also deployment and documentation managers, and a host of others depending on the scope of the project. In reality, only a few healthcare organizations, even vendors, have such an expanded complement of healthcare ICT implementation managers, and they are typically those that develop proprietary software and other healthcare ICT products. Most general practitioners would get by with a little help from IT consultants implementing these technologies. There is no doubt that their efforts in not just improving their service offering s to their clients but also contributing to the overall e-Health implementation goals of their country would be worthwhile in the end. In Canada for example, E-health or health-oriented information technology is improving the way Canadians receive medical care. One technology that is gaining even wider acceptance is telehealth, or medical care at a distance, ranging from a 1-800 number for answers to health questions to remote surgery. Every Canadian province now has telehealth in one form or another. There is teletriage, telepsychiatry, telehome care, even telerobotics. This is possible partly due to the steady advance of broadband access, even into remote parts of the country. Now, individuals living in remote communities without a doctor can receive diagnosis via videoconference and need not make a long trip to the nearest city to see a doctor. Diagnosis is one of the biggest uses of telehealth technology, but there are other equally valuable uses. Telehealth does not replace your family doctor, but it makes the everyday work of health workers much easier, and it allows patients to receive medical care without having to travel or even leave home. Telehome care might involve giving a patient a monitor that sits in their living room, connected to their blood pressure cuff, and transmitting information to health-care workers as they perform their other duties. The values of IT in healthcare delivery notwithstanding, there are lingering issues regarding how health technologies can safeguard privacy while making the information more accessible Some hospitals have consolidated their printers, copiers and fax machines into multi-function devices, using for example Lexmark technology, bidding farewell to the manila folder. In the old system, a porter, a hospital employee, would go to each nursing station and take orders down to the pharmacy. Other hospitals had vacuum tubes and other fax the documents. However, Lexmark technology for example, makes it possible to send a digital image down to a printer in the pharmacy, and the printer beeps so the pharmacist knows an order came in. Many hospitals are also implementing a barcode assigned to a patient on admission, which carries the patient's name, and possibly prescription and allergy information. The system prints bar-coded labels for the wristband, the bedside, and the pill bottle. A nurse would scan the medication and the patient's wristband, making sure it matched. The bar code helps to reduce errors, and errors can no doubt cost lives. Machine-readable patient identifiers have gone beyond barcodes, with able to have radio-frequency chips decodable for valuable point-of-care information implanted under their skin. Dedicated medical-record and data management software continues to change how hospitals manage information. Oacis, for example, software developed by Dinmar, an Ottawa-based company, shows health workers all the information available for a patient, such as for medications and laboratory tests, including for previous hospital visits. This information links to the hospital's medical-imaging database, which enables a doctor to look up a patient s record and see previous X-rays and blood test results. The system even highlights abnormal lab results. Health workers are able to access a hospital's information system from wherever they are through rolling wireless terminals or handheld computers. The dawn of wireless phones in hospitals helps staff find one another quickly, and means that patients call buttons can beep the nurse s phone directly, not a desk down the hall. You could not use cellphones in hospitals a decade ago but now you see clinicians using wireless phones almost everywhere in most hospital because they are on the right frequency and do not interfere with hospital equipment or communication systems. These are just a few of the ways healthcare ICT is changing healthcare delivery. The onus is on all of us to embrace these technologies and make e-Health work, something we are most unlikely to regret we did.

References

1. Available at: http://www.fda.gov Accessed on April 22, 2006

2. Available at: http://www.medicalnewstoday.com/medicalnews.php?newsid=42061 Accessed on April 22, 2006

3. Available at: http://www.medicalnewstoday.com/medicalnews.php?newsid=42040 Accessed on April 22, 2006

Conclusions

W e have come to a stage in healthcare delivery that we are no longer able to deny the immense benefits we could derive from implementing healthcare information and communications technologies, hence moving forward e-Health as a crucial underlying infrastructure for any modern healthcare services. The interests of governments particularly in the developed countries in investing in healthcare information technologies attest the appreciation of the increasing role of these technologies in not only providing qualitative healthcare but also in containing skyrocketing health care spending by governments, companies, even individuals. Considering the need to achieve these objectives, it is imperative for us to continue to work toward the widespread adoption, implementation, and use of healthcare ICT, in order to make e-Health work. Canada Health Infoway is the federal agency given $1.2 billion to accelerate the adoption of EHR and achieve the objective of half of Canadians having EMRs by 2009. The deputy Health Ministers of Canada define its role and dictate policy, while its board implement the policy, which is currently to provide the infrastructure, the highway, not give physicians subsidies, although many are calling for a policy change, which they argue would facilitate the achievement of the objectives of the agency. Some believe that giving such subsidies is the surest way to secure physician involvement in the program. This was what Alberta did. The province apparently is serious about meeting the commitment its Premier, Ralph Klein, made to Albertans that every one of them will have an electronic medical record by 2008. Besides being the first province in Canada to implement a provincial EHR, the province has since established a $66 million Alberta Physician Office System Program in collaboration with the Alberta Medical Association. Every physician in the province is eligible to $7,700 in each of four years to install, undergo training in, and start to use electronic medical records (EMR) in their practice, and about 40% of the doctors have so far done so, the numbers rising. The EMRs in doctors' offices integrate with the provincial EHR, the perfect scenario for a fully digitalized and modern healthcare system. Considering that, primary care physicians constitute the bedrock of the province's healthcare system, as it is indeed the case in all other Canadian provinces,

Alberta is on the right track towards improving healthcare services to its peoples. Will other provinces adopt its program of assisting physicians to purchase and implement EMR? There is no doubt that this program has facilitated the adoption of EMR in the province and increased utilization of the provincial EHR. By adopting Alberta's approach, other Canadian provinces, and territories will also facilitate healthcare ICT diffusion and the pace of reform and improvement in the quality of service provision, and ultimately the overall health of all Canadians. The Health Council of Canada supports the idea of all Canadians having an EMR, and wants this to happen by 2010. It contends that the benefits of EMR such as improved quality of care, patient safety, and cost saving, are too important to ignore. EMR can save the federal government up to $1.3 billion annually for example. It can save provincial and territorial governments money too. It is a win-win situation for every stakeholder in the health arena to support the implementation and utilization of EHR and EMR. There are challenges in the way, for examples, changing entrenched attitudes, changing demographics and technology costs, among others. However, these are surmountable challenges as our discussion in the e-book shows. Each province and territory will have to identify and address its challenges. No matter how difficult, it is our obligation, governments and peoples alike, to join hands in promoting health, preventing disease, and ensuring accessibility to equitable and qualitative health services throughout Canada. Understandably, other countries should do the same. In fact, both government and private organizations should collaborate in encouraging healthcare professionals to adopt and implement healthcare ICT, and we must commend the efforts made in other countries such as the U.S., and the U.K, too. Some may object to what might at first appear to be pampering these healthcare professionals, but considering the stakes, whatever efforts to ensure that e-Health works would likely turn out to be worth the while in the end.

Indeed, many physician practices, solo, or group, would have been thinking about implementing an electronic health record system someday, although perhaps not sure precisely when due to cost considerations. Implementing EHR clearly has its pros and cons, one of the latter being that they generally tend to be beyond the reach of most small practices, and even larger group practices. All that may already be changing, albeit with a little help from well-meaning sources in the public and private sectors as mentioned above. Furthermore, while implementing EHR may still represent significant projects for many practices, there is evidence from vendor surveys that the average total cost of ownership for a typical three-doctor practice is under $10,000 per doctor per annum, increasingly coming within affordable reach of many small medical practices after all. Indeed, vendors are reporting increasing sales of integrated or stand-alone EHR, and predicting that sales will continue to soar. Coupled with other developments in the healthcare ICT industry such as the falling prices of computers and peripherals, many practices will likely be getting on the EHR bandwagon sooner than they envisaged. Let us face it, medical practice will have to employ increasingly, cutting-edge technology to prevent medical errors, enhance patient safety, and improve healthcare delivery in general. These are the core elements of the value propositions healthcare professionals offer their patients, and society. They will surely like to deliver on their word. This is why doctors and other healthcare professionals need to embrace ICT even more and faster than they are currently doing. Every day of delay in taking this decision may be another day of unnecessarily mounting morbidity and even mortality due to medical errors, and crucial patient information not being available at the point of care, for examples, problems that ICT would have helped prevent. Implementing an EHR is one major step toward contributing your quota to improving your profession and saving your patients lives, and moving widespread e-Health adoption forward. For healthcare professionals ready to implement healthcare ICT, you first need to do a number of things to get started with an EHR project. Discuss the project with your partners and staff. Find out if they are interested and if not why. Find out what their concerns are and establish potential sources of resistance down the road. Allay their fears, for example, your secretary may think, automation means the end of her job. Let everyone know the goals of the practice and the benefits of the proposed technology to the practice, patients, and even the staff members themselves. Buy them into the project from the start. There are certainly going to be changes in certain operational aspects of your practice due to implementing EHR as we noted in our discussions in this e-book. You should optimize the chances the change process creates for service improvement including incorporating the exercise in your quality improvement (QI) program if you had any in order to set up the EHR to meet your benchmarks and in turn to ensure your practice emerges with higher quality operations. Depending on the size of your practice, you and your partner may oversee the implementation yourselves, or you may need to assemble a project team, or the services of an ICT consultant. There should be personnel in charge of the project, the clinical, business, and technical aspects, respectively although one person may perform dual or more roles. An important aspect of any ICT implementation is to know your needs. Implementing ICT to meet your needs is preferable to first purchasing technology and then looking for what to do with it. Needs assessment is sine qua non for cost-effective ICT deployment. Know what your practice needs in all the functional areas first, examine your workflow processes and identify their bottlenecks, and then the requirements for ICT will follow, after which you can begin to build or buy the relevant ICT. You may already have the resources with which to embark on the EHR project, in which case, you can skip this step otherwise you will now need to look for the right approach to financing the project and go for it. You should also make the necessary arrangements for maintenance of the EHR if not already included in the contract with your vendor. In this regard, you should also be ready for data loss and system failures, with appropriate measures in place to mitigate such risks and contingency plans to tackle the problems. By implementing EHR, you just may be taking the first important step toward modernizing your practice, improving the quality of the care you give your patients, and preventing avoidable medical errors. You will also be contribution to the increasing use of e-Health. These are all no doubt noble objectives every doctor should aspire to achieve. Our effort to promote the pervasive deployment and use of healthcare should also target other healthcare stakeholders, including the public. This includes the development of novel technologies to facilitate healthcare delivery. For example, there remains a wide information chasm for many even today despite the Internet being so seemingly ubiquitous, and these peoples not all live in developing countries where the lack of the necessary infrastructure understandably compromises ICT diffusion. There are also many people in the developed world, that still lack access to the Internet, mostly those living in rural and remote areas, where service providers do not often consider profitable enough for them to run high-speed links. Microsoft is coming to the rescue of these remote areas. Microsoft Research is collaborating with seven universities in the US to develop Mesh Connectivity Layer technology that will make it easier and more affordable to provide people living in remote areas with faster Internet connections. This would likely make more people benefit from the many initiatives on health services provision delivered via the Internet, for example targeted health information, and even encourage them to place their personal health records (PHR) securely in cyberspace, where authorized personnel, including their healthcare providers could access them readily. There are also developments in the hardware end of health information technologies and they are likely to increase the usage of these technologies. Portable PCs could be running for eight hours in another three years. The current lifespan of notebook batteries is four hours, after which the batteries need to recharge or the notebook shuts down automatically. The improvement in battery life is evidence of the frenetic pace of activities taking place in the chip and notebook manufacturing industries. Notebook manufacturers are making them ever thinner and lighter to meet consumer preferences and maximize profits regardless of battery life but also due to pressure from chipmakers such as Intel for thinner and lighter notebooks with 8-hour battery life. Intel for example is giving notebook manufacturers until 2008 to comply with its demands. Intel and other chipmakers and notebook manufacturers are particularly interested in the notebook market. With the notebook market gulping almost a third of all PC processors and notebook processors generally costlier than those for desktops do both industry sectors have much to lose not revisiting the issue of battery life. Even the current 4-hour battery life standard is not always realizable depending on usage and, how new the batteries are. Progress in battery manufacturing is lending a helping hand it would seem, in making the 8-hour notebook battery a reality. For example, Zinc Matrix Power is fine-tuning methodologies for producing longer lasting batteries from zinc alkaline than conventional lithium ion batteries yet occupy just as much notebook space. Pionics is sticking with Lithium ion batteries with a similar lifespan. Thin and light notebooks weigh less than 5 pounds and usually have batteries with 58-watt energy-hours capacities, and with average power consumption of 12 watts last no longer than four hours. Notebooks will soon be packing 72-watt hours and some contend much lower average power consumption, between 8 and 9 watts. Improvements in LCD performance, with power consumption of new LCD panels now typically only 3watts, also contribute to the overall increased efficiency in notebook power consumption. This is an important contribution as LCD panels use up about 30 percent of overall notebook power. Intel's Display Power Saving Technology enables added lighting via wider opening of pixels in a digital picture or graphic image, but prevents the extra light washing out the picture as would normally occur because the chipset also turns down the light source inside the panel. This is a significant power-saving parallel development in notebook technology. It confers on the notebook an added benefit of lower overall power consumption, while maintaining the quality of the image. Intel also has a new, chip, the Yonah notebook chip, expected to use up much less power than Pentium M processors, and Via Technologies, the C7, a new power-conserving notebook chip. Samsung recently announced it has developed a new hard drive that first stores data in flash memory, enabling the hard drive to hibernate most times, thus conserving energy, and extending the notebook's battery life. Hard drive usually use up close to eight percent of a notebooks power supply. Samsung claims its new hard drive would give notebooks half an hour more of battery power. These developments in notebook energy efficiency can only increase the already high profile of these handy devices. There is no doubt about the positive effect of these and similar developments in software and hardware technologies would have on the widespread adoption of healthcare ICT, which would further enhance the chances of making e-Health work. We have discussed extensively the benefits of these technologies in this e-book. We have also discussed the issues surrounding their widespread adoption, including those fostering and hindering it. The benefits derivable from these technologies are simply too important to ignore. They are not just important to the delivery of qualitative healthcare, they are also crucial to our efforts to curtail spiraling healthcare costs. Besides, these technologies offer opportunities for the improvement of the quality of both the ill and healthy. Consider the elderly for example, who even free of any chronic debilitating illness knows he/ she is secure living alone because of a wearable technology with which he/ she could seek instant help in case of an emergency. Is this not going to improve the quality of life of the senior? There are innumerable such benefits of healthcare ICT, too many to mention in one e-book. However, we have all to continue to seek ways to assist in the development of even newer and more valuable such technologies. There is no going back on e-health now. We all know its benefits are immense and capable of helping solve many of the problems our health systems confront today and will face in the near and long terms. Making e-Health work is work in progress. With health parameters such as disease prevalence and outcomes, so fluid, and dependant on technologies to elucidate the natural histories of diseases for examples, and with other factors at play in determining the nature, scope, and financing of health service also changing, so must e-health initiatives and the technologies to accomplish them. The continuing appraisal of these factors and of the efforts to ensure the institution of the necessary actions to ensure the continuity and improvement of our e-health programs is our collective responsibility to humankind.